Unchallenged Violence

Unchallenged Violence

AN AMERICAN ORDEAL

Robert Brent Toplin

Greenwood Press

Westport, Connecticut ● *London, England*

Library of Congress Cataloging in Publication Data

Toplin, Robert Brent, 1940-
    Unchallenged violence.

    Includes bibliographical references and index.
    1. Violence—United States. 2. Crime and criminals—
United States. 3. Cities and towns—United States.
I. Title.
HN90.V5T66   301.6'33'0973   75-72
ISBN 0-8371-7748-0

Library of Congress Catalog Card Number:75-72
ISBN: 0-8371-7748-0

First published in 1975

Greenwood Press, a division of Williamhouse-Regency Inc.
51 Riverside Avenue, Westport, Connecticut 06880

Manufactured in the United States of America

CONTENTS

Part II   *Sources*

Part III   *Conclusions*

PREFACE

Early in 1974 I dined with a friend who exuded excitement about one of the most enjoyable trips of his lifetime—he had just discovered San Francisco! The town was "fantastic," he said, an urban spectacular of mountain and bayside views, daring architecture, and quaint shops. But most important were the people. Their diverse styles reflected Frisco's extraordinary ethnic and cultural mix. The people were warm and open in their relationships with each other, my friend commented. Folks in San Francisco exhibited a special spirit, a zest for life that seemed contagious in a highly cosmopolitan and friendly environment. The gleam in his eye betrayed thoughts he revealed later. He considered Frisco about as ideal a place for settling down as anywhere in the United States.

This was a familiar description, this oohing and ahing over California's Bay Area. Many times before I had heard friends rave about metropolitan San Francisco as the epitome of the best American civilization had to offer. They talked about the town in such glowing terms that I often wondered why each didn't just hurl caution to the winds, pack his bags, and venture forth toward his Eden. In fact, several of them eventually did resettle. How many others shared the dream? It appeared that soon a very sizable chunk of the United States population would have postal zip codes in the 9400s.

Just a few weeks after I spoke with my friend, San Francisco received nationwide headline news attention as a city trapped in urban nightmares. Its confident and congenial people noticeably turned nervous and testy. These reactions developed especially after a night of bizarre slayings. During a two-hour period, gunmen shot down five citizens, killing four. The murderers did not attempt robbery or sexual assault, and they apparently chose their targets at random. Their victims had only one thing in common: they were white. Policemen and journalists expressed great worry as they placed events in this night of bloodshed against the background of other incidents in the area: six similar random slayings in the previous two months, abduction by gunpoint of the daughter of newspaper publisher William Randolph Hearst III, fatal ambushes of policemen, and the shotgun assassination of Oakland's superintendent of schools. Terms like the Symbionese Liberation Army and the Zebra Killings became household words. Actually, the developments boded ill for Bay Area citizens of all colors. For example, the school superintendent was an "Establishment" black, a noted educator whose appointment had been angrily criticized by some community members. Moreover, many black residents worried about public over-reaction to the new dangers. "I'd hate to see somebody get blown away just because he made a false move," commented a black man, referring to the growing suspiciousness of whites. Indeed, hundreds of whites in the region reacted to the news reports by rushing to gun stores to purchase their first firearms. Citizens harbored frightening visions of facing in real life the kinds of confrontations that wrecked their dreams at night. Eden seemed to be turning to hell. San Francisco was in trouble. America was already in deep trouble.

The San Francisco situation was only one small aspect of a fast-growing problem that greatly disturbs Americans in the 1970s. A once proud and confident people seem increasingly worried and uncertain about their future. More and more they turn inward, searching not only for ways to keep their own lives free of violence but also for means to ease their minds and achieve at least a feeling of security. Given the immensity of their difficulties, their desire to escape from the harsh realities is certainly understandable. While escapism has its virtues on the individual level, its consequences on the collective level are troubling. Instead of confronting the problem of violence, Americans are accommodating their lives to it. They are learning to live with their growing difficulties rather than challenge them. In the short run their posture may engender illusory comfort; in the long run it appears likely to produce bigger problems and greater anxiety.

This study represents an attempt to understand the nature of the current problems and the attitudes that have fostered an uncharacteristic fatalism in the American public response to them.

ACKNOWLEDGMENTS

Many people from a variety of professions and academic disciplines were generous with their time and thoughts during the preparation of this study. Since I do not wish to name some while overlooking others, I prefer a general statement of sincere gratitude for their help. In a slightly more specific way words of thanks may be directed to two groups. At Denison University 205 students labored superbly as Devil's Advocates and contributors of information and ideas in two classes on "The Problem of Violence in American History and Culture." Their perceptions helped me greatly to question, revise, and expand many interpretations that appear in this book. Furthermore, I developed a deeper *feeling* for the issues through conversations with prisoners sentenced for crimes of violence. Their mature and probing observations about their pasts made a strong impact. The prisoners seemed to have a better understanding of how environmental experiences helped to place them behind bars than many of those who comment about them from outside the penitentiary walls. I am also indebted to the National Endowment for the Humanities and Denison University for financial assistance that made this work possible. During a year's leave under a N.E.H. Younger Humanist fellowship, I found opportunities to work on the book while engaging in another, related project. Summer grants from Denison University facilitated completion of the study. Finally, Betty Pessagno deserves a word of appreciation for her excellent editorial assistance.

Houston, Texas
November 12, 1974

CAVEAT EMPTOR

Before delving into specific problems of current life, a few words of caution. Certainly, there are enormous pitfalls in dealing with a topic so large and controversial as the role of violence in American society. At first glance the task of assessing the impact of violence on something as amorphous as "American civilization" seems downright ludicrous, if not impossible. How do we get a grip on the concept of civilization, much less speculate on the rise or decline of one? How does violence affect the quality of civilization? What can be done to alleviate the problem of violence? Before tackling these general questions, some precautionary notes are in order. With a proper understanding of the limitations in such a broad-based study we shall feel freer to face the large issues without embarrassment.

To begin, a word about definitions: "violence" is a very general term, and people preoccupied with a variety of different concerns can easily relate it to the specific cause that interests them. The meaning is so broad in popular usage that we even speak of one individual's idea doing violence to another's. Many view scandals such as Watergate or mischief involving large corporations as forms of violence. Others emphasize society's injustices, considering oppression of the poor as a type of violence. From an opposite perspective, some people complain more about the "violent" way poor people protest their condition by destroying property.

The definition I want to emphasize here is narrower and deals more specifically with the condition of human life. What motivates this study is the threat to life posed by violence—the threat of physical harm or even death at the hands of other people. There is something particularly horrifying about people consciously meting out physical injury or taking the lives of others. At the risk of sounding insensitive, I would say that a news story about the loss of lives from criminal violence or warfare is more disturbing than news of even a greater number of deaths from earthquakes or tornadoes. The spectacle of one person purposefully violating the life of another surely must be the most outrageous of all forms of violence.

The problem of violence obviously goes far beyond actual physical harm. A fear of victimization by violence increasingly plagues Americans, sapping the lives of the many people it troubles. What good are the amenities of urban civilization if we are afraid to go out and enjoy them? What is lost from democratic politics when most of the population expects more assassinations of leading public figures? These and related worries greatly expand the list of the casualities of violence. We need only to begin talking openly to discover how prevalent this fear has become in America.

Since the 1960s there has been much more writing about violence in America than ever before. Students of American history and culture who had long neglected this research field suddenly rushed into a publishing revolution that began exploding in the late sixties. Generally, these new works fall into two categories. First, there are the myriad special studies that examine particular problems such as urban riots, assassinations, media violence, homicides, and criminal justice. Some of these investigations narrow their focus quite specifically to consider the relevance of particular case studies to the larger issues in question. Among these contributions we find, for example, psychological analysis of individual murders, evaluation of the historical role of violence in Southern culture, and reports on the motivation and activities of violent street gangs. Although the quality of these works varies greatly, anyone looking into the literature on violence in America is likely to feel indebted to the many authors who have clarified specific problems through careful monographic studies and news reporting. Much of their research has been in the best tradition of academic and journalistic investigation. Today, someone beginning to study violence in America can get a very useful head start from these works hardly available to students just a decade ago.

The second category of recent books on violence—the general, broadly encompassing studies—is hampered by many more difficulties than the monographic studies. These are works that weave together diverse information to construct highly interpretive syntheses. Often these grand, sweeping analyses fail to achieve credibility. Sometimes their difficulties lie in the questions asked and at other times in the answers posited.

Many of these broadly interpretive books suffer from what may be identified as the Handkerchief Approach. Such studies produce long catalogues of atrocities from American history to convince readers what bloody, bloody people Americans have been. From the Pequot War to Kent State and beyond, they condemn society for indulging in immoral bloodshed. Overall, they appeal more to a sense of guilt than to an understanding of the complex reasons that drive diverse groups to settle their differences violently. The pathos of these accounts certainly has its place, but hopefully not at the expense of sophisticated evaluation. Jeremiads are not enough.

Furthermore, Handkerchief Approaches are quick to bore. The long list of horrors soon becomes tiring, because it suggests the wrong questions. We need not ponder incessantly over the issue "How big is the problem of violence in America?" Anyone familiar with history books or large city newspapers should know the vastness of the problem. But to leave the question there closes some of the principal avenues to understanding. For example, how can we intelligently judge the significance of a problem's size without a frame of reference? Violence is not a uniquely

American problem. If, indeed, we find that America is more violent than many other societies, we face several new questions. For instance, why does so much violence arise in a highly "developed" country like the United States? What special conditions in America generate its particular forms of violence? And beyond those inquiries lies another vexing question: Why have Americans done so little to deal with their problems of violence in basic and effective ways?

Another genre of broadly interpretive books suffers from what we may call the Ideological Approach. These works usually offer neat, supposedly air-tight explanations that require acceptance of a few fundamental assumptions. Once we agree, for example, that American society is basically racist or fascist or, viewed from the other side, that it has been spoiled by naive liberals, anarchistic radicals, or permissive judges, explanations of violence fall nicely into place. For those who feel more comfortable with faith than understanding, the intellectual strait jackets provided by these explanations should be quite appealing. After all the praise one hears for American pragmatism, however, this penchant for treating complex issues with simpleminded labels is disappointing. The precise meaning of *conservative, liberal,* or *radical* with respect to the diverse ramifications of violence is not always clear. What *is* the "conservative" perspective on assassinations or the "liberal" perspective on movie violence? Of course, some topics lend themselves to ideological approaches. Despite some confusion, the public has a general idea of what a liberal or conservative position might be on a subject such as "criminal justice." Still, these generalizations are grossly inaccurate when we consider changes over time and the diversity of opinion on particulars.

More annoying is the fact that popular ideological labels subtly encourage analysts to subscribe to party lines. How often does a "liberal" seem ready to offer a distinctive approach to the problem of violence, then fall back from his statement, apparently thinking, "I can't say that. I'd sound like a conservative"? Or the reverse concerning thoughts of a conservative? Such ideological partisanship only obfuscates the issues with artificial taxonomy. All groups—conservative, liberals, and radicals—are tempted to dilute their valuable insights with sizable doses of philosophical nonsense. A more realistic approach requires greater independence of thought and less party-line rhetoric. Analyses of violence need not be stamped in capital letters: CONSERVATIVE, LIBERAL, or RADICAL.

Finally, Disciplinary Approaches constitute another genre of broadly interpretive books that suffer from major pitfalls. In these analyses specialists from particular disciplines tend to explain varied manifestations of violence under the rubric of their favorite professional subjects. Some psychologists tell us that almost all violence relates fundamentally to personality makeup. Ethologists point to instincts as a common denominator. Economists frequently see most violence resulting from personal frustrations and failures in a tough, competitive capitalistic society. Sociologists often point to status frustration. And a good number of political scientists attribute much of the violence to shortcomings in the political system. Apparently no gynecologist has yet issued an overview of violence, but when one does, we may expect some new and interesting perspectives.

Today's scientists of human behavior (and, no doubt, tomorrow's too) cannot produce precise answers to our questions about violence. They can offer speculations on the problem —hopefully intelligent, well-documented speculations. Students of violence need not be intimidated by the professional auspices under which theories appear, for even "scientists" are fallible. The best we can do for their theories is to treat them with critical respect. The worst we can do is to accept them without question.

It should be evident that analysis of so broad a topic as violence in America calls for a multidisciplinary approach, not a partisan interpretation operating on a priori considerations. The task calls for choosing from the evidence and arguments of various disciplines, judging both their quality and their relevance to the problems at hand. From history to psychiatry, all the disciplines are necessary to the task of explaining violence. The real challenge seems not to point out the importance of one over the others, but to discover their interrelationships.

Thus, readers ought to beware that this investigation represents a conscious effort to avoid some major pitfalls of the

Handkerchief Approach, the Ideological Approach, and the Disciplinary Approach. Such an effort is bound to annoy everybody in some way. Many readers will be irritated with what they consider to be abundant contradictions in this study. They will complain that many comments about violence swing between strong, opinionated statements and wishy-washy, neither-here-nor-there assessments. Grumbling about inconsistencies in treating the issues, they will charge that the analysis sometimes is intolerant of compromises and half-way solutions while in other places it compromises too much with pragmatic concessions to supposed reality. There will be irritation over a tendency not to label heroes and goats consistently or to take firm ideological stands. In some places readers will detect the voice of a liberal, but in other sections sounds of conservative thought. In fact, they will observe this fluctuation in the comments on nearly every group discussed in some detail. Many, no doubt, will complain that, while the study criticizes every group specifically, almost in the same breath it eschews hunts for culprits and tries to apologize for just about everybody. In attributing responsibility for violence they will find that the essays both blame and exonerate groups such as the rich and poor, whites and blacks, gun fanatics and gun controllers. Finally, they will complain about inconsistencies in the tone of analysis, noting that comments vary from the light, waggish, and sarcastic to the heavy, serious, and moralistic. May I say that I concur on all of these charges. There is a catch, however. I would attribute the wavering tone to irony rather than to inconsistency. The issues associated with problems of violence in America bubble over with irony, contradictions, and paradoxes, because both the causes of violence and potential solutions are infinitely complex.

Of course, eventually one must take a stand. It would be difficult to do otherwise with so controversial a topic. Not surprisingly, debates on violence in America tap enough sensitive nerves to bring out the opinionated best in each of us. Consensus will stretch only so far when delving into emotion-laden subjects like the nature of man, movie violence, civil disobedience, the role of the police, or gun controls. Differences of opinion on these matters do not call for polite apologies. Though debates can go on forever, each of us must at some point speak his own mind. Those who await definitive answers from "unimpeachable sources" had better pray for immortality. Given the absence of infallible assessments in our own time (and probably well beyond), it is reasonable to venture forth with very subjective observations. Certainly some commentary will lapse into moralizing over the current state of affairs. What can one say about this tendency to be preachy?

Before closing, a few more specific precautionary notes. Lest the wording in this study inadvertently lead some women to jump to false conclusions about piggish prejudices, a brief explanation is in order. Wherever comments about violence in "man" appear, the word "man" is intended to connote people in general. Since it is awkward to speak of "people in general," "humankind," "the human race," or whatever, I have retained the old-fashioned terminology. I hope that women will understand that this wording does not reflect the spirit of grating male chauvinism. Also, lest residents from diverse sections of the United States feel slighted by a paucity of material herein about violence in their own regions, the pattern of illustrations in this study should be explained. While the analysis contains references to events in many large cities across the country, it skews the examples in favor of two East Coast towns: New York and Philadelphia. During the course of this investigation, I began collecting information on incidents of violence from many daily newspapers. In a short time the abundance of information became overwhelming, a reflection of the pervasiveness of the problem in American cities. To make the project more manageable, I decided to concentrate on New York and Philadelphia, two large cities with which I had the closest personal familiarity. I also selected these two cities for their lack of distinction; i.e., they were not the most extreme examples of violence available. Had I been looking for the highest rates of homicide, I would have focused on a place like Detroit, sometimes called "Murder Capital, U.S.A." If I had been searching especially for examples of bizarre murders, I probably would have chosen metropolitan San Francisco.

So much for warnings. No approach to the problem can be entirely objective, and I recognize that it is necessary to exercise considerable discretion. Certainly no one can agree with everything said here. I can only hope that, if all the answers do not seem satisfactory, at least I have tried to ask the right questions.

Part I
Problems

1
THE PROBLEM

In 1973 I received a letter from a young lady who had recently moved with her husband from a small town to a medium-sized (645,000 population) American city. After only a few months, she felt growing discomfort and nervousness with her new home. The city turned out to be a real "bummer," she wrote, and as soon as possible, she and her husband intended to return to a small town. That is, if they weren't "shot, stabbed, drowned, raped, mugged, [or] beaten" first, she pointed out half seriously, half in jest. "At *least* 5 people die that way *every* nite here," she reported. "It's great for the population [problem], not so good for the security and well-being of all us innocent *people*."

Was this young lady "running away from reality," as a colloquial expression goes? If the violence she associated with life in the new city was "reality," her response was understandable and excusable. Few people *want* to live in a violent environment. When they have an opportunity, most usually move out quickly. This is a familiar pattern in America. More and more people are on the run, seeking safety in the suburbs, the countryside, or in heavily guarded residences in the city. Yet they are also discovering that the problem is difficult to escape, for violence cannot be contained easily. It has become hauntingly pervasive in American culture, reaching out to people from all locations, classes, and ethnic backgrounds. No longer just a threat to specific individuals, it is a menace to the entire society.

The idea of living in a society plagued by violence is so unappealing that Americans tend to hide from facing this thought just as they try to run away from specific threats of aggression. Again, the response is understandable and excusable. It is discomforting enough to view individual confrontations with violence; how much more unsettling is the realization that we live in a pervasively violent society? Perhaps for our own sanity we avoid trying to put the pieces together and attempting a larger view. Mundane, day-to-day headaches of compensating for the cost of living or maintaining social prestige are sufficiently taxing to make an obsession with violence seem highly unattractive. Even many who worry seriously about the "larger issues" of ecology, energy crises, poverty, or ethno-racial injustice do not want to add anxiety about violence to an already heavy burden of concerns. Violence is a problem, they admit, but let us keep it "in perspective."

There is an interesting, subtle attitude in American culture that pressures against accepting violence as a pervasive problem. People frequently brand efforts to describe the issue broadly as alarmist. Complaining about specifics is all right; worrying about a general malaise seems out of place. Perhaps Americans do not realize that the very nature of their problem of violence may contrive to make proposition of larger questions unpopular. Violence is so integrated into the culture, so apparently part of the "way of life," that Americans often view frightened talk about it as unfashionable, as unnecessary queasiness, as manifestation of a fear to face reality. Perhaps this refusal to deal with the larger implications of violence openly reveals an aspect of the Americans' *macho* ethic, an attitude that sanctions violence more than Americans care to admit.

A visitor to America, an outsider, could probably point out salient aspects of the problem with more assurance than a native American. Often foreigners can collect cultural insights in brief visits that hardly occur to citizens who live in the society all of their lives. Keen observers such as Hector St. John de Crevecoeur, Alexis de Tocqueville, and James Bryce left valuable historical notes on American civilization that outlined the forest where others could only see trees. Without making any pretentions of joining the company of such stellar figures, we might nevertheless ask what visitors might especially notice today in looking for the salient characteristics of American life. What are the culture's sharp points and rough edges? How does America stack up as a civilization?

There are many ways to evaluate the character of a civilization, but the one we shall especially stress here involves the quality of relationships between people. This aspect, as many argue, should take priority over matters of material wealth and technological development as the principal test of success. In this context respect for human beings and a show of concern for their well-being constitute the noblest aspects of a civilized spirit. On the other hand, callousness toward the lives of others and indifference toward pain and death represent the antithesis of a civilized attitude. For what is the value of civilization, anyway, if it does not work toward removing fear, discomfort, and suffering from people's lives? The vast apparatus of technology helps to protect against nature's threats to comfort. What a pity if man perpetuates these troubles for himself. A truly civilized people cannot manifest widespread indifference to pain and death. John Donne's compassion well summarizes this ethic of Civilized Man —the idea that "Any man's death diminishes me, because I am involved in Mankinde."

The present American scene, then, looks disturbing in view of popular attitudes about violence. Indeed, many Americans seem all-engrossed with the matter. Their interest shows in myriad, complex ways across the breadth of national life. Often they accept violence almost insouciantly as "part of life." One puzzles over the apparent Womb to Tomb emphasis on violence in American society. Some little scenes are difficult to put out of mind, like the picture of a father beaming down on his newborn son in the hospital, boasting to friends, "That kid's gonna be tough . . . Hiyah, killer." Nor is it easy to forget the funeral for a

Vietnam War victim, where friends of the deceased boasted of his bravery and readiness to "die like a man." For life along the way from cradle to grave, one notices other common-place but un-forgettable examples of the extraordinarily pervasive interest in things violent. There are those fascinating toy collections of American youngsters, playthings ranging from gun-shaped teething rings to realistic arsenals of imitation pistols, rifles, bazookas, and cannons. And, of course, the clever little games like "The Pendulum," an assemble-it-yourself guillotine kit complete with simulated human organs decorated imaginatively with drip-ping painted blood. Moving on to view the leisure interests of teenaged Americans, we may consider the tremendous populari-ty of rock music sensation "Alice Cooper." "Alice" off stage is not at all the wild character he makes himself out to be when under show business lights. It seems that Alice, the son of a minister, was just another aspiring leader of a low-budget rock group, dogged-ly running the concert circuit until he found gold in a violent motif. Songs like "Killer," "Love it to Death," and "Dead Babies" put his albums in the feature displays of record shops across the country. It was "Dead Babies" that catapulted Alice to stardom. As most American teenagers knew, when Alice Cooper gave a live performance of "Dead Babies," he hacked a doll to pieces on stage with an axe, drawing a shower of simulated blood. Then, for the *pièce de résistance,* he hurled limbs to a howling audience.[1]

Trying to set our minds at ease, we might reason that Alice Cooper and "The Pendulum" are just symbols of a make-believe world. These may look like illustrations of sadistic infatuation, but surely such grotesque attitudes do not work out very often into actual behavior. To maintain confidence in this optimistic view, we had better avoid the newspapers. Daily periodicals reveal too much about the frequency of senseless and bizarre murders. The papers are full of blood-curdling stories, so many in fact that often they are reported in capsule form only. One can pick up a big-city newspaper at random and easily find a small catalog of true horror stories. Trying the experiment with *The New York Times,* I drew a copy of the August 22, 1973 edition. It contained references to the following cases:

—A man entered a bar on 73rd St. with a toy gun and announced a holdup. An off-duty policeman at the scene shot the robber dead.

—A seventeen-year-old youth died on the streets of Brooklyn from stab wounds, following a gang fight.

—A street argument in Brooklyn resulted in gunshots and the death of one man.

—A twenty-two-year old paroled ex-convict admitted to killing an eighty-six-year-old semi-invalid in a midtown church rectory during a holdup attempt.

—The prime suspect in two murder cases involving nine victims including men, women, and children failed to show up at a hearing where he was to be indicted by a grand jury.

—An angry crowd of 500 citizens besieged a Lower East Side police station for two hours, demanding the officers turn over a man they believed was responsible for the mutilation killings of four young boys. Each youth had been found dead with an "X" mark carved on his chest. Police insisted the man the crowd wanted was not the suspect.

The abundance of this kind of information in newspapers suggests a lesson from American history. Perhaps a compendium of recent newspaper accounts of violence could be as instructive in sharpening awareness as a nineteenth-century document on slavery. In the 1830s abolitionist Theodore Dwight Weld prepared a book called *Slavery As It Is,* composed entirely from the clippings of Southern newspapers. Weld intended to show slavery in its everyday form, not as an attractive "way of life" as slaveholders described it, but as a brutal institution held together by lash and chain. Weld did not load his book with emotional appeals. He simply let the newspaper facts speak for themselves. One wonders what a modern-day book called *Violence As It Is* might do for the American public who consider violence just "part of life." Might the easily collected list of macabre incidents prompt people to raise more serious questions about the nature of "life" in their own culture?

Though most Americans know about a few sensational cases

of murder involving famous people, they do not pay much attention to related occurrences each week, affecting a host of obscure people. The public showed great interest in reports of gory slaughters by Charles Manson and his strange "family," not only because of odd relationships among the murderers, but also because the case involved the death of a celebrity, pregnant movie star Sharon Tate. In fact, many identified the whole affair as the Sharon Tate Murder Case, a title that left out a gesture of respect for other victims of the Manson gang. On the other hand, few people know about or give much attention to hundreds of other grotesque murders each year. Many could outline the Sharon Tate Case; we would have to search long before finding someone who knew about, say, the Isadore Selez case. A group of youths beat the sixty-year-old junk dealer to death with sledgehammers, then cut off his head with a hacksaw.[2] Selez was just one name from a long list of victims of blood-curdling sadism—a list which could form a handsome collection called *Violence As It Is.*

Skimming over a jigsaw puzzle of murders in the United States, it is easy to become disturbed about the pattern of senseless, brutal crime. In other cultures criminals who commit violence often do so for material gain: poverty motivates the killer, a desperation to obtain money for food and shelter, or to gratify a desire for some lavish material goods. In the United States, however, a significantly large proportion of murderers kill without expecting material gain. Murder for profit is bad enough, but what of murder without apparent functional utility? Why did the young men who held up Senator John Stennis outside his Washington, D.C., home believe that taking a billfold and watch was not enough? After receiving the goods, one of the robbers pointed a revolver and announced, "We are going to shoot you anyway." He promptly fired, leaving Stennis in critical condition.[3]

Perhaps "senseless" is not the proper word to describe this kind of crime, since if we could effectively probe the gun wielder's mind, it would probably be possible to understand many of the psychological components of such behavior. People who shoot when violence is not necessary may derive some inner satisfaction from their act, some sense of personal gratification, some fulfillment of psychic need. Without total insensitivity to possible psychological difficulties of such murderers, however, we ought to worry about the consequences of insecurities being worked out in lethal confrontations. We can appreciate the psychic pain of Arthur Bremer, who admonished himself in his diary, writing, "Just another god Damned failure." Yet Bremer's attack on Wallace was a totally unacceptable means of working out these frustrations. And, still, the pattern of murders for psychological gratification grows. A Santa Barbara, California, police detective recently stated the worry as well as anyone: "We're all used to murder that falls into four broad categories—revenge, anger, fear or greed," explained the detective. "But in the last five years . . . the thing that has become so prevalent is murder for pleasure."[4]

The large record of murders resulting from more traditional situations is also disturbing. Whether killings result from alcoholic intoxication, jealousy, temporary fits of anger, rattled nerves during a holdup, or whatever, most need not occur. A special NBC television program on these "traditional" murders, which showed the indifference of people to the increasingly common occurrences, described the problem well. The television special, called "Murder in America," reported on several day-to-day episodes in a large, rather typical American city. By following policemen on their rounds in Denver, Colorado, through several months, NBC reporters found what they described as an "epidemic" of homicides. Most of the murders reported seemed to be incidental to the performance of a robbery, or accidental consequences of emotional confrontations (often between inebriated individuals). Murders were so common in Denver's inner city that neighbors described them as if they were merely local cases of chicken pox. Witnesses talked of homicide in a manner one could expect from someone describing a minor traffic accident. In one unforgettable interview, police described their answer to a call reporting a murder in a combination bar and dance hall. When they arrived, they found customers drinking, the band still playing, and dancers going through their gyrations, all practically ignoring a body lying in the middle of the floor.

While studying this melange of bizarre, senseless, emotional, and accidental killings, we may develop an eerie feeling about the paucity of sorrowful expressions offered for the victims. Witnesses don't want to discuss what they see, and murderers frequently comment on their acts as if they had simply erased a number rather than destroyed a life. Obviously, it is their own skins that killers worry about; the lives of their victims, even if taken over insignificant disputes, seem highly expendable. A sociologist's interview with a convicted murderer reflected this attitude poignantly. When asked whether he was sorry for his behavior, the young killer responded, "Am I sorry? Are you nuts? Of course I'm sorry. You think I like being locked up?"[5]

An observer expects to find much more compassion among the noncriminal, "law-abiding," mainstream elements in American society. At first glance their thinking and behavior appear quite civilized. They verbally endorse a basic biblical commandment, "Thou shalt not kill." They do not scurry about mugging people in the dark of night. And they believe in a respectable burial for the dead. Scratching through that veneer of a civilized mentality, however, observers can begin to discover some troubling symptoms. The more we catch on to subtle qualifications in the supposedly pacific and humane character of mainstream attitudes, the more we may question the alacrity to label their values "civilized." Many middle- and upper-class Americans show a strange preoccupation with toughness that makes them sound like cheap imitators of General George S. Patton or John Wayne. They appear to want everybody to know that they can't be crossed, that they intend to be and remain "Number One."

This egocentric thinking, which leaves little place for concern about the poor souls who get in their way, becomes especially evident in discussions about foreign policy. During the Vietnam War, mainstream America sharpened its words and swords while moving towards an intense belief that a small, distant people were, somehow, their mortal enemies. Mainstream America adopted a classic we/they mentality toward people about whom they knew almost nothing and applauded saturation bombing on them as a show of America's "determination." It became a Holy War against "gooks." Even many of the nation's brightest technocrats and leading politicians accepted popular hate-filled assumptions. They added their own vocabulary to the wartime jargon, reeling off euphemistic statements about "pacification" and "protective reaction strikes" when all along they were speaking of blood and destruction. How far can hatred and acceptance of violence "for the cause" carry "civilized" people in wartime? Despite all the evidence of extremes, it is still difficult to believe how many Americans defended Lt. William Calley, Jr.'s crimes as a fully acceptable response to the uncooperative behavior of Mai Lai villagers. During the Vietnam War years, we/they thinking reached great intensity *within* the United States, too—even to the point where millions heaped abuse upon groups of the nation's own youngsters loosely categorized as "hippies." Kent State became the classic example of we/they thinking directed within. Numerous mainstream Americans excused the shootings as an inevitable consequence of intemperate action by students. Their easy rationalization of violence stirs thoughts about the future. If politics become similarly strained in another era, might the hatreds of the Vietnam War period easily be evoked again?

It appears that much of this readiness to sanction violence derives from an "eye for an eye" mentality. Rather than bemoan tragedies of violence and search for ways to prevent recurrences, Americans seem anxious to meet crises with cries for vengeance and bloodshed. In the 1960s many who saw pictures of teenage rioters looting stores and walking off with TV sets under their arms urged the police to shoot offenders against property. "Overkill" seems to be the most descriptive word for this kind of reaction—a tendency to respond to problems of violence with the deterrent of greater, even more outrageous violence. For a verbally dramatic, extreme example of this reaction, consider a ludicrous comment from an Alabama businessman on hearing news of the assassination attempt on Governor George Wallace in Maryland. "It's awful, and we wish we could blow up the whole state of Maryland," bellowed the incensed businessman.[6] It is not that we should interpret the Alabaman's statement literally. His response is relevant not because he really wanted to wipe out the population of a state, but because it reveals how an angry and frustrated citizen couches his emotions in violent terms. It is a typical response: violent thoughts to meet violent challenges, tough talk in reaction to tough problems.

For all the toughness Americans boast about, for all their outspoken confidence in the effectiveness of violent deterrents, we find that, below the surface, Americans are an extremely nervous and fearful people. Increasingly they hide behind locks, gates, guards, and walls. Many keep guns at home or work for "self-defense." Some belong to vigilante-style groups dedicated to counter-terror against the violent people who threaten their safety every day. Watching all this nervous, frenetic activity, which belies declarations of confidence, one cannot help thinking that, given modern-day conditions in America, such responses are to be expected. People are fearful because the danger is real. Since *society* does little to combat the problem in an organized way, the *individual* has to fend for himself in the best way possible. No wonder he turns to locks, alarms, guns, and vigilante groups, trying anything he can to protect himself against danger. The more uncontrolled violence grows, the more obsessed individuals become with two extreme options: to run away completely or to make a stand by "fighting fire with fire."

In view of this situation, simple distinctions between guilty killers and innocent victims no longer seem applicable. Now most killers look like victims too. They are victims of an environment that places extraordinary stress on violence as a means of confronting problems and settling scores. They grow up as students in a "school of violence," for violence oriented values are an important aspect of the American way of life. In this sense it is appropriate to feel compassion rather than contempt for many of the violent criminals in America. One can appreciate, for example, how easily a young man, particularly a poor young man, can become involved in petty crime without realizing that his first minor confrontations with the police mark the beginnings of a career in crime. A criminal record can easily throw him into a vicious circle. Efforts to reform his life may only bring frustration. Job opportunities and social elevation do not come easily to people with criminal records. Finding little hope in mainstream society and becoming increasingly spiteful toward its Establishment, this angry individual frequently turns to more crime as the clearest avenue toward money and, possibly, some measure of self-fulfillment.

Once a young man decides to engage in criminal activities, guns become a likely appurtenance of his trade. Giving little thought to the potentially serious consequences of equipping himself with a lethal weapon, he sets out mobilized for the challenges of a gun-wielding society. His potential victim also loads up. In this buildup toward a confrontation, the young man prepares himself either for a trip to the hospital or morgue or for a deeper commitment to violent crime. And, on the other side, the person who anticipates attacks ready with his own arsenal risks precipitating his own death or becoming a killer himself. These are buildups toward unnecessarily deadly confrontations between attackers and defenders, both victims of a violent environment, both entrapped by situations where bullets often bring quick and final solutions to minor problems. Sooner or later the armed attacker or the person who fears him may have cause to fire away. When this day of reckoning arrives, when the criminal shoots the defender or the defender beats him to the trigger, serious violence occurs with instant fury.

An isolated news story illustrates the tragic occurrences which easily develop in violent societies. It involves three men, all of them victims of a pervasive malaise. The first, an eighteen year old, fell into a life of crime. During an armed robbery, the second, his accomplice, was shot to death. Later, the third man, a brother of the slain man, watched calmly at the teenager's trial. After a six- to twelve-year sentence was pronounced, the bereaved brother rushed up, pulled out a concealed pistol, and shot the youngster to death. He then prepared for his own homicide trial.[7]

How can we evaluate such a triple-victim episode? Who should be blamed? Who should be forgiven? Actually, there should be sympathy for all three. We can understand how the teenager fell victim to a social milieu in which armed robbery had become an increasingly popular profession for urban youth. The slain man became victim of the rampant crime which now paralyzes much of urban life. And his brother fell victim to his own exasperation, an uncontrollable anger at the pain of being left with the consequences of violence and no means of attaining satisfactory retribution or compensation. All three were victims of pervasive violence. All three were caught up in a society troubled by killers, the killed, and citizens who want to kill the killers.

Without being alarmists, from the diverse examples we can draw some conclusions which are far from optimistic. We know that violence is not unique to America, yet we cannot deny the prominence of bloody thinking and action in what is supposedly the world's most developed nation. It is not that Americans are a naturally bloodthirsty bunch; indeed, they show much humaneness in their character. But somehow we seem to have lost control. It is disconcerting to see unmanaged conditions and attitudes that reflect a sense of drift and fatalism.

Can the roots of the present problem be summarized succinctly? Although any listing of a few broad generalizations cannot apply to every person in the society, we can at least try to delineate what appear to be some major sources of difficulty. The list might look like this:

Why Violence Plagues Americans
1. Americans usually refuse to acknowledge that violence is a pervasive problem in their society until a shocking occurrence shakes their confidence.
2. When an event does stir them into complaining about violence, they show tremendous disagreement about its causes.
3. Lacking consensus about the causes of violence, they cannot decide upon effective solutions.
4. Since they have no solutions, Americans rely on the hope that somehow the society will muddle through and that they, personally, will find ways to avoid becoming victims of violence.

While we would like to be optimistic about the future of American society, the implications of this little list does not inspire confidence. Surely we cannot say that greater problems in the future are inevitable. When people themselves create a problem, outcomes are anything but inevitable. Nevertheless, a candid observer cannot erase the impression that people's ostrich-like escape efforts and laissez-faire responses spell continued trouble. Americans seem quick to resign to conditions with a *que será será* attitude. Instead of expressing confidence that things can be different, they talk of violence as an unfortunate "reality," as "part of life," or as something that cannot be expected to go away. They appear to be so enmeshed in a violent culture that they cannot recognize how problems of violence contribute to the decline of civilization. No wonder they cannot see violence as representing the very antithesis of civilization.

2
FEAR

In 1964 Americans were shocked to learn the horrible fate of a twenty-eight-year old woman outside her home in a staid, middle-class section of Queens, New York. While thirty-eight residents of her apartment unit watched from their windows, a man stalked and stabbed Kitty Genovese in three separate knifing attacks. On several occasions, Miss Genovese gave blood-curdling screams as she attempted to fend off the attacker and crawl toward a door to her apartment building. Most of the witnesses just looked on as if they were watching a television thriller. Some called out, imploring the attacker to stop. Yet none called the police. Shortly after Miss Genovese's body turned cold from the final attack, someone notified authorities. Police arrived on the scene within two minutes. Had anyone called them during the victim's thirty-seven minute ordeal, she probably could have been saved.[1]

How could it happen? Why didn't witnesses do something? In a more primitive society some witnesses might be expected to refrain from action because any involvement would require substantial personal risk from physical intervention. But in the modern metropolis, onlookers were only a telephone call away from demonstrating even the most modest form of responsibility.

After publicity on the Genovese case, social scientists and laymen conjectured on how so many could watch brutality without responding to help the victim. Some thought the witnesses' reaction reflected conditions of life in a metropolis. People lack feelings of community closeness, they said, and city folk have difficulty empathizing with the problems of a total stranger in a population of millions. The Genovese case could not have occurred in a small town, they asserted. Others suggested that witnesses reacted to crisis with numbness because they had been long exposed to such violence through the media of TV and film. Just as they had been passive witnesses to an astronomical number of crimes presented as visual entertainment, so they remained passive witnesses when confronted with the real thing. Long conditioned to watching fictionalized murder unblinkingly, they could not change roles quickly enough when faced with a true crisis.[2] These interpretations probably hold considerable validity, as suggested by discussion in other sections of this study. But there is another element in the Genovese case which highlights, in extreme form, a feeling which increasingly overwhelms and incapacitates Americans in cities, large and small. It is the element of fear.

In the Genovese case and others like it, witnesses to violent crime worry that their intervention can, in some way, make them victims as well. This fear was probably unjustified in the Genovese case, but it apparently was very present in the minds of witnesses. Could they be certain that the vicious attacker would not go after them if he learned their identity? One angry letter-writer to a newspaper revealed this concern unabashedly, claiming that in situations like the Genovese incident, the police will give names of informants to the newspapers, "with danger of reprisals always present."[3] Newspaper editors clarified the issue, assuring readers that the police did not release informants' names for publication. Still, the perception of a loss of anonymity is significant. As psychiatrist George Serbans reflects on this phenomenon, "It's the air of all New York, the air of injustice, the feeling that you might get hurt if you act and that, whatever you do, you will be the one to suffer."[4]

Such fear is more valid in the frequent cases where witnesses are not in easy reach of a telephone and are realistically frightened and intimidated. The abundant examples of passenger reaction to brutal behavior in subways reveals very calculated assessments of the possible dangers of intervention. These situations are similar to a scene in the film *The French Connection* when one passenger tries to stop an armed troublemaker, only to be shot down. Such slaughtering of good samaritan interveners occurs in real life too, as in the case of Arthur Rubinow. A kindly man, he admonished a tough who was bothering subway passengers. The tough shot him to death. This incident realizes some of the most horrible thoughts of witnesses to subway violence who have no immediate protection for themselves. One wonders what the panicked passengers on a New York BMT train were thinking as they watched seven youths rampage through their car, then surround and knock down a seventy-nine-year-old man and take $5 from him. Not only did the passengers decide against aiding the man, but when a newspaper reporter interviewed him, he asked that his name not be printed.[5] Another scene involving several passive witnesses ended tragically. On a subway platform in North Philadelphia four youths approached two Temple University students and asked for a cigarette, then demanded some change (reports of the amount varied from fifty cents to a dollar). When the college students said they had no money, the youths attacked them, leaving one wounded and the other knifed to death. More than a dozen persons watched the incident—about five or six standing on the platform where the knifing occurred and the remainder watching from a platform across the tracks.[6]

Like New Yorkers who agonized over the Genovese case, the Philadelphia subway episode produced complaints and explanations from many worried Philadelphians. Numerous citizens criticized the witnesses for their cowardice. This is a popular response, yet it is not difficult to imagine still more tragic consequences resulting from the intervention of just a few unarmed witnesses, male and female, of varying physical condition.

A newspaper editorial expressed sympathy for the harried subway patrons, saying, "No one who has stood on a lonely subway platform can doubt that fear of crime is one factor in the decrease of seven million subway fares last year." Another editorial commented that, "for too many of these subway riders, the ordinary act of taking the subway to work or to shop requires a disproportionate display of courage. This is no way for a city to live."[7]

As reporters interviewed friends and students in the area, evidence of strong fears extending well beyond the subway station came to light. One coed who had given up on the rapid transit system because "the subway isn't safe" found that driving to school did not alleviate her tensions. At night she had to be escorted regularly from school to the parking lot. "I hold my breath until I get into the car," she admitted. A male student who resided in the same building as the subway platform victim said he had been in fear of his life since he moved into the apartment house. "This is the only place I could find, and it's out of the area that the Temple security guards patrol." The situation being what it is, one ought to sympathize with the nervous security guards as well as the frightened residents.[8]

Stories of rampant violence and widespread fear in Philadelphia are personally troubling, for I recall many enjoyable experiences made possible by the city's transit system during my first seventeen years as a Philadelphia resident. Of course, there were times when adolescents had aggressive encounters with each other, but these were usually minor incidents. Citizens, young and old, black and white, were not plagued with the fear of imminent danger that plagues Philadelphians today. In the 1950s youths frequently took the "El" during the day or night to enjoy center-city attractions. Guys and their dates rode the transit system together to visit the theater, to attend a baseball or football game or to enjoy a shopping adventure. Thoughts of assault hardly crossed their minds, and uniformed policemen were certainly not familiar figures among the passengers. By the time of the subway platform murder, Philadelphia's law enforcement authorities had 117 patrolmen and twenty police dogs assigned to its transit unit. When the public expressed outrage over the knifing incident, Mayor Frank Rizzo said he hoped the federal government would honor his request for funds to hire 900 additional policemen (many of whom could help beef up subway security).[9]

As big-city residents know, expansion of police forces does not necessarily bring greater confidence and security. Nervousness continues to mount, despite substantial improvement and enlargement of law enforcement agencies. In a Gallop poll released in April 1972, for example, statistics showed extraordinary increases in the level of tension. Forty-one percent of those polled said they were afraid to walk at night in their neighborhoods. Fifty-eight percent of the women admitted they were afraid to go out alone at night. Figures for a variety of other categories measuring insecurity were sharply higher than those reported for the same questions in a 1968 poll. And, significantly, increases were much higher for smaller cities (population 2,500 to 50,000) than for larger ones.[10] This increase in fear cannot be dismissed as paranoia. Increases in the rate of violent crime give substance to such fears. During the 1960-1970 decade the nationwide rate of violent crime rose 156 percent, according to the FBI's Uniform Crime Report. This figure accounts for the population increase; the absolute increase was 176 percent.[11] The figures for violent crimes continued to rise sharply in the following years, even when the reported increases for other kinds of crimes began to slow. Moreover, as we shall discuss later, the actual level of violent crime is much higher than the FBI reports indicate.

Whatever figures are accepted, numbers alone cannot adequately portray the human consequences. Who are the people behind these statistics? What is the nature of their tragedies? A glance at some individual cases from one category, homicide connected with robberies, offers perspectives which numbers can never provide and a clearer understanding of why fear of violence increasingly haunts urban residents.

Violence, when committed against the good and the kind, holds special poignancy. The name of Dominick Nanna, a New York A&P store manager, does not stand out in the galaxy of American folk heroes, but to the customers who knew him Nanna was a special, unforgettable individual. He was the man who gave dignity to life in a crowded city. Nanna took time out to put away boxes for the neighborhood kids' hamsters, he advised customers carefully on the best kind and size of turkey for Thanksgiving, and he helped the blind make collections. He would always flash a smile to break the boredom of customers waiting in long lines at the checkout counter. "There are few people in this world who practice goodness and morality and he was one of them," said a client after Nanna's tragedy. "When he appeared in the store, it was like the sun came out in the room," she said. "There was nothing too much for that man to do . . . He wasn't just a shopkeeper. He was so human." Another customer attested, "This was one of the most marvelous men who ever lived," and a fourteen-year-old girl agreed in her own language: "He was really cool."

What snuffed out the life of this special person? A robbery accompanied by an act of violence far out of proportion to any-thing the robbers needed to protect themselves or extract profits from their victims. In June 1970 four men moved in on Nanna's store in an attack plan befitting a major bank robbery. While one posted himself outside, three entered in the presence of about twenty customers and approached the manager. They demanded he open the safe. Nanna smiled in apparent disbelief. "I'm not kidding. Move to the safe and open it," one insisted. Nanna was still smiling when a blast from a sawed-off shotgun ripped into his chest. As the would-be robbers fled, Nanna's fourteen-year-old son pursued them down the street. He caught one and tangled with him until a second culprit pounded the youngster on the head four times with a revolver, knocking him to the ground.[12]

Let us look more closely at another "statistic." Psychiatrist Richard Stamm should also be remembered in a special way, though his name, too, is obscure. For years Stamm and his wife had been civil rights activists and dedicated friends of the poor. The Stamms counseled people in trouble and gave them money when they needed legal counsel. In November 1972 Richard Stamm was involved in one of his typical projects—he was on his way to deliver bail money in a poor neighborhood in Bridgeport, Connecticut—when someone mugged him near his car and ran off with his watch and wallet. Stamm refused medical help when he was found in the lot dazed and beaten. He went home, talked about the experience with his wife, and expressed no resentment or bitterness about what had happened. But a short time later he succumbed to head injuries. Another good man lost, another statistic in the curve of criminal violence.[13]

There are many others like Nanna and Stamm. Big-city newspapers contain numerous reports of these incidents every day—so many that often each case is relegated to a back section of the paper designed to concentrate listings of violent crimes.[14] From these short descriptions of cases involving elderly people, for instance, we wonder why thieves resort to brutal acts in carrying out petty crimes against mostly defenseless victims. We question how necessary it was for a robber to slay ninety-two-year-old Michael Kochmanowicz, a popular old soul in his Philadelphia neighborhood, known for his love of flowers and children. The thief got off with Kochmanowicz's wallet.[15] And what of the life of a seventy-eight-year-old woman robbed of $1.75? She died of a heart attack after a thief beat her. Or the life of an eighty-three-year-old Philadelphia man strangled by an intruder who ran off with his jar of pennies and TV set?[16]

The increasing brutality accompanying petty crimes is the most distressing aspect of America's much-discussed "crime-wave." It is a frightening problem familiar to those who have lived and worked in America's big cities. I recall one particularly informative discussion about the changing character of crime with a physician who worked the night shift in a Cleveland hospital. The doctor gave bone-chilling reports of cases brought for his attention, cases in which victims of petty street robberies were frequently rolled into the emergency room with critical gunshot wounds. In earlier years thieves usually tried to scare victims into handing over a pocketbook or a wallet, the physician said. Sometimes they would wallop you over the head in order to gain the desired goods. But now the confrontations are very different, he commented, shaking his head. Thieves carry guns, and they are not hesitant to fire them. From the many cases he had seen, it appeared that most shootings during robberies were completely unnecessary. The mere threat of a gun was enough to make victims entirely cooperative. Yet, somehow, armed robbers seemed to feel that violence was necessary to complete a crime. This pattern is very familiar to authorities associated with the law enforcement and judicial branches of government. A Chicago public prosecutor comments bluntly, "When I was a kid a guy would stick you up, take the money and run. Now they'll *kill* you. It's just wild. These f——ing kids will kill you."[17]

What compels the robber to commit these extreme acts of violence? In many incidents sadism and calculated self-interest so overlap that it is difficult to separate one from the other. For example, was it sadism that moved an ex-convict to blind a girl by tearing her pupils with broken glass or was it, as he claimed, to avoid identification after he stole a record player and a tape recorder?[18] In many cases of violent robbery it appears that armed intruders do, indeed, kill to avoid identification by the victim, however remote the possibility. Human lives become highly expendable in successful rip-offs.[19] Sometimes too it appears that violence takes place out of the sheer thrill of inflicting pain.

It is the violence in these crimes that most alarms the public. City dwellers worry about purse-snatching and wallet-stealing but most of all about the danger of being injured and killed in the process. In an outstanding study of the problem, *The Mugging,* Morton Hunt speaks of the "devastating" impact of violent crimes on American civilization, observing sadly that the "great cities sink slowly into medieval savagery."[20] This fear of becoming victim to violence eats away at the fabric of American life. As "unpredictable violent attacks upon one's person become an ever present and uncontrollable danger, the great mass of citizens lose their faith in the integrity and viability of society," says Hunt.

Those who live with this fear daily are best able to describe it. Louis S. Campbell, a thirty-nine-year-old Brooklynite of black and Puerto Rican parentage, grew up among fighting gangs and developed his physical fitness in the military service. As he walked home from evening college in years past, he worried for the safety of his family, but not for himself. All that has changed, as he explained in a letter to a newspaper:

Now I'm afraid, really afraid, because I can see my number coming up, and feel absolutely helpless . . . I am no longer a cocky combat-ready ex-Marine infantry sergeant. I am a frightened man returning home from work at night, looking behind me, to the side of me, to the front of me, wondering if tonight is the night I will get it . . .

One of these nights I will not be coming home to my wife and four-year-old son. I will have been the victim of one of the numerous packs of muggers that have turned the streets of Bedford-Stuyvesant-Williamsburgh into an asphalt jungle filled with terror and violence for my fellow black and Puerto Rican neighbors and myself and my family.[21]

In time, the cancer of mugging and its attendant fears have spread from the streets and into the city's business places and public buildings. At Lincoln Hospital in New York, for example, the staff only used to fear commuting to and from work. Once inside the hospital doors, however, they could breathe a sigh of relief; it seemed they had crossed the mugging frontier and entered the fort. But, by the early 1970s, fear began to permeate all levels *within* the hospital itself. From the elevator operators to the medical doctors on staff (not to mention security officers), workers worried about being victimized while walking the *hospital corridors.* "Many people just come in to see what they can carry out and sell, and if we ask what they are doing here, many threaten your life," reported a security officer. Surgeons operated behind locked and barricaded doors. One physician was so shaken that colleagues suggested a vacation so that he could regain his composure. Two other doctors refused to report to work until they could be guaranteed protection on the evening shift.[22]

What can nerve-racked city dwellers do in the face of such daily challenges? Some choose to grit their teeth and wait out the storm. This is the kind of steely determination shown by millions of urban Americans who refuse to surrender to omnipresent threats. Their spunk is admirable, but their long-term possibilities for success are doubtful. Even the most dedicated citizens can lose heart after a while. Such a test of will challenged a group of young idealists in New Brunswick, New Jersey, who tried to put their humane philosophy to work in a city plagued by crime. Graduates, undergraduates, and college dropouts from Rutgers University opened a nonprofit grocery store in an old neighborhood to service poor blacks, Puerto Ricans, and whites with food items at very reasonable prices. Local merchants grumbled that their project was a harebrained "hippie" scheme. The idealists persisted in their enterprise while suffering tremendous difficulties—not from competing merchants or lack of customers but from urban crime. In their first seven months of operation, the young merchants became victims of four armed holdups (including one at shotgun point), about a dozen burglaries, and countless shopliftings. Some of the workers fell to pistol-whippings and beatings by holdup men. Whether the "People's Store" could survive these constant threats was by no means certain. Unless there could be greater safety, it appeared that harsh realities would eventually defeat even the most determined idealists.[23]

Many prefer flight to fight. When the opportunity arises, they quickly migrate to the suburbs in search of both physical and mental security. As long as life in the metropolis remains precarious, who can blame them? The migratory patterns of New Yorkers and varied local responses to these demographic changes represent the trends in many other cities. For example, when newspapers report on New Yorkers who plan to move away because of fear, almost invariably someone writes a letter asking that the individuals manifest confidence in urban life and show the courage to stay. One New Yorker, Andrew Vascallaro, announced he was leaving "this jungle city" for the South to start a new life in a small town after his eighty-six-year-old father died from a mugging incident. The chairman of the Association for a Better New York wrote giving a typical pep talk: "I urge Mr. Vascallaro to reconsider. I want him to stay. New York needs him to fight back against those who are trying to rip this city apart."[24]

In another case a New York woman determined to move, despite appeals from friends, after her husband was robbed at knifepoint. Despite thirty years of enjoying the rich cosmopolitan life of New York, she did not feel guilt or shame about moving away. "Some of my friends, people who sound just like I used to sound, tell me I ought to stay and fight," she explained. "I don't want to stay and fight. I don't feel like fighting at all. If people want to kill each other, let them."[25]

Reactions of winners in the New York State lottery illustrate the magnitude of the urge to flee the city at the right opportunity. A *New York Times* random sample of twenty lottery winners in New York City who won $100,000 or more showed that eight had moved to another part of the country shortly after receiving their prize.[26] If such samples could be followed up after a few years, perhaps much more than 40 percent of the winners could be counted among those who decided to start a new life elsewhere. Though fear is not the only motivation for these people to resettle outside of New York City, it certainly appears to be a major one.

The rush to the suburbs has been so great in recent years that the movement has produced a major historical and demographic watershed. In the 1920s America became what may be called an urban nation, as reflected in census returns. For the first time in its history, the majority of people in the United States lived in cities and towns rather than the country. The 1970s brought a tripartite breakdown which reflected another historically symbolic statistical change: Americans became a people of the suburbs first, the urban cities second, and the countryside third. The 1970 census showed an absolute decline in the population of many large cities across the nation. The same census showed tremendous gains for suburban communities immediately across the city lines. The new Great Escape broke all previous records.

The escape to suburbia is often illusory. The first major shortcoming new suburbanites usually notice relates to employment. Home is in the outskirts but many of the better jobs are downtown in the metropolis. Hence, asylum now appears only partial: it applies more to their leisure activities, while vocational pursuits send them back into the "jungle." They hope their commuting can be fast and safe, for they want as little contact as possible with society between home and work. As the Violence Commission pointed out, city expressways have become high-speed, patrolled corridors connecting safe areas for these commuters.[27] These corridors too, can seem threatening to those who lose the mobility of their vehicles. One resident of a suburban

Chicago apartment reports carrying a gun in his car because he is afraid to stop with a flat tire on the Eisenhower Expressway.[28] Others choose to forego the job benefits of the center-city labor market because they feel the dangers far outweigh higher earnings. For example, during the 1971 job recession the executive director of Washington, D.C.'s Building Owners and Managers' Association reported: "Not long ago I ran an ad for a secretary and got 100 responses. But more than half the applicants would not even come by for an interview when I told them the office was downtown."[29]

The escape to suburbia is also illusory because crime and violence are spreading there along with the population. Thousands move to the suburbs hoping to free themselves of fear, but, in time, it catches up with them. The FBI Uniform Crime Reports, which are probably under-recorded anyway, show crime rising in the suburbs at three times the rate of large cities.[30] This startling figure can partly be attributed to its relatively low crime rate in earlier years; the increase began from a much smaller base figure than the one for larger cities. But in recent years the problem has mushroomed to serious proportions. Now suburbanites are beginning to experience the effects of ingenious criminal visitors, including the "commuter burglars." These residents of the inner city take daily commuter excursions to the wealthy suburbs, make their unappointed rounds, and return to the metropolis with their loot after a day's "work." In Scarsdale, New York, one of America's richest suburban communities, numerous residents have installed "panic buttons" in their homes for personal protection. These buttons send an alarm directly to police headquarters, thus providing a means for fast communication as well as psychological comfort. Others in Scarsdale have fortified themselves with locks, fences, or walls to the homes they once considered havens from the madness of the city. "More burglar alarms have been installed in Scarsdale than in any other community in America," conjectures one observer of the town's crime problem.[31]

Alarm systems such as those in Scarsdale are costly for both citizens and the police. Initial expenses for a good system range between $1,000 and $3,000; costs for leased telephone lines and maintenance run around $10 a month.[32] Police find the new, sophisticated alarm systems a nuisance. In the posh suburb of Englewood, New Jersey, the police chief reported on a typical month's problems: 155 alarms, of which "only a very small percentage were real." In a two-week period in New York City, of 8,602 alarms received, only 141 turned out to be valid. The New York City Police Department indicated 8,461 man-hours lost on false alarms during the period. Despite these problems, the manufacture of electronic detection devices and sophisticated alarm systems continues to boom, thanks to suburban nervousness. Some of the new systems are extraordinarily complex and impressive. For example, a former NASA engineer designed a floodlit golf course for a housing project featuring a $200,000 computerized warning system.[33] Not surprisingly, Merrill, Lynch, Pierce, Fenner and Smith made bullish predictions on the electronic warning system industry.[34]

For those who prefer more traditional security approaches, there are many other expensive options. New housing projects feature huge walls and guarded "checkpoint entrances." Some even include moats. Old-fashioned manned security also remains a big business. The mere supplying of security guards for offices, stores, parking lots, banks, and factories is a $3.3 billion a year industry. National estimates place the number of private policemen at twice the number of public law enforcement officers. Clearly, the search for security in America is very expensive. [35]

For the many Americans who cannot afford electronic alarm systems, walls, moats, or guards, personal "defensive" measures have become popular. Many prepare to meet threats of violence with counterviolence. Throughout the cities books and courses on judo and karate attract large numbers of people preoccupied with self-defense. Many keep guns for security. Public opinion polls indicate that more than one-third of those questioned report keeping firearms in the house for protection against criminals.[36] These protective weapons sometimes prove quite dangerous. In San Bernadino, California, for example, a husband left the house after his wife thought she heard prowlers. He returned to assure her there was no difficulty, but his jittery wife was unprepared for his early return. Hearing noises, she grabbed the family's .38 caliber pistol and fired four shots at a dark figure entering the front door. Both went to the hospital—the husband to have two bullets removed from his abdomen and the wife to be treated for shock.[37] In another case an armed defender's mistake almost proved tragic to youths on a rescue mission. When three Cincinnati teenagers saw flames going up in a multi-unit apartment building, they rushed in and began pounding on doors to alert residents. One occupant mistook the noise for a break-in attempt. He fired a bullet through the door, narrowly missing one of the boys. Because of the youths' bold deed, all but one of the residents escaped safely. The quick-triggered apartment defender escaped without harm after almost killing those who saved him.[38] Clearly, the security fetish not only costs much money; it can also cost lives.

Americans' fear of violent crime is costly too in its diminution of the quality of life. Visits to the home of a security-minded apartment dweller leaves one wondering about the degree to which people will enslave themselves in their quest for safety. Institutionalized paranoia greets a visitor at almost every turn. The home has become a fortress, protected by multiple defenses at various stages of entrance, analogous to the protective obstacles constructed for medieval castles or checkpoints limiting access to the Pentagon's inner rooms containing top-secret material. At the entrances of some apartment buildings, for example, guests are met by guards stealthily giving them the once-over for clearance. Inside, security men in para-police uniforms stand casually scattered about the lobby. In facilities with less manpower, one may enter what could be called a sub-lobby, where a telephone is available for making initial contact. After facing a television camera and conversing through an intercom system, the host recognizes his guest and produces a buzzing sound to indicate that the iron gate is ready to be opened. After an elevator ascent the visitor finally reaches the apartment entrance where his host doublechecks the doorbell with glimpses through a tiny peep hole, then unlatches the bolts and double locks. At last the door swings open. With all these elaborate preliminaries, one expects to be greeted by a mysterious character sitting at a huge desk, saying, "Come in, Mr. Bond. I have been expecting you." But this is not a movie fantasy. It is a *common* aspect of urban living—for those who can afford it.

A visitor to a city can notice abundant examples of nervous living, situations often unremarkable to city dwellers because they are so common. Public buses and delivery trucks display warnings with big letters, "Driver does not carry cash." Taxis contain thick glass and caging wire to separate driver from passenger. People erect barriers everywhere to protect themselves when making contact with the most dangerous form of life in the cities—other human beings. The comment of a New York delicatessen owner reflects the mood that makes these barriers necessary. When asked about working conditions in a bullet-proof booth he had constructed for his cashier after two late-night robberies, the proprietor admitted the new cramped, confining quarters could be uncomfortable for an employee, commenting, "I've been in the cage myself . . . there's no question about it. You feel like an animal. But what can you do? These are the times we live in."[39]

As these examples show, the cost of fear cannot be calculated simply in dollars and cents; it results from what is missing, what falls short in the everyday lives of people. No monetary outlay can fully counteract the price of fear. Americans talk about reordering priorities to spend billions on fast, new urban transit systems. Will the huge investment be worthwhile if the public is afraid to use the facilities once they open? Americans speak about ridding themselves of urban blight and replacing dilapidated buildings with beautiful city parks. Will many people *use* the parks, however attractive, if they fear violence? The changes in Morningside Park in New York are instructive. A black resident of the city reports that when she arrived in New York in the 1940s streets and parks were relatively safe. She very much enjoyed the urban environment during her youth by dancing in the casinos and sometimes sleeping all night in Morningside Park. When community leaders debated ways to improve facilities in the park in the 1960s, an angry woman loudly testified to the tremendous deterioration of city life just a quarter of a century later. She scoffed at the debates as irrelevant, pointing out that "everyone in the community knows that unless one wished to be mugged or knifed, no sane person would go near the park—night or day."[40]

A visitor from the country or small town is frequently surprised at the degree to which urbanites not only are afraid to use the city facilities, but also to talk with strangers.[41] To the outsider, those in the core area of a large city often seem to be a conglomeration of distrusting people. If a stranger begins a conversation spontaneously, many city dwellers are put off-guard. Some try to end discussions brusquely. Others are more polite, yet they exchange words with great caution, ever careful not to disclose any clue to their identity—a name, an address, a place of work. Many social scientists contend that an urbanite's craving for anonymity in the crowd is a product of his crowded environment. Perhaps so, but only to a degree. Probably more important is the urbanite's *fear* of the possible consequences of identification. He worries about a stranger's ulterior motives, and is concerned lest discussion lure him into a trap, revealing information that can make him a victim of armed robbery, sexual assault, or other criminal violence. These fears cannot be dismissed as unwarranted or paranoic. The record is frightening enough to excuse cold or rude responses to the inquiries of strangers. In some situations caution and discretion are preferable to the dangers of openness.

When future historians assess the course of America's troubles, they will probably conclude that the quality of urban life became one of the biggest victims of violence. As the Violence Commission reported, "Fear is destroying some of the basic human freedoms which any society is supposed to safeguard—freedom of movement, freedom from harm, freedom from fear itself."[42] In a most fundamental way, America's urban citizens are losing their freedom to enjoy life. They are losing a precious right to pass their days at work, at home, or at leisure in comfort and safety, to express friendship to acquaintances, and to find that expression reciprocated. They are losing the delightful freedom simply to walk out into the street and enjoy the sunshine, the night lights, or even the darkness without being followed by the shadow of fear.

3

CRIME

Although deeply troubled by violence, many Americans deny that the growth in criminal violence is any cause for alarm. Despite multitudinous evidence of very serious problems, they often go through complicated mental acrobatics to assure themselves that the difficulty is no worse than before and, perhaps, is getting a little better. Some note that criminal violence has been a perennial problem in America and warn the frightened against acting as if they had just discovered the problem. Others say violent crime will always vex society because it is a natural consequence of life in heavily populated urban environments. Some try to settle fears by citing the government's inaccurate crime statistics to argue that the wave of violence has already crested. All of these approaches represent head-in-the-sand attitudes toward an epidemic of criminal violence that badly needs treatment.

Placing violent crime in historical perspective has long been a popular way of quieting cries of outrage. Reports on present-day crime waves can be treated as alarmist when viewed alongside the numerous historical examples of previous crime waves in

American history. Descriptions from very sophisticated historians may easily be twisted to support contentions that violent crime will always be with us. For example, Carl Bridenbaugh's comment that colonial Boston showed steady increases in "assault, arson, breaking and entering, embezzlement, fighting and brawling, manslaughter, theft, and the reception of stolen goods" can be misconstrued to minimize recent reports of the same behavior.[1] Historian Charles Lockwood's findings can also easily be misinterpreted. Lockwood tells us that in the 1870s New Yorkers feared an "atmosphere of highway robbery, burglary and murder" throughout the city. *Wood's International Handbook of New York* (1873 edition) warned visitors to avoid "walking late in the evening, except in the busiest thoroughfares of the city," and in 1897 an observer reported that "human life is rather more secure in Arizona than in the streets of New York."[2]

Appreciating the recurrent nature of crime waves, many Americans viewed the evidence of mounting troubles in the 1950s and early 1960s with only a modicum of excitement. No need for panic or hysteria, they cautioned; we have seen this pattern many times before. Even some of the most respected social scientists added their skeptical observations, drawing amusement out of the hypothesis that conditions in modern times are no worse than before, and, perhaps, even a little better. Developing a persuasive analysis from this theme, sociologist Daniel Bell spoke of "The Myth of Crime Waves." Bell emphasized that "today the United States is a more lawful and safe country than popular opinion imagines." In fact, Bell found the contemporary homicide rate to be lower than that of a quarter century before. Then why the great clamor about crime? Because people *felt* that modern life was more violent than ever before. It was a matter of perception. In modern times there is greater "show" of violence through literature, newspapers, plays, and movies, explained Bell. With help from the media, citizens become more familiar with violence and crime, even though it is less prevalent in day-to-day life in America than 25, 50, or 100 years before.[3]

Daniel Bell's smooth, relaxed, and clever interpretation of *organized* crime anticipated the pooh-poohing of fears about crime that became fashionable in later scholarship. Bell especially enjoyed poking fun at the Cassandras of violent crime by questioning popular images of the Italian gangster. He spoke of the "legend" and the "myth" of the Mafia and asked whether such a violent and clandestine organization really existed. If some Sicilian gangsters had made news in days past, that was a case for the history books, Bell concluded, "for the mobsters, by and large, had immigrant roots, and crime, as the pattern showed, was a route of social ascent and place in American life."[4] In the early 1970s elaborate in-depth studies by Francis Ianni and Gay Talese expanded Bell's thesis to show that the sons and grandsons of mafiosi leaders had worked their way into the professions; they had become doctors, lawyers, college professors, and business executives. In short, the pattern reflected the progress of family generations in America—from the first immigrants' highly competitive "anything goes" struggle to the second and third generations' ensconcement in the Establishment. Of the remaining figures who had engaged in organized crime through earlier decades, their activities were now much more legitimate. Long ago they had forsworn violence, and now most of their income came from respectable sources.[5] This, in Bell's terms, was the "Embourgeoisement of Crime."

In 1971 the Mafia image once again looked much more like reality than legend, and by 1972 the "Embourgeoisement of Crime" thesis drowned in a pool of blood. During the second annual "Unity Rally" of the Italian-American Civil Rights League, reputed Mafia leader Joe Colombo fell unconscious with three bullets in the back of his head. Over the next year mafiosi henchmen gunned down more than a dozen gangland figures in struggles linked to competition between the Colombo and Gallo families. Revenge occurred when gunmen calmly mowed down Joe Gallo in a twenty-bullet execution at Umberto's Clam House. The war raged on. Just a few months later four Colombo men were targeted as they sat at a front bar in the Neopolitan Noodle restaurant. When they moved to a table at the back of the restaurant, four unfortunate businessmen took their seats. Within minutes a man walked in, pulled out two guns and fired away, killing two of the mistaken victims and leaving the other two seriously injured. So much for the "death of the Mafia." Crime-watchers simply had not appreciated the dogged persistence of violent tactics. Like guesses about violent crime in general, wishful speculation about the decline of bloodshed among "professionals" turned out to be precisely that—wishful speculation.[6]

What *was* happening in these years? Just in terms of general figures supplied by the FBI's Uniform Crime Reports, the trend looked quite serious. For the period 1960-1970, even with the general population increase taken into account (as in all of the rate figures listed below), curves rose sharply. For example, larceny and theft (defined as unlawful taking or stealing of property or articles of value without the use of force or violence or fraud) soared to a 204 percent increase during the decade. Another "nonviolent category," burglary (unlawful entry of a structure to commit a felony or theft even though no force is used to gain entrance), increased by 113 percent in the period. As mentioned earlier, figures in the category of violent crime increased generally at a rate of 156 percent during the decade. Robbery (which implies the use of force or threat of force) rose at the disquieting rate of 186 percent. In six out of ten cases the robber used arms. Among reported cases of armed robbery, 63 percent involved firearms, 24 percent a knife or other cutting instrument, and 13 percent blunt objects.[7] For a glimpse at the number of people involved, consider the following rounded figures from FBI reports for a later period, the decade 1962-1972. In 1962 police agencies reported 8,460 murders; in 1972 the number was 18,520. In 1962 17,400 rapes were reported; in 1972, 46,400. Robberies more than tripled during the decade from 110,300 to 374,600; aggravated assaults more than doubled, from 163,000 to 389,000.[8]

It is little wonder that presidential candidate Richard Nixon received nods of agreement from audiences who heard him campaign in 1968 with the claim that "crime is rising nine times faster than the population." Nixon's charge that "Lawlessness is crumbling the foundations of American society" sounded very plausible to millions of voters who went to the polls hoping the Republican candidate would "do something" about crime and violence.[9]

During the Nixon years in the White House, some real gains did develop in the struggle against crime in the streets but not nearly as much as political spokesmen tried to suggest. From 1969 to 1974 police forces beefed up their numbers and trained their officers in modern techniques of law enforcement and methods to improve community relations (training that owed a great deal to the recommendations of President Johnson's Commission on Law Enforcement and the Administration of Justice). Reorganizational efforts began in other sectors of the government too. The courts experimented with ways to expedite trials, and Supreme Court decisions, such as the one which determined that a verdict need not be unanimous in certain kinds of criminal trials, enabled faster decisions. At the community level, groups experimented with diverse approaches such as planning new youth activities and organizing vigilante committees for citizens' protection. Overall, these represented holding actions, piecemeal efforts, with inadequate remedies. Nevertheless, news of such efforts on many different fronts, *in combination* with reports on improvement in the FBI statistics, tricked the American public into believing that, at last, there was light at the end of the tunnel.

The Nixon Administration congratulated itself for effecting an "improvement" in the war against crime based on the FBI's Uniform Crime Reports. Spokesmen for the Administration, as well as Nixon himself, bragged about the data which, according to their claims, showed that the rapid crime rise was finally slowing down. Their interpretation was sadly amusing. Yes, the overall rate of crime continued to increase during the first four years of the Nixon Administration, they admitted, but the *rate* of increase had declined year by year. In contrast to the whopping 17 percent increase in 1968, crime increased by only 6 percent in 1971, and the rate for 1972 decreased by 2 percent.[10]

In some speeches Nixon particularly emphasized Washington, D.C., which was expected to be a model of improvement under the President's experiment with a tougher "law and order" program in the Federal District. Boasting that Washington "is one of the safest cities in the country for the millions of tourists who come here," Nixon claimed that the crime rate in Washington had been "cut in half" during the first three years of his Administration.[11] Yet, about a year later visitors were still being warned of the dangers of walking near the White House or the Capitol at night, and Senator John Stennis was robbed and critically shot outside his Washington home. Furthermore, when a Washington newspaper asked newly elected congressmen how they felt about the safety of Washington, thirty-four replied they believed the city was not as safe as their home communities, while only three said they thought it was as safe.[12] Apparently, the new congressmen did not share the President's confidence. Nor did many Americans believe the optimistic figures about the country in general, judging from chatter about the frightening incidents of violent crime that they knew about from friends' reports or from personal experience.

How could crime and violence appear much more serious than years before when the statistics showed no major increases during the Nixon Administration? Was the "feeling" just an illusion? Apparently not. Much of the difference between what was apparent and what reports indicated arose from sloppy and biased means of collecting data. For a modern nation with a highly advanced technology, America's compilation of national crime statistics is appallingly backward and laden with potential for error.

What are the shortcomings? First, various police departments have varying notions about categorizing crimes. Although the fundamentals for definition are spelled out on paper, police agencies differ greatly in recording the seriousness of a particular incident. Second, the FBI figures show crimes *reported* to the police, figures that may be very far from the actual number committed. Some people are afraid to "become involved;" many others feel crime is so widespread and out of control that their information is worthless. Believing the police have little chance to solve most crimes, they despairingly accept their loss of property or personal injury as a *fait accompli.* Third, and perhaps most important, the police themselves knowingly influence the statistics they report to the FBI. Celebrated reports of "declining increases" in the crime rate look less impressive in view of the tremendous political pressures on precinct officers to show decreasing crime rates in their communities.[13]

During the years of the Nixon Administration, local statistics became politically volatile material, subject to manipulation by the agents who collected and reported them. Mayors, police chiefs, councilmen, and other community officials, as well as the national political leaders in Washington, D.C., had vested interests in the situation and very much wanted to see data trends that could mollify an angry public. Amid this great apprehension over the "crime wave," apparently many police departments purposely downgraded their reports on serious crimes in order to appear successful in their war against crime. In Baltimore, for example, citizens hailed a report that the crime rate for their city had dropped 15.1 percent in the first six months of 1972—a figure which went on to the FBI for compilation in the Uniform Crime Report. Suspicious journalists for the *Baltimore Sun* discovered, however, that in 102 larceny reports the police failed to record assaults in nine out of ten cases. The Baltimore Police Department followed up with an investigation of itself and found that in 50 of a sample of 191 larceny reports the investigating officer failed to note actual or threatened assaults on victims. In one of the typical cases reported as simple robbery of less than $50, they found that the victim's claim of having been repeatedly hit in the face and the fact that his head was wrapped in bloody bandages during the police interview had been omitted from the report.[14]

In 1973 the Census Bureau added to the skepticism about local data collection with an eye-opening report on its first, tentative findings from a special pilot study. Working through the Law Enforcement Assistance Administration, the Bureau tried to measure the extent of crime in America without depending on police department figures reported to the FBI. Through extensive surveys of victims in the sample cities of Dayton, Ohio, and San Jose, California, census officials found that robberies and rapes occurred at *twice* the number reported to the police and aggravated assaults occurred at *five times* that number.[15]

In April 1974 the Law Enforcement Assistance Administration released still more devastating information, since the new report was based on careful study of crime in the nation's five largest cities—Philadelphia, New York, Chicago, Detroit, and Los

Angeles. During 1973 the agency had questioned people directly in 25,000 households and 10,000 businesses regarding their personal experiences with crime in the year 1972. The results showed actual crime much greater than the amount reported by police in the five cities. Figures from Philadelphia were the highest and most surprising: the study found that about 80 percent of Philadelphia crimes went unreported. Philly's embarrassed "law and order" mayor scoffed, declaring the study "farfetched." Overall, the investigation revealed some startling statistics about the size of the victim populations. For each thousand residents there were 68 violent crimes in Detroit, 63 in Philadelphia, 56 in Chicago, 53 in Los Angeles, and 36 in New York.[16]

Even the figures released by the FBI in 1974 showed significant increases. The Uniform Crime Report showed serious crime up by 6 percent for 1973. Moreover, FBI computers showed a spurting 16 percent increase for the last quarter of 1973 and a 15 percent increase for the first quarter of 1974. Perhaps the publicity about inaccurate reporting was prompting local police departments to turn in more realistic figures.[17]

In view of the political manipulation of local crime reports and the failure or reluctance of many people to report crimes to the police or other authorities, it is outrageous that political leaders should attempt to interpret minor changes in the present Uniform Crime Reports as accurate indications of major trends. Potential fudge factors and margins of error are so great in the FBI reports that a sophisticated statistician would be nauseated by popular efforts to draw optimistic conclusions from these data. Clearly, the FBI figures could not pass rigid statistical "tests of significance." As the Uniform Crime Reports now stand, they are worse than useless on the question of whether crime is rising or falling. The much discussed reports of declining crime "increases," or even actual decreases in the 1960s and 1970s, were probably far from the truth. We may make a respectable guess that during the period in question, crime in general actually increased steadily, and violent crime in particular accelerated at an extraordinary rate.

It is time that a modern nation with a serious crime problem learns to plot its data accurately so that its people can know the true dimensions and character of their difficulties. No matter how carefully the FBI's computers calculate percentages, the resulting figures are dubious if original data are inconsistent and only partially valid. As the President's Commission on Law Enforcement and the Administration of Justice commented in 1967, the government should be able to plot levels of crime in a city or state as precisely as the Census Bureau and the Department of Labor plot rates of unemployment.[18] The seriousness of violent crime calls for more sophisticated recording so that reports can be free of political influence.

While politicians and social scientists will, no doubt, continue to disagree over trends of rising or declining crime rates, almost all can agree on the geographic concentration of violent crime. There is an extraordinarily disproportionate incidence of violent crime in large cities. Crime rates for the metropolises are approximately eight times greater than rates for small towns. Occasionally, statisticians of crime play some amusing games with these figures, indicating, for example, that if you live in a metropolitan area, your chances of becoming a victim of homicide, rape, assault, or robbery are 1 in 125 each year. Any person walking the streets in a high-crime area at night does not need probability ratios to alert him to his precarious situation.[19]

Why so much criminal violence in the cities? Long before Americans had even the incomplete Uniform Crime Reports at their disposal, observers of the crime problem commented frequently on its particularly urban nature. They considered violent crime as an extreme example of the antisocial behavior typical of a large metropolis. Commentators on city life noticed this relationship long ago, as, for example, in the Biblical prophet Ezekiel's observation, "The land is full of bloody crimes, and the city is full of violence." The long-familiar correlation seemed to suggest that a concentration of people in urban centers contributed to the difficulty. "Cities give not the human senses room enough," noted Ralph Waldo Emerson in an intuitive explanation. In the twentieth century scientific researchers explored this idea more methodically. Ethologists, psychologists, and biologists found the correlation between population concentration and violent crime very enticing. According to some of their explanations, even the lower forms of animal life, such as worms, give off lethal toxins in overcrowded conditions. Studies reveal also that relatively small doses of amphetamines can kill rats confined in a cage with many other rats, but rats kept in isolation can survive doses up to four times higher. This evidence suggests nature may have its own chemical controls to help prevent over-population.[20] Zoologist Desmond Morris imaginatively speculates on high population density for human behavior in his book *The Human Zoo*. Referring to the city as something akin to a "human zoo," Morris comments:

> Under normal conditions, in their natural habitat, wild animals do not mutilate themselves, masturbate, attack their offspring, develop stomach ulcers, become fetishists, suffer from obesity or commit murder. Among city dwellers, needless to say, all of these things occur. Does this, then, reveal a basic difference between the human species and other wild animals? . . . The zoo animal in a cage exhibits all these abnormalities that we know so well from our human companions. Clearly, then, the city is not a concrete jungle, it is a human zoo.[21]

After comparing the behavior of city dwellers with that of captive animals, Morris concludes: "We think of claustrophobia as an abnormal response. In its extreme form it is, but in a milder, less clearly recognized form it is a condition from which all city-dwellers suffer."[22]

Many social scientists, studying people rather than animals, also worry about the way overcrowded cities may aggravate human aggression and violence. Rejecting theories which relate antisocial behavior to animal instincts, psychologist Elton B. McNeil sees city life as an important factor. "Man's animal nature is a feeble excuse for violence; a more reasonable explanation is that the seemingly senseless violence of humans is one of the costs of urban living," says McNeil.[23] Many social scientists describe how crowded urban conditions produce social disintegration and anomie (the condition of an individual in which normative standards of conduct weaken, leading to personal disorientation, anxiety, and social dislocation). They worry about the impact of demographic trends on urban populations in the future. America is already predominantly urban, and scientists speak with concern about the growth of future "megalopolises"—huge urban areas, such as the region between Boston and Washington, D.C., that will soon seem like one long, stretched-out urban complex. Every year additional thousands of people relocate in large cities. "What will be the consequence for mental health of a continuing massive increase in human populations?" asks George M. Carstairs. He answers with disturbing uncertainty: we simply do not know.[24]

Still, American cities need not head straight toward civil Armageddon. Even population density does not fully explain the increase in urban violence in America, since, for a great number of large cities, population has remained steady or actually declined in the last decade. Americans are spreading out; they are spilling into ever-expanding suburbs. Resident population within the basic city limits is, in many places, less than it was earlier. Though one might counter this observation by noting that the daily influx of suburbanites into the city proper greatly augments its population in daylight hours, this point hardly explains the greater incidence of urban violence in residential neighborhoods (where there are fewer commuters) and at night (when most commuters are outside the city again).

Anyone familiar with various foreign countries knows that large cities do not have to be "jungles," "zoos," or whatever. The violent crime records of other advanced nations make interesting comparison. For example, gun murders in the United States averaged about 6,500 per year when the nation's population stood at 200 million, while England, Germany, and Japan with a total population of 214 million averaged about 135 gun murders per year.[25] Violent crime is not a serious problem in great cities like Tokyo and London. Orange County, California, averages almost as many homicides per year as the entire Greater London area, which has a population ten times larger.[26] "People can still walk abroad in London at night with little fear of being molested," reports London Police Commissioner Sir John Waldron.[27] This comforting feeling is one of the pleasures of an American's visit to England, Denmark, Germany, or Japan.

We should also note that within American cities, various social groups show strikingly different tendencies toward violence, a pattern that suggests population density alone does not necessarily lead to trouble. The relationship of nonviolent behavior to economic status is especially obvious. Among upper-class residents of urban complexes, the likelihood of engagement in violent crime is miniscule in comparison with the probability for lower-class city dwellers, even though both may experience equal population density. Congestion, depersonalization, and other consequences of city life may heighten the irritability or nervousness of wealthy urban citizens, but these conditions do not produce many dangerous characters among them anxious for criminal assault. An urbane millionaire mugger is scarcely to be found.

Age seems to be another very important factor in violent crime. The record of involvement among young people between the ages of fifteen and twenty-four is strikingly serious and far out of proportion to the records of other age categories.[28]

Finally, various ethnic groups in urban areas have extraordinarily clear records for violent crime, a pattern that further undermines the population density theory. For instance, Japanese-Americans show very low incidence of violent crime, although a disproportionate number of them live in the cities. Even when Japanese-Americans were very poor (as most of them were when they first came to America as immigrants or after World War II, following confiscation of their property and release from detention camps), they maintained a record of good citizenship. Their experience in America, therefore, is more than just an economic success story. Amid rising urban violence, Japanese-Americans strengthened their community ties and remained impressively nonviolent. In Los Angeles County, for example, their small crime figures actually decreased over recent years while the rates for both white and black Americans soared.[29]

The spiraling rates of violent crime that frighten Americans need not be accepted as inevitable consequences of urban life. People *can* live in cities and deal with each other in a civilized manner. But this potential for progress offers little immediate solace to the many who must live daily with the reality of robbery, brutality, and killing. Americans are a highly nervous people, anxious to find some sense of relief. Often they consider the most attractive deterrent a combination of toughness, counter-violence, and hard-line political stances commonly identified as a "law and order" approach.

4

LAW AND ORDER

"Law and Order" has become a household term in modern America, an intensely controversial phrase that stirs great emotion among citizens who support or condemn it. Advocates of Law and Order approaches to violent crime believe that tough policies are necessary to set back the rising crime wave. Authorities must not "coddle" criminals, they say; it is time to round up the troublemakers and set an example for others with criminal intentions. Law and Order spokesmen recommend a variety of ways to implement their conclusions. Among the most controversial are neighborhood vigilante activities, tougher police practices, faster and more frequent criminal convictions in court, capital punishment, and imprisonment of more individuals deemed dangerous to society.

From the other side of the fence, many Americans see the Law and Order approach as frightening and dangerous. It represents a police-state mentality, they say, an inflexible and insensitive posture toward the problems of crime that can seriously abuse precious, hard-earned civil liberties. Constitutional rights must not be endangered just because citizens are upset about crime and violence and want to punish the offenders. If we begin seriously compromising our sense of justice, warn the critics, the end-product can be a serious abridgement of everybody's freedom and, perhaps, the arrival of a totalitarian state. Instead of screaming for hard-line crackdowns on crime, we should concentrate on "preventive medicine" for the diseases of poverty and despair, and on rehabilitating convicted criminals.

Who is right in this debate over Law and Order? Should we choose a "hard-line" or a "soft-line," greater rigidity or greater flexibility? Actually, the choices may not be so stark. Both sides in the dispute offer perceptive comments on the problems as well as some exaggeration and shortsightedness. If the debaters could listen to each other more openly and tolerantly, acknowledging a degree of substance as well as shortcomings in each other's arguments, they might develop a more balanced understanding of their troubles. With understanding comes the basis for solution.

Among the many Law and Order responses to violent crime, vigilantism represents the most spontaneous and dramatic development of all. Many Law and Order enthusiasts *talk* about tough anticrime policies, but it is quite another matter when citizens take the law into their own hands and activate "tough" solutions themselves. This is precisely what has happened in many crime-plagued areas, where residents have opted to fight violence with violence. Some Americans respond to news of this resurgence of vigilantism with surprise and worry; others, particularly residents of troubled city neighborhoods, condone vigilante approaches without embarrassment. Faced with extraordinary problems of violent crime and inadequate law enforcement, they consider their situation an emergency. Vigilantism seems necessary in the absence of other viable defenses against violent crime.

Many people associate "vigilantism" with anarchism and violent disruption, yet the term looks less frightening and its current revival becomes more understandable when viewed against its historical and social background. Over the course of American history, vigilante movements often developed in reaction to significant increases in crime and violence. Local, para-police groups grew out of the need to establish tranquility and reduce crime. Richard Maxwell Brown, the foremost historian of vigilante movements, points out that vigilantism was often a positive force in the short run, even though its precedents for violent reprisals could undermine law and order in the long run. Brown notes that in the nineteenth century many typical vigilante leaders were not ruffians; rather, they often represented upper crust society, which produced a natural leadership in times of trouble. When conditions got out of hand, as in the early years of lawlessness in San Francisco, these figures stepped in to fill the absence of legitimate law enforcement authorities. Since new cities as well as frontier areas often lacked a necessary complement of sheriffs, judges, and other agents of the law, vigilantism served to protect the citizenry against rowdy, disruptive, or criminal elements. New elites led the vigilante movements, motivated by the protection of life and property and the securing of order. In time, as law enforcement became more institutionalized and violence subsided, vigilantism faded. In light of this pattern in American history and the rise of new fears of lawlessness in recent times, it is clear why historian Richard Maxwell Brown told the Violence Commission that "a new wave of vigilantism is a real prospect today."[1]

Recently, vigilante activities have appeared in a number of cities. The case of New York City is instructive. For example, in sections of Greenwich Village, once a comfortable and exciting hub for middle-class New Yorkers, a spate of robberies, muggings, and drug-related incidents of violence turned the usually liberal community into a hotbed of Law and Order sentiment. When the high incidence of violence and murder continued after abundant calls for better police protection, citizens began organizing voluntary associations. Defense-minded block associations formed, and some neighbors agreed to operate on a whistle system. At the sound of the recognized distress signal, they would blow their own whistles to alert others, then rush to aid the person in trouble. Even the avant-garde newspaper, *The Village Voice,* began featuring articles that sanctioned the self-help approach and criticized people in the neighborhood who typically mouthed antipolice rhetoric.[2]

In another section of New York, East Flatbush, vigilante sentiment gained support after the tragic "Apple Pie Murder." Mr. and Mrs. Beno Spiewak, survivors of the Nazi concentration camps, had come to New York in 1949 and eventually purchased a candy store with their savings. The Spiewaks planned to retire in Israel once their nineteen-year-old son completed college. One day in 1971they were tending their store when two young men entered the shop and asked for apple pie. Mr. Spiewak said he had no pie but could offer Danish pastry. Then, in a senseless and savage act, one of the intruders shot the storeowner to death while his accomplice wounded his screaming wife. A few days later a large procession followed Mr. Spiewak's body, as both white and black mourners trailed behind the hearse. During the solemn event, an older man from the neighborhood announced his readiness to support the militant Jewish Defense League. "I'm past 72," said Rubin Wollman; "but I'll join the JDL. I was in World War I and II, and I am still handy with a gun." Wollman said there were no racist overtones in his decision, referring to the fact that the shooting suspects were black. He asserted that he held no dislike for his black neighbors and close black friends, and that his anger was directed at anyone from outside the neighborhood who would intrude to commit robbery and violence. Wollman was one of many who announced their enthusiasm for the JDL following the Apple Pie Murder.[3]

A series of incidents in black Harlem inspired similar interest in neo-vigilantism. Beginning in 1962 residents of a 1,272-apartment low-income housing project known as the Man-hattanville House fell victim to several attacks of criminal violence. In 1962 the fatal stabbing of a twelve-year-old girl in one of the buildings deeply shocked the apartment community. As the years passed, robberies and stabbings in the project occurred so frequently that frustrated residents no longer even bothered to report all such incidents to the police. Their living conditions became extremely intolerable. As one tenant described life in the Harlem project, "The tenants are afraid to leave their apartments at night and they are not safe in the afternoon either." Finally, tenants in one of the buildings formed a committee to keep a twenty-four-hour vigil in the lobby, hoping to counteract the threats to their daily lives. As in Greenwich Village and East Flatbush, vigilantism became necessary for the security of Harlem citizens.[4]

In 1973 New York City residents showed great enthusiasm over news of dramatic efforts by town citizens to take personal action against crime. Reports on these efforts excited some New Yorkers to speculate that the indifference and noninvolvement characteristic of witnesses in the Kitty Genovese case might, at last, be passing. It seemed many irate citizens were now prepared to act spontaneously and apprehend suspects on their own.

In the first case that attracted public attention in New York, fifty citizens surrounded a taxicab carrying three suspects who were attempting to escape the scene of a crime. The crowd succeeded in holding back the cab until police arrived. Witnesses said the suspects appeared relieved to put themselves in police custody after being held by an angry band of residents. The next night a state Liquor Authority commissioner, a Democratic party district leader, and a businessman passed the scene of a mugging, where they found a store-owner dazed and bruised and two suspects in flight. The three citizens took off after two of the suspects, wrestled with the men, and held them until the police arrived. Some weeks later two more dramatic examples of vigilantism appeared in New York newspapers in a single day. In the first incident a crowd of residents from West 134th Street beat a gunman unconscious after he shot one neighbor and wounded two. Just a few hours later thirty cab drivers chased suspects in the robbery of a gypsy cab, cornered them in the Bronx, and beat them severely before the police arrived.[5]

Modern urban life is replete with other examples of neo-vigilantism—from the bloody KAP programs (Kill A Pusher) to the more "respectable" efforts of the director of the New York Academy of Trial Lawyers to form a civilian anticrime corps.[6] To some degree these aggressive programs should be appreciated as serious attempts by normally law-abiding citizens to counter very real dangers in their daily lives. Troubled by rampant crime and violence, many urban citizens do not believe the police can give them adequate protection. A controversial motion picture, *Death Wish,* described urban vigilante behavior in extreme form, but the film touched sensitive nerves with relevant points about the frustrations of victims. New York City theater audiences applauded loudly as the story's pacifist-turned-vigilante shot down several muggers.

Nevertheless, we should recognize that there are long-term dangers in neo-vigilantism. Any movement that encourages people to take the law into their own hands may produce unfortunate byproducts, since violence can become habit-forming as a means of resolving problems. The aggression of a KAP group or a JDL agency can carry over into its dealings with other groups where the issues go beyond the control of local crime. Chances of uncontrolled violence developing out of emotional, ideological, or political confrontations increase with the buildup in angry attitudes and weapons for conflict. Whenever possible, it is preferable that the police assume responsibility for law and order.

Violent crime has become so pervasive and serious in many places, however, that the police, too, sometimes act like uncontrollably violent vigilantes. Police can threaten even law-abiding members of the community they are supposed to protect. Such a problem developed in Detroit, where a get-tough police program called STRESS (Stop the Robberies—Enjoy Safe Streets) indulged in several excesses. The special STRESS units were created as a police reaction to public clamor for action against Detroit's accelerating crime rate, especially after Detroit achieved one of the nation's highest homicide rates for large cities. To combat the problems, an elite corps of about 100 STRESS policemen concentrated on some of the city's most troubled areas. They were an ultraviolent group, as evidenced by their first fifteen months of operation when they accounted for about 40 percent of all killings by a 5,000-man Detroit police force. STRESS members became edgy and began overreacting after a series of violent attacks against police by blacks in late 1972 and early 1973. In one incident a black youth jumped out of a car and began firing at officers, leaving four policemen wounded. A few days later two officers spotted a suspect along with two other men wanted for another crime. The suspects fired away, pumping one officer's body with bullets well after he was dead and leaving the second in critical condition. The shootouts could not be explained entirely in terms of racial hatreds, since the suspects were also wanted for the murder of a black man.

News of these tragedies, occurring on the heels of a long series of criminal outrages, provoked a rampage by the Detroit police. Led by members of the STRESS units, officers began bursting into homes in a wild hunt for suspects. In the process they frightened several innocent citizens, got into unnecessarily dangerous confrontations, and accidentally killed one innocent person. Plainclothes officers broke into one resident's home by mistake at 4 A.M. by kicking down his door, pointing a loaded gun, and warning, "Nigger, if you breathe loud I'll blow your brains out." In another Hollywood-style broken-door entrance, officers disguised in old blue jeans and overalls pointed rifles at a woman and forced her to disrobe during a search. Commenting on her upsetting experience later, the woman described the plight of Detroit's innocent and harried citizens by saying, "I don't know what this city is coming to if you can't sit in your own house and be safe."

The tattered nerves, egregious errors, and fatal accidents developing out of operations by Detroit's STRESS units point up the dangers of relying heavily on the police in the fight against rampant crime. When they are called in for emergencies, the public expects them to wage a tough campaign to bring about order and security. But the almost inevitable mistakes, shakeups, and antiviolence violence that result from these efforts are rightly criticized. As Detroit Police Commissioner John F. Nichols describes the officer's dilemma: "If you do not police those areas, you're not providing the services. If you do come in, you're an occupying army. How do you police a whole community without alienating some elements? You can't do it."[7]

With the number of criminals increasing greatly, and enmity for the police *per se* becoming fashionable in various sectors of the urban community, nervous policemen are likely to commit many more abuses against the innocent citizenry. Officers are embittered by the hostile reception they get from community members and they are highly nervous about the dangers they face on the job. These tensions often make them "trigger happy." Moreover, many policemen do, no doubt, harbor prejudices against the minority groups they are assigned to protect. The Kerner Commission reported what was common knowledge to black inner-city residents—that the police often acted in a belligerent, discriminatory, and racist manner toward members of the ghetto communities. Some ghetto riots, in fact, began from residents reacting to incidents of gross police injustice.[8] Similar difficulties have continued to occur. In 1971, for example, a white policeman shot and killed a fifteen-year-old black boy whom he suspected of stealing a car. The automobile actually belonged to the dead boy's father. This grotesque mistake brought a rampage of looting and fire bombing which cost $500,000 in property damage and led to the arrest of 300 persons.[9]

Special studies confirm the impression that many policemen are indeed prejudiced, poorly trained, and, sometimes, dangerously impulsive. In a major report to the Violence Commission entitled *Law and Order Reconsidered,* researchers noted that, across the country, police officers tended to be white, middle-class, resistant to change, and distrustful of blacks and other minority groups. The study found that policemen were also poorly prepared to handle volatile human relations.[10] This shortcoming came out even more glaringly in the Commission's famous *Walker Report (Rights in Conflict)*, which investigated causes for rioting during the 1968 Democratic National Convention. Although investigators learned that protestors bitterly taunted policemen, the actions of dissidents were hardly sufficient to provoke the indiscriminate gassing and clubbing by uniformed officers. Based on evidence of assaults on sixty-three reporters and photographers, as well as hundreds of students, the *Walker Report* described Chicago's melee as a "police riot."[11] Revelations of widespread corruption within police departments have further undermined public respect for the police. Particularly disturbing was New York City's Knapp Commission study which slowly unfolded a pervasive pattern in the police force of payola and cooperation with criminals.

It is against the background of such abuses and corruption that policemen have become favorite targets for criticism by intellectuals, civil liberties spokesmen, social reformers, as well as many white and black militants and radicals. While the police deserve much opprobrium, the alacrity to attribute crime and violence to their failures often goes beyond reason. Police critics have sometimes found themselves enmeshed in contradiction: By placing disproportionate emphasis on police wrongdoing, while pointing to police failures as a major stimulus to violent behavior, they also insist that urban violence develops most fundamentally from poverty, poor education, and unequal employment. Much as do the Law and Order fanatics, these critics overestimate the power of the police to curb rising violence. Excessive concentration on the role of the police can detract attention from the more important and basic urban problems.

Alphonso Pinkney, in *The American Way of Violence,* shows this kind of inconsistency when he attacks the police in a chapter suggestively titled "Police Violence." In a manner typical of lopsided views on the police, Pinkney describes officers as agents for the ruling class who help maintain the status quo. "In this role they have permitted themselves to be turned against the people," claims Pinkney, "and have gone to any length, including 'murder,' to serve the interests of their employers."[12] In *Police Power: Police Abuses in New York City,* Paul Chevigny gives us his personality profile of the typical cop. Why be shocked by stories of police atrocities, Chevigny asks, when we already know the mentality of the people in question? "The tendencies in police behavior which give rise to abuses do form a sort of 'police character,' " explains Chevigny. He describes this individual basically as "a man suspicious of outsiders, who is concerned with order, reacts aggressively to threats to his authority, and regards every attempt to control that authority with cynicism." Given these unenviable traits, police excesses can be expected. "It is not for nothing that ghetto people have chosen police abuses as the symbol of oppression; it is because they actually *are* acts of oppression." In less sophisticated street language this assessment of law enforcement officers often appears in the one word epithet "pig."[13]

To a degree, critics like Pinkney and Chevigny do illuminate police shortcomings. Much can be done to change the mix of characteristics that frequently leads to trouble. Policemen can profit greatly by improved education, including special training in psychology, sociology and criminology. Officers also could learn to be less abrasive in their dealings with the community. And certainly police could become better models for the citizenry by setting their own houses in order. More careful screening of candidates and removal of criminal connections within departments are among the first priorities. Municipal governments can help by providing higher salaries and better working conditions so that there will be less temptation for the policeman to supplement his income with illicit activities.[14]

Even with extraordinary police reform, however, police abuses, violence, and difficulties with the communities are likely to remain serious problems until the dangers of violence against police can be reduced greatly. In view of the threats that many officers face daily, it is understandable that many have turned increasingly nervous and trigger-happy. By the 1970s a policeman's job had become a tension-filled occupation that did not offer recompense commensurate with the tremendous dangers he faced. We can imagine what ran through the minds, for example, of three Chicago police officers who found themselves trapped in the elevator of a housing project for more than an hour while some residents tried to set the elevator afire with molotov cocktails. Policemen deserve greater public sympathy for the extremely difficult and often thankless tasks they perform. As Henry A. Singer, executive director of Westport, Connecticut's Institute of Human Resources, notes, the popular picture of the cop as borderline criminal is inaccurate and shows lack of appreciation for his position:

During the last four years I have worked with many policemen and I have found some who conform to this stereotype. But I have also discovered many more who are among the most dedicated, hard-working, committed individuals I have ever met.

The job of a policeman in our society is by far one of the most frustrating, enervating, distressing, and least financially rewarding of any municipal function. . . . The policeman is one of the few agents of society who is required to perform the unpleasant tasks that none of us would do for three or four times his salary.[15]

We should not forget that his blue uniform often marks a policeman as a hated man among many white and black residents in a large city, particularly those between twelve and twenty-five years old and those involved in crime. While frightened citizens try to stay off the violence-filled city streets at night, it is specifically the policeman's *job* to walk the beat and look for trouble. Often he finds it, as is evidenced by the record number of police officers killed on duty between 1961 and 1973. The number of police homicide victims climbed more than 300 percent during the period, an even higher rate of increase than for the population in general. The following figures tell the story:

Policemen Killed in the United States

1961——37		1968——64
1962——48		1969——86
1963——55		1970——100
1964——57		1971——125
1965——53		1972——112
1966——57		1973——127
1967——76		

In several cities policemen have held elaborate funeral services for some of these victims in dramatic attempts to draw public attention to their plight. An impressive gathering of thousands of uniformed men for the funeral of two slain colleagues in New York City in 1971 was typical of these campaigns to publicize the personal tragedy behind spiraling statistics. Officers gathered to honor Wavery Jones, a thirty-four-year-old black, and Joseph Piagentini, a twenty-eight-year-old white. Both were married, both were fathers. They had been killed in seemingly senseless acts, ambushes for which the motive appeared to be simple hatred for anyone in the official blue uniform, whatever his color. Just a few days before, two other New York City policemen had been relatively "luckier." After they stopped a car for a minor traffic violation, a blast of machine gun fire left them in critical condition.[16]

In addition to publicity as a recourse, police departments have worked on self-defense. Their programs include special training in avoiding sniper attacks, learning how to spot ambushes, and reacting to booby traps. The New York City Police Department even resorted to the drastic measure of arming hundreds of specially trained officers with highly lethal shotguns.[17] Baltimore policemen, too, adopted a more militant approach by forming special shotgun squads.[18] Despite considerable public outcry about the legality of such countermeasures and the possible dangers they posed to innocent bystanders, the police defended their move as necessary in an otherwise impossible situation.

There has been very strong support for the decisions of police departments to reemphasize the "get tough" attitude toward criminal violence. The successful mayoralty race of Philadelphia "Super-Cop," Frank Rizzo, showed the public's growing impatience with problems of violent crime and strong interest in Law and Order politics as a countermeasure. Rizzo had established a controversial reputation as a hard-line police chief who worried little about restraint when facing anyone he judged a troublemaker. He organized fast-moving patrol systems in Philadelphia which rushed in with superior force as minor incidents developed. This system helped prevent further upheaval by breaking up crowds before agitation could gain momentum. By the time of his election, Rizzo had not succeeded in making Philadelphia the "City of Brotherly Love," but he did help the city to achieve a favorable anticrime image. Some columnists and politicians exaggerated the meaning of Rizzo's eye-opening mayoralty victory, worrying that Philadelphians were slipping into a fascist mentality. But it was not totalitarianism that made Rizzo appealing. It was the beleaguered citizens' desperate search for someone to bring a measure of security to their lives. Rizzo did not become a model mayor, and his answers to the problems of crime and violence were far from complete. In fact, his political influence quickly dissipated amid charges of favoritism, corruption, and falsification of crime information. But the sentiments which helped place him in office were unmistakable.[19]

If tough cops are increasingly popular with some in America, it is because the public is frightened and is desperately searching for symbols of relief from anxiety. It has been said that people hate tyranny, but they hate anarchy even more, for anarchy is the worst tyranny of all. Public clamor for tougher attitudes toward criminals reveals the popular desire that authorities show greater concern for the masses of people who are victims of crime and give them hope that their lives *will* be more secure in the future. It is inappropriate and unfair to label those who voice these worries and demands as ultraconservatives, police-state fanatics, fascists, or racists. Though many of their proposed remedies for the problems do, indeed, tread heavily on civil liberties, a counteranswer that simply recites the Bill of Rights does not constitute a satisfactory reply to their questions. There *is* a severe problem of law and order in America; it is not just a figment of popular imagination. If those most threatened by the problem frequently suggest muddled solutions, their confusion is understandable. Even some of the best minds in the country are without persuasive answers; one cannot then expect the average citizen who has limited acquaintance with the issues to respond only with cool rationality.

Just as Law and Order sentiment calls for "tough" cops, it also cries for "tough" judges. Widespread criticism of Supreme Court decisions for "tying the hands" of judges in rulings on criminal cases developed out of the frustration from soaring crime rates. An angry public wants convictions. Why do so many criminals seem to get off scot-free, they ask? Perhaps court rulings are to blame, reason the Law and Order spokesmen.

Two decisions of the Warren Court particularly attracted critical attention: the *Escobedo* decision of 1964 and the *Miranda v. Arizona* decision of 1966. Essentially these decisions sought to insure that the poor could avail themselves of their basic constitutional rights when they were apprehended as suspects in a crime. In actual practice the poor often did not use their constitutional rights because of their ignorance of the law or inability to afford a lawyer. The controversial rulings required police to inform suspects that anything they might say during an investigation could be used against them in court and that they had the right to remain silent and secure a lawyer who could be furnished to them free of charge. The aim of the Supreme Court and the advocates of these changes was, of course, to make constitutional guarantees more effective. Too frequently the poor and uneducated had been pressured into confessing under conditions of duress and confusion (sometimes even confessing to crimes they had not committed), while wealthier and more sophisticated suspects understood their rights and could afford the legal assistance necessary to face charges effectively. The new rulings pointed out that the prosecution was expected to establish guilt by evidence gathered freely and independently, not by reliance on tricks and coercion against the accused. Former Attorney General Ramsey Clark conveys this notion of justice succinctly by asking, "If we are to accord rights to all our citizens, should we be embarrassed to say so?"[20]

It is not surprising that, when these Supreme Court decisions coincided with a rising crime rate, many claimed the new rulings would hamstring the law enforcement agencies in their efforts to convict dangerous criminals. If the police had to warn suspects about their right to remain silent, they said, confessions would become extremely difficult to obtain. Prosecutors would find it much harder to prove guilt, since suspects would be less likely to talk, and the evidence they needed would be harder to find. Much information about names, places, and dates, which often came out in confessions and helped police and prosecution to "nail down" their case, would not be available. Moreover, many violent crimes take place under conditions where there are no witnesses, said the critics. Hence, confessions become especially important to the prosecution for proving guilt. In short, critics of the new decisions charged the Court with showing more interest in protecting the criminal's rights than the rights of law-abiding victims. In a society plagued by violence, victims might be left dazed, injured, or dead by criminals who could walk off free on a legal technicality. Alabama Governor George Wallace epitomized this angry reaction with an oft-repeated statement in his campaign speeches. He said people in the audience might get hit on the head on the way home by a thug who would probably be out of jail before they got out of the hospital.[21]

The strong emotional commitments of each side in this serious debate are quite appropriate, since each position is partly right in its principal complaints. At the same time, both sides suffer from extremist argumentation that blinds them to some kernels of truth that the other group has to offer. One-sided, biased, and short-sighted assessments are familiar in the heated controversy.

On the one hand, spokesmen who favor court rulings such as *Miranda* and *Escobedo* may take pride in supporting what a true constitutional democracy ought to do, that is, put the Bill of Rights into effect. The old system was reprehensibly negligent in the way it allowed police and prosecutors to violate due process and equality before the law. Cases like *Miranda* did not just suddenly "happen" in the Supreme Court. They culminated a series of decisions over many years which aimed at implementing some of the most important principles laid down in the Constitution. The record of police abuses in obtaining confessions—long hours of interrogation, glaring lights, and physical beating—was well known. A civilization of laws could not allow these abuses to go on without challenge.

On the other hand, the courts' new rules can, indeed, help to free some guilty criminals. One can hardly argue that criminal prosecution is aided by the denial of opportunities to capitalize on a suspect's readiness to confess. Both sides in the debate produce evidence which purportedly shows that convictions in various places rose or declined after the controversial rulings. But logic, common sense, and frankness would require civil libertarians to admit that, overall, the decisions contained real potential for reducing rather than facilitating criminal convictions. While *Miranda* and *Escobedo* have, no doubt, helped to protect some innocents, these rulings have also probably authorized the release of many suspects who were, in fact, criminals, and who might indulge in illegal violence after their release. Studies conducted both before and after *Miranda* show that law enforcement agencies have great difficulty in solving crimes and punishing the guilty. One report on ten million serious crimes committed in a year following the *Miranda* decision indicated that only 12 percent of the cases resulted in arrest, 6 percent in conviction, and 1-1/2 percent in actual incarceration. In view of such statistics, a leading student of the crime problem commented, "It should be hard to argue that crime does not pay."[22]

Though one could easily sentimentalize the true story of an innocent man convicted unfairly (a popular theme for movie sagas as well as debates about court rulings), we should remember that one could just as easily reconstruct the sad case of a victim slaughtered by someone who might have been behind bars were it not for the difficulties of conviction. Newspapers are filled with such stories. William A. Stanmeyer gives a graphic example of one in a hard-hitting plea for strengthening the position of public prosecutors. He refers to the case of four-year-old Joyce Ann Huff. The child was playing in the yard of her Los Angeles home when suddenly three men drove by; one fired a shotgun at her, driving forty-two pellets into her small body. Joyce Ann's mother held the bleeding child in her arms, where she died within five minutes. When police finally apprehended the prime suspect, they discovered he had been arrested several times before for attempted murder, assault with a deadly weapon, robbery, burglary, arson, and narcotics trade. This time, thrill-killing seemed to be his aim. Why do the laws help to release this kind of person, asks Stanmeyer. "If there must be a tradeoff," he insists, "we should be more concerned about the civil liberties of little children than about those of accused murderers who already had been arrested for six previous felonies and yet, incredibly, still roam the streets with their shotguns."[23]

As could be expected, renewed interest in heavier jail sentences has accompanied the rising violent crime rate. Public frustration over the expansion of very serious crimes often manifests itself in calls for the extreme forms of punishment. Former Governor of New York Nelson Rockefeller voiced this concern in a highly controversial Law and Order statement of 1972 when he addressed the New York legislature about drug abuse. Rockefeller requested mandatory life sentences for all hard-drug peddlers or for addicts who committed violent crimes while under the influence of narcotics. For drug traffickers associated

with organized crime Rockefeller suggested a final solution: the
death penalty. Why the request for such extreme deterrents?
Because "the citizens in our state are terrorized," he explained.
Rockefeller said he supported the extraordinary measure
because "I am convinced after trying everything else, that
nothing else will do." Strong punishment was necessary, he insisted, since the rights and security of the general citizenry
deserved priority over the right and security of highly dangerous
criminals. After many unsuccessful efforts to combat the drug
problem it seemed that only radical deterrents could work. As
Rockefeller explained, "So often we are so focused on protecting
the rights of the individual involved in an affront to society that
we tend to lose sight of our paramount responsibility to protect
society itself." Though many New Yorkers recoiled at the
suggestion of such severe penalties, polls of legislators and their
constituents revealed the governor had surprisingly strong
support—especially in view of the harsh reception his speech
would have received just a few years before. Many legislators
applauded his address at the time it was given. The mood had
clearly changed and Rockefeller's political antennae were well
placed. He knew public patience was wearing thin.[24]

Evidence of increasing public frustration over the failure to
slow down serious crime and signs of growing interest in capital
punishment as a deterrent surfaced quickly around the country
in the months following Rockefeller's controversial address. One
case in Pennsylvania was particularly important because it raised
the difficult question of what could be done to challenge violent
criminals when almost all deterrents short of execution had been
exhausted. The situation involved a bloody incident at the state's
Holmsburg penitentiary, the overcrowded quarters for many
convicted murderers and men awaiting trial for murder. In 1973
inmates slew two prison officials. Short of especially cruel
treatment within the prison, which could be ruled unconstitutional, what could authorities do to frighten or deter homicidal inmates from committing further murders? Threatening them
with longer sentences would do little, since many already
expected to spend decades or their entire lives behind bars. In an
extraordinary session which reflected public disgust over the

whole epidemic of violent crime, the Pennsylvania House voted 172-20 to restore capital punishment. This bill was particularly significant for the crimes it listed as punishable by execution in the gas chamber—crimes considered among the most appalling, dangerous, and difficult to deter. The list included execution for murder while serving a life term; killing a fireman, law enforcement officer, or prison guard while in the performance of official duties; paying or being paid to kill someone; murdering a hostage, a victim during a hijacking, or a bystander during or after a felony. In 1974 the Pennsylvania legislature overrode Governor Milton J. Shapp's veto to reinstitute the death penalty. Pennsylvania joined several other states in restoring the extreme measure, leaving a Supreme Court ruling as the principal protector of many inmates on "Death Row."[25]

The justification for capital punishment that interested the Pennsylvania legislators was, of course, deterrence. Advocates of capital punishment, in growing numbers, postulated that a person who intends to kill will think about his act more seriously if he realizes execution can be the ultimate punishment for his deed.

Is the assumption correct? There are thousands of statistical and written materials on this question, and both sides in the debate contend with vigor that the preponderance of evidence is clearly on their side. Opponents of the death penalty point to evidence from various countries which abolished capital punishment yet recorded fewer murders after the decision. Advocates of the death penalty point out that this evidence involves countries which were already reducing their violent crime anyway. Moreover, they claim that statistical data are often mis-leadingly interpreted. On the other hand, critics of capital punishment argue that most homicides take place under intense emotion, when the murderer loses rational control over what he is doing. Such people cannot calculate the possible consequences of their acts. In response, supporters of capital punishment insist that assumptions about a murderer's irrationality are made too easily. Perhaps the prospect of punishment by death can cross an enraged person's mind more forcefully than many are inclined to believe. Furthermore, defenders of capital punishment point out that just the potential effect on the many who attempt voluntary, premeditated manslaughter could make a death penalty worthwhile.

Although this old debate is not likely to be settled conclusively to the satisfaction of either side, we can acknowledge a degree of validity in each position. Overall, it seems reasonable to claim that the threat of capital punishment probably can help *sometimes* to deter murders, but the price society pays for living with the death penalty is very dear. It is not just a matter of considering the possibility of error in a guilty judgment (a horrible thought, since the human injury in this case is irreparable and final). It is also a matter of values. The entire problem of violence is related to the values, the attitudes, or the ethos of a culture. Resolution of the problem of violence calls for fostering much greater respect for the sanctity of human life. Certainly capital punishment undermines that respect. The whole idea of forcing an individual to wait for his fateful date on the calendar, then placing him at the disposal of executioners who prepare the noose, gas, or electric wires in front of a glaring crowd of newspaper reporters reminds critics of an *auto da fé* out of the Middle Ages. Moreover, when the sad realities of culpability for violence are realized, the gory injustice of "final solutions" looks especially distasteful. For we should remember that murderers themselves are often victims too—victims of forces in society which make violence common.

As morally repulsive as capital punishment may be, Americans will probably clamor for it increasingly, and, if the tide of violent crime continues to rise, passage of the death penalty for certain kinds of crimes may be in the offing. Already public support for capital punishment has shifted significantly with the wave of much-discussed violence. There is growing evidence of willingness to risk errors in accusation as a necessary trade-off for deterring violent crime. The public seems prepared to live with the unattractive implications of this choice in order to achieve what they believe to be a greater measure of security. In 1972 a Supreme Court decision signaled the possibility that, in time, some forms of capital punishment might once again receive legal sanction. The Court decided against the death penalty by a slim margin of 5-4, but the appointment of new justices in later years could bring a reversal. Gallop polls over several years have shown that if the Court did change, a preponderance of the public might support it. In 1953 Gallop interviewers found generally strong support for the death penalty: 68 percent. In the following years the idea began to lose favor. By 1966 only 42 percent favored capital punishment while 47 percent opposed it. Then opinion swung around again as Law and Order concerns intensified. By 1972 the polls revealed an extraordinary transformation in public sentiment: as many as 57 percent supported capital punishment while only 32 percent opposed it.[26]

Imprisonment also figures prominently in Law and Order sentiment. Many nervous citizens would like to see more of society's criminals behind bars, and for longer terms than inmates typically serve at present for various crimes. Some want longer sentences because they hope the experience will deter any further crimes. Many more want criminals under lock and key to keep them "out of the way" where, it is believed, they cannot do much harm. From this perspective, prisons look like another solution to the problem of violent crime.

If prisons represent an "answer" to the problem, they constitute a quite appalling solution. Prisons in America have long had an ugly record. Taxpayers are reluctant enough to pay for programs that benefit themselves; they are especially niggardly about programs to watch over (or care for) people identified as threats to society. In America, as in many other countries, the public prefers to forget about prisoners—to put them out of sight and mind financially, psychologically, and ethically. When citizens occasionally get an opportunity to glimpse behind penitentiary walls, they usually find the view repulsive. Stories about the worst prison conditions in America rival tales about wartime concentration camps (for instance, the discovery of mass graves in an Arkansas prison or the exposé on syphillis experiments with inmates in an Alabama prison).

Even reports of the better, "model" prisons frequently point out the narrow limitations of rehabilitation and reform. The systems usually cannot bear true liberalization, for if they could they would not be prisons. Serious efforts at prison reform often backfire. For example, a campaign to improve the living situation in the New York State penitentiary system helped to stir the expectations of inmates and heighten their frustrations, contributing to unrest which led to strikes, riots, and takeovers within the prisons at Auburn and Attica. In efforts to counteract the inmates' taking of hostages and frightening acts of defiance, state authorities overreacted at Attica. In an uncalled for display of brutal "toughness," officials permitted the use of firepower to meet the crisis. Indiscriminate shooting led to the unnecessary deaths of eleven hostages and thirty-two inmates. Sadly, the upheavals at Attica, Auburn, and elsewhere set back many of the reform efforts, led to greater restriction of prisoners' freedom, and added further tension to an atmosphere already badly strained by suspicion, fear, and hate.

These prison rebellions and the fierce Law and Order reactions to them suggest the formidable difficulties involved in prison reform. Certainly the drive to liberalize and improve treatment of inmates must go on despite the dangers. But even with better funding and greater commitment, these improvements will constitute only minor gains because of inherent contradictions between the twin goals of punishment and rehabilitation. Each works against the other. Efforts to *combine* the discomforts of incarceration (to impress inmates that crime does not pay) with programs to reform habits, mold character, and train inmates for responsible citizenship often produce predictably poor results.

Prisons do not provide solutions to the problems of violent crime. Rather, they are more frequently "schools for crime" where novice miscreants hobnob with more vicious offenders and learn to handle more ambitious adventures upon "graduation." Some would hope that vocational training and personal counseling could set the inmate in a different direction—toward becoming a responsible contributor to society after his release. Training programs are usually poor, however, and even when inmates learn a new skill, their knowledge may be useless when they enter a society with millions of unemployed and little demand for men previously convicted of serious crimes. Finally, and very significantly, prisons fail miserably because of severe overcrowding. Facilities are already heavily overtaxed from inmate populations well beyond numbers considered the acceptable maximums. In the meantime, the public cries for incarceration of more criminals and judges know very well that they could easily find abundant additional candidates if they wished to press sentencing. America's prison population could quickly be doubled or tripled if facilities were available, a thought that hints at the relationship of prison overcrowding to larger questions about crime and violence in the country.[27]

We can best view prison problems in the broadest possible way, considering not only what the sad state of American prisons tells about society's treatment of its criminally disobedient or how this condition reflects the failures of American penal institutions. The problem also suggests the general failures of society to deal effectively with crime and violence. Like problems with the police and the courts, many of the difficulties of prisons develop out of the sheer size of criminal violence in America. Corrective institutions cannot be very helpful under present circumstances. Some frustrated and angry citizens burst with impatience over the high incidence of violent crime, commenting, "They ought to put all the damned criminals in jail." Such casual, unthinking remarks overlook the harsh fact that if society were really to implement this demand, thousands more would be behind bars and governmental spending on prisons would rival defense and welfare expenditures. One of the most disturbing threats in the whole criminal justice tangle is that judges increasingly send potentially dangerous people back into society because they realize that incarceration of every criminal would require taxpayers to support a new penitentiary construction program of monumental proportions. And judges feel that massive new prison expenditures would not be worth the price. The government would only be putting away thousands of individuals who might better reform their lives outside of penitentiary walls. High return rates show how little institutions that congregate felons in a "school of crime" can do to give society long-run protection. Instead, it is necessary to deal with the fundamental reasons why there are so many candidates for prison in the first place.

One of the major morals in this story of overcrowded prisons in America is that the serious crime problem cannot be resolved solely by a hard-line, Law and Order approach. America's law enforcement authorities, judicial agencies, and penal institutions cannot function effectively when the number of criminals is so great. Police could double or triple their forces in every large city, yet violent crime would continue. Judges, too, could be doubled or tripled in number and be required to work longer hours, yet the results would still not be satisfactory. Already dockets are so huge that trials must be delayed months or years. Among those formally accused of crime, many more choose to settle out of court with a plea of guilty than bring their case to trial. As Morton Hunt notes, "The criminal justice system would collapse if the courts had to try all, or even a substantial minority, of the indicted."[28] Finally, by pleading guilty (often to lesser offenses), the accused usually receives a shorter sentence than could be expected from a conviction in court. This compromise not only brings a measure of relief to the accused but also to the heavily overpopulated penal systems, which cannot accommodate more criminals serving longer terms (even though a longer sentence might, according to law, be more appropriate, given the seriousness of violent crimes).

Whether there are more police on the streets to round up suspects, more judges to sentence criminals, or more prisons to confine them, these measures do not offer effective remedies for violent crime, because they do not drive at its sources. Until there is effective action against the major *causes* of crime, the police, courts, and prisons will remain deluged with work and continue to perform their duties in ways that do not satisfy justice and public security. If violent crime continues to increase, however, the public will clamor for even tougher Law and Order responses.

Because the fears of the people arise from very real threats, those who criticize their wavering sense of justice or attacks on civil liberties must quickly deal with the fundamental causes of violent crime. If they do not, the future will surely bring further deterioration of the principles they cherish. In time, if the crime wave cannot be reversed, Americans may see the abridgement of many precious civil liberties.

5

BLACKS AND WHITES

Never underestimate the capacity of a race-conscious people to obfuscate the realities of a social problem like violence. As long as people view themselves in terms of starkly different categories, such as black and white, there is bound to be considerable confusion. In popular American attitudes about the way so-called racial groups view violence, stereotypes of heroes and goats typically dominate thinking. Some blame blacks for problems of violence, pointing to the angry militancy of the publicity-seeking "revolutionaries;" others rail on about the abuses of white racism that provoke violent language and action. Some point out the high involvement of black youths in urban crime; others stress the lack of action against the poverty that makes ghetto environments conducive to crime. This pendulum motion in debates that tries to point out culprits obscures the fact that both sides have their heroes and villains and that the problem of violence is much larger than a racial question.

To examine this tendency toward racial scapegoating more closely, let us first focus on some of the gross simplifications in popular attitudes among whites, then move on to assess stereotyping among blacks.

It is no secret that many white Americans tend to make blacks scapegoats when assessing the problem of violence. Although they do not associate all antisocial violence with blacks, they do attribute an inordinate amount of it to them. In middle-class and upper-class homes, discussions about crime, muggings, murders, or civil disorders too frequently operate with the tacit assumption that these problems relate specifically to the black community. Whites talk as if violence were someone else's doing, not their own. They make the difficulty appear to emanate from a foreign culture, not mainstream American teaching, values, and failures.

Discussions about the role of blacks in crime and violence often fail to recognize historical or current perspectives. When whites blame blacks primarily for modern-day troubles, they take a short view of American history. Through glimpses of very recent and general information, they select evidence to confirm their suspicions and reinforce their prejudices. They learn, for example, that the arrest rate for teenage blacks in cases of aggravated assault, forcible rape, and criminal homicide is many times higher than for whites in the same age group. Although some apologists try to discount these figures by arguing that differences relate to the greater readiness of the police to arrest black rather than white youngsters for suspected crimes, this disclaimer is not wholly convincing. Hence the scapegoating. Many see statistical contrasts as evidence that blacks have a greater inclination for violence than whites do.

Abundant historical and sociological research shows the shortsightedness of this view. The records reveal that, over American history, high crime and violence rates tend to concentrate among people who live in congested inner-city neighborhoods, especially the poorest sections. Furthermore, individuals from families that are new arrivals to these areas show a higher involvement in crime than members of older, more settled urban families. In short, high incidence of crime and violence usually correlates with residency in the inner city, status as a recent immigrant, or low socioeconomic class. We might also add that through history this antisocial tendency has been disproportionately strong among males in their teens or early twenties.

In earlier decades it was not the blacks but youngsters from other ethnic groups who matched this profile for urban crime and violence. During the nineteenth century, for example, the Irish and Italians contributed disproportionately to the violent criminal population in New York City, and, indeed, they ranked among the poorest and most recently uprooted classes. Gangs of white youths as well as white organized criminals also caused considerable trouble. Violent clubs such as the Dutch Mob, the Molasses Gang, and the Hartley Mob roamed New York's streets. The Whyos gained an especially notorious reputation for pillaging and murder before their movement dissipated in the 1890s.[2]

In the twentieth century many blacks fell into a pattern similar to that of earlier groups in urban environments. The period of their heavy concentration in large cities has been relatively recent. Blacks began moving to the North and Far West particularly during World War I and its aftermath. The pace of migration to urban areas accelerated after World War II. In a sense, then, America's black ghettoes became the home of its latest "immigrants." It is not surprising that many youngsters from recently uprooted families, particularly males in their teens and early twenties and individuals from broken homes, have engaged heavily in crime and violence. Their behavior has followed historical and sociological patterns, not racial peculiarities.

Many whites, showing a proclivity for stereotyping, generalize excessively about black attitudes toward violence. They forget too easily that all blacks do not share the same ideas about violence. *Neither* blacks nor whites have achieved consensus on the topic. This fact is so elementary that one hesitates to mention it, yet stereotyping continues to interfere with appreciation of the complexities of the violence problem. Emphasis on the concept of race in popular thought leads many people to gloss over important distinctions in behavior between classes within the black community. For example, popular stereotypes give little recognition to differences of attitude between the employed and the unemployed, middle- and lower-class individuals, and even between those who are resigned to their plight and those who aspire to climb the social ladder. When it comes to discussion of violence, surely there is no typical black man just as there is no typical white man.[3]

Although blacks differ in their views about violence, it is important to remember that a substantial majority of them condemn it. Even in 1968, during the heyday of popular black militant rhetoric urging bloody revenge upon white racism, nine-tenths of the blacks interviewed for a CBS poll disapproved of violence. Many black city residents fear the rise of violence much more than their white suburban counterparts precisely because they live in the middle of the rundown, high-crime districts. Crime statistics show that it is they, much more than whites, who are the likely victims of robbery, assault, or homicide.

This daily danger of falling victim to violent crime is difficult to face. "It's a heavy scene here," reports Camille Billops, a black artist in New York. "I used to think I was safe because I was black," comments Billops. "Well, that just isn't true. Black people are getting ripped off left and right. I even have fantasies of doing junkies in, of trapping them in hallways and ripping them off right here. I've had it," he says sadly. "I'm so tired of being scared."[4] Because of these hazardous living conditions, many black city residents endorse Law and Order solutions and demand better neighborhood police protection. As one black policeman notes, "Black people really need and want good police protection because of the gang terrorism and the crime within the community."[5]

The hunger of the middle-class blacks to leave the ghetto and resettle in the suburbs should be observed with understanding, not the mockery and abuse that both whites and fellow blacks often pour on them. Their drive to migrate is motivated by much more than just a search for grass to mow or a prestigious address. Fear figures among their prime motives. They want out; they want chance to live in a safe community where they can enjoy life relatively free of the fear of crime and violence.

Many white residents of Philadelphia's Wynnefield section learned about this attitude of middle-class blacks from personal experience. As blacks began to settle in their neighborhood, the whites became apprehensive. But soon they learned that the migrants to the attractive area shared their own concerns. The new residents were especially vocal in condemning crime and violence and asking that bars and other potential trouble-spots be kept out of the neighborhood. "You work all your life to come to a place like this," explained a forty-eight-year-old carpenter, "and you don't want the rough element around." A fifty-year-old white resident viewed the new influx of middle-class blacks to Wynnefield as the latest development in an old pattern. He observed that the blacks "considered Wynnefield as an escape from the jungles of West Philadelphia just as the Jews found it a refuge in the 1920s."[6]

If white residents sometimes react emotionally and unfairly against permitting middle-class blacks to integrate their neighborhoods, it is important to recognize the confusion and uncertainties that often plague their minds. To dismiss their behavior as racism is to evade the central issue. Often their intolerance relates much more directly to a general fear of crime and violence than it does to specific, unbending hostility against non-Caucasians. It is worry over personal security that frequently makes them hyperdefensive, not a hangup over skin pigmentation. They become extremely tense about possible incursions of inner-city troubles into their suburban sanctuaries. This fear fosters the stereotyped thinking for which they are so well noted. Aware of the disproportionately large role of black youths in urban crime and violence, they often generalize this condition to all blacks. Their attitudes leave little room for appreciation of the same kinds of class and cultural distinctions among blacks that characterize whites. Out of fear over very real problems, they become emotional, intolerant, and prejudiced. Appreciating this difficult situation should suggest what society can expect from middle-class Americans, be they white or black, who face influxes of individuals suspected of crime and violence. If the "undesirables" are poor, have a criminal record, or display the swagger and tough language of a roughneck from the inner city or hill country, both white and black middle-class suburbanites are likely to impede their entrance into the community.[7]

Who can condemn them fully for such resistance? Improving the lot of the criminal and violent cannot be placed in the laps of suburbanites. The intense resistance of many middle-class *black* suburbanites to the incursion of dangerous groups into their neighborhoods powerfully illustrates that this tension is first and foremost a class rather than a racial problem. Contrary to popular commentary, a black worker who struggles successfully through his lifetime to lift his family out of the ghetto is not hypocritical when, after reaching his suburban Eden, he turns around and tries to fence out the violence-prone individuals of his own color. Such a man is not an intra-racist or an "Uncle Tom." He merely exhibits a common characteristic of the pragmatic man—the one who does not try to sweep back the ocean singlehandedly and, possibly, to sacrifice himself and his family in the process.

After a decade of confrontation rhetoric in which militant blacks frequently made excuses for criminal behavior by black youths, tolerant language became less fashionable. Black leaders began organizing a direct assault on black crime. In 1974 they planned a series of meetings throughout the country to heighten their communities' awareness of the difficulties. Through the Commission for Racial Justice, black community organizers, churchmen, elected officials, and lawmen drew attention to the crime statistics. For example, blacks living in urban settings ranked unusually high as mugging victims, and a disproportionately high percentage of their muggers were blacks. "For years we have shied away from the problem for fear of being accused of joining the establishment," explained Charles E. Cobb, a leader in the United Church of Christ. But Cobb and others were prepared to address the issue openly in 1974, undaunted by the familiar charges of being racial traitors.[8]

NAACP leader Roy Wilkins recommended similar self-criticism for the black community in 1964, but the rising militant mood gave many listeners the impression that his comments were out of tune with the times. Wilkins spoke out when a dispute developed over reactions to newspaper reports of black gangs terrorizing subway passengers in New York City. While many whites as well as blacks placed the blame on society, describing the violence as forms of demonstration against unequal education, employment, and housing, Wilkins reacted with more than just sociological observation. "A punk is a punk" regardless of color, he insisted, and black "hoodlums" were no less deserving of excuses than white youths who acted in the same way. Alluding to the active civil rights movement of 1964, Wilkins claimed that public concern about news media reports on subway terrorism was "undercutting and wrecking gains made by hundreds of Negro and white youngsters who went to jail for human rights." "They are slowing down the drive for employment of Negroes," said Wilkins. "Who wants to hire wild people?"[9]

The ghetto riots of the 1960s and tough talk from black leaders at the time of the riots contributed also to white backlash. A 1966 poll by *Newsweek* magazine revealed significant changes in white attitudes toward blacks compared to previous years. Eighty-five percent of the whites polled in 1966 thought the civil rights movement was moving too fast, while only 49 percent thought so in 1965 and 34 percent in 1964. Comments from interviewers showed that worry over the recent ghetto riots weighed heavily in the responses. This reaction influenced a dramatic reversal in the civil rights gains of the 1960s. After history-making decisions to guarantee blacks rights to public accommodations and voting in 1964 and 1965, Congress scuttled an important open housing bill in 1966. The national mood became more hostile to civil rights pressures, and the glory days of the rights movement's legislative successes passed quickly.[10]

The tough words of militant blacks gave additional force to white backlash. During the tumultuous 1960s Eldridge Cleaver wrote, "America will be painted red. Dead bodies will litter the streets. . . ." The Black Panthers warned they were going to "get whitey," and Malcolm X preached about the dangers of working with "white devils." Indeed, Malcolm X well understood the purpose of the strident voice. As biographer Peter Goldman notes, Malcolm conciously used harsh language in public to assert black confidence and pride, and to "frighten whites out of their shoes."[11] The aggressiveness had a point, but not to the degree of diminishing returns. Malcolm X, who died in 1965, did not live to observe the full impact of reaction. By the late 1960s and early 1970s the civil rights movement was in decline. The potential of violent language and behavior for provoking anger and dis-illusionment among whites and despair and confusion among blacks figured significantly in the reversal.

In sum, the tendency of both blacks and whites to stereotype and scapegoat each other produces considerable emotion but little progress toward eliminating violence and inequality. In the broad view no group has a special claim to innocence or guilt in contributing to the difficulties. The problem of violence defies simple black and white explanations.

6

YOUTHS

In 1974 New York City police pondered over ways to handle the growing incidence of violent crime committed by youths less than sixteen years of age. In some cases police took seven-year-olds into custody for rape, robbery, and assault and attributed murders to eight- and nine-year-olds. Most of the new examples of youth violence involved groups. Boys, and sometimes girls, operated in packs of two, three, or four. Some of their murder and mugging victims were children of their own age. Others were men and women in their seventies, eighties, and nineties whom they beat, stabbed, and shot to death. Because New York State courts tended to treat guilty youths under age sixteen with short or suspended sentences, many young attackers continued their string of crimes without fear of being caught. "We can do this until we're 16 cause the Court won't do nothing to us," they told police. In one case three youths who killed a taxi driver had a record of 42 previous arrests, including charges of robbery, grand larceny, burglary, and shoplifting. Two of them had been arrested for holding up a taxi driver three days before the murder. These are just a few examples of the rising tide of youth violence that stirred great concern among the police and the public in New York as well as other cities.[1]

Not many years ago, many viewed movies about teenage violence as portrayals of small but potentially serious problems. They believed films like *West Side Story* and *Blackboard Jungle* identified the behavior of a dangerous minority that might grow in numbers in the future. The future has arrived, and it makes the old movie scenes look tame by comparison. Many of today's city streets and schools have the appearance of war zones, places where people fear imminent outbreaks of violence. The warriors in these battle zones are not seasoned soldiers, of course. They are belligerent youngsters who are only a few years away from the age when most young men lose interest in the ruffian image, unclench their fists, and hang up their weapons. How to protect these violent youths from harming others as well as themselves before that time comes remains a formidable challenge.

We will be wise to examine only a few salient manifestations of this growing popularity of violent behavior among youths. The literature on adolescent violence is so vast that it cannot be given the attention it deserves in this brief discussion. Rather than attempt a survey of important topics in the field, this chapter will focus on two problems that are particularly severe today: violence in the schools and the behavior of violent inner-city gangs. Through these two foci perhaps we can more clearly view the larger problem.

Violence in the Schools

A century ago Eliza Cook spoke hopefully of the school's potential for preventing crime. "Better build schoolrooms for 'the boy,' " she said, "than cells and gibbets for 'the man.' " This statement succinctly expresses one of the major expectations of schools in poor urban neighborhoods. In addition to educating individuals for a career, schools should serve as civilizing agencies. They should be oases of culture in environments devoid of almost all other civilizing stimuli. Schools should take youngsters off the streets, teach them manners, and instill an appreciation of mainstream values. Education should encourage its clientele to eschew the driftless life of the criminal for the goal-directed life of a respectable citizen. Or so folks said.

Today many public schools in big cities are hard put to resist the invasion of street culture into the classroom without even the possibility of teaching underprivileged youngsters the skills they will need to compete in the market place. In these troubled buildings the idea of school-as-civilizing-force is being undermined severely by increasing violence, intimidation, and fear. Far from inculcating young people with the values of civility, the environment in many schools trains students for bullying, gang warfare, robbery, vandalism, and defiance. Like prisons, their buildings have become schools for crime and violence, gathering together an amalgam of antisocial types under one roof and providing them opportunities for mutual antagonism or encouragement of gangsterism. The lawlessness of street life has permeated many classrooms, bringing attendant hells into the very buildings designed as educational sanctuaries from the madness outside. As one fifteen-year-old New York City student commented, "I go to school for an education, not to be robbed and stabbed." He said he was "scared of walking down the halls." Even seven-year-olds face lunch money "shakedowns" in the corridors. Teachers, too, frequently fall victim to robberies in the schools, including holdups by intruders who appear unabashedly in front of packed classrooms. One visitor walked up to a New York City instructor with a gun during a session and announced, "There are a lot of children in your class. Walk behind your desk and sit down. If you move, I'll blow your brains out." In many cities both students and teachers face constant fear of falling victim to serious physical attack. In San Diego, for example, there were three times as many assaults on teachers in 1973 as in 1972 and twice as many assaults on students. The situation produced swelling enrollments in parochial schools as nervous parents withdrew their children from public institutions.[2]

Still more dramatic are numerous incidents of school bombings. In 1972 school administrators from thirty states gathered in a purposefully unpublicized meeting in Denver to talk with bomb experts and compare notes on means to protect their schools from these threats. In the previous year the Bomb Data Center had received 2,585 reports of incidents involving school bombings.[3]

These and other examples of violence indicate that many educational institutions have turned into teenage battlegrounds. As the Law Enforcement Administration pointed out, "Today, when newspapers speak of mugging, vandalism, rape, robbery at knifepoint, assault and rape, they do not refer to the underworld but to our schools, our children."[4] Long gone are the days when infractions in city schools typically meant chewing gum, smoking in the lavatory, or going up the down staircase.

This tough reality makes much of the debate about reforming educational techniques in city schools sound like irrelevant theorizing. After all, how effective can even the most ambitious programs to upgrade inner-city education be if violence pervades the laboratories for change? Educators' disputes over the advantage of different curricula, general versus vocational training, or the influence of family background, income status, and peer group relationships in school success lose their import when tension over violence troubles students and teachers daily. In many inner-city schools the violence of the youth culture operates as a far more serious detriment to learning than limitations in the students' social backgrounds. Learning becomes secondary when survival is the primary concern. Relationships often operate by the code of the jungle.

As with crime in the streets, society has responded to growing crime in the schools with cries for law and order. Parents and teachers frequently criticize administrators and city governments, demanding better protection on the schoolgrounds. In response, officials have assigned security guards to patrol halls and have sent policemen to watch over the school environs. Many teachers readily accept the measures as necessary for security, even though administrators sometimes resist such drastic policies. "Think carefully before you turn the high school into an armed camp," one principal warned his impatient staff. But these teachers *wanted* an armed camp.[5] So did many parents of their students. For example, Philadelphia's superintendent of schools

responded to their outcries by asking for $500,000 to hire uni-
formed guards to line "safety corridors" to and from the schools
in violence-infested neighborhoods.[6]
Even the most stringent security measures are likely to fail
when students are more deeply impressed by the education they
receive on the streets than the education they receive in the
classroom. Peer group attitudes provide the main cues for
behavior. For a substantial number of city youths in America
today, social acceptance within the tough value system of the
streets is far more meaningful than success according to the value
system they learn in school. The violent subculture's tremendous
influence on city youth is particularly evident in the thinking and
behavior of teenage gangs. Understanding the motivation of
these gang members can help to clarify the rising violence among
teenagers in various schools.

Teenage Gangs

Gang   members   deserve   more   understanding   than
mainstream Americans often accord them. The destruction and
bloodshed caused by teenagers running in wolfpacks do have
meaning. Abundant sociological research confirms that the
desire to achieve status and self-esteem is one of the most important motives of youths who join gangs. Display of toughness,
so typical of inner-city gang members, helps individuals to overcome feelings of insecurity during their difficult adolescent years.
By showing bravado, by advertising an eager readiness to fight,
the unemployed, the unskilled, the school dropout, the ne'er-do-
well in mainstream society's eyes can become a success in his own
eyes and in the eyes of his friends. Boasting about one's fighting
talents expresses machismo. It is a demonstration of no small
importance to a teenager struggling for manhood and group
acceptance. Approval by the group for acts of violence provides a
valuable sense of belonging. Few adolescents have the individual
fortitude to go it alone, particularly when they are so ill-equipped
to break from the influences of a ghetto environment. As one
big-city administrator explains the situation, "The whole at-

mosphere is geared to crushing a person's spirit, and most people don't have the kind of strength to resist."[7]

For youngsters of low socioeconomic background with few opportunities to make it in the competitive market place, violent gangs offer particularly attractive routes to status. "Gangs give folks something to be proud of," explains a member of Chicago's tough Black Disciples, who notes that, "My parents couldn't afford to put me in the Boy Scouts."[8] Though they lack marketable skills and good education, these youngsters, too, yearn for personal fulfillment and dignity. But they know they cannot find personal satisfaction by working through regular channels as do many of the more privileged youths. In lieu of following the traditional work ethic, they turn middle-class values upside down. Rather than seek psychic gratification according to Establishment criteria, to which they are unlikely to measure up, they make their own rules, giving the greatest honor to those who are most successful in doing precisely what is not "cricket." Harassment, vandalism, burglary, and robbery range among the most frequent of these antisocial acts. Especially in recent years, acts of violence have become very important marks for elevation in the status system of youth gangs. Young men can gain respect from their friends, enhance their reputations, and find opportunities for mobility within the gang subculture through participation in rumbles, beatings, shootouts, and similar activities. Thus, violence per se has become a major factor in the gangs' ethos.

Today's gangs engage in much bloodier activity than did gangs of past years. It is difficult to measure degrees of gang violence over the long course of American history, but the trend through recent decades is quite clear. An upsurge of gang activities in the 1950s stirred considerable public concern. Some of the most perceptive studies of the gang phenomenon appeared during this period. Among them were books such as Lewis Jablonski's sociological classic, *The Violent Gang*, and artistic portrayals such as the beautiful and touching Broadway show, *West Side Story*. Gang activities waned in the 1960s as drugs, the civil rights movement, urban rioting, and other matters temporarily dominated the attention of inner-city youths. By the late 1960s, the violent gang movement became popular once again, paralleling the increased violence in other sectors of society. But the new movement took on a much bloodier form than did the earlier one of the 1950s.[9] By the 1970s urban citizens had a serious new youth problem on their hands. It was new in terms of youth involvement in very lethal confrontations. For example, Philadelphia recorded 43 gang-related deaths in 1971 and 39 in 1972. Many of the victims were children, and the average age of both victim and killer was only a little over sixteen.[10] The gang-infested Bronx scored an even worse record in 1972, considering its smaller population. Official counts associated gangs with 30 murders as well as 10 rapes, 124 armed robberies, and 800 violent crimes of different types. Unofficial estimates placed the figures much higher, since many crimes went unreported.[11] Many other urban residents were casualties of a different sort—victims of profound fear of gang activities. Millions of unidentified urban residents suffered from the debilitating worry that they might become prey for teenage wolfpacks.

The increase in bloodspilling from gang activities demonstrates the growing influence of a popular ethos of violence that glorifies toughness as a route to peer acceptance. This increase has been facilitated by the availability of sophisticated weaponry. During the 1950s, gangs fought with fists, bottles, clubs, chains, knives, and a variety of makeshift weapons. Though these instruments of combat were hardly innocuous, they were not nearly as lethal as the trusty Saturday Night Specials as well as rifles and shotguns now popular with youths. Once guns became common on the streets, they made other weapons seem obsolete. An arms race began which could not be stopped. "Nobody wants it," said one Philadelphia gang member, of the rush to obtain firearms, "but everybody's doing it." Callous attitudes about murder accompanied the proliferation of guns and the increase in shootings. One *New York Times* reporter claimed the spate of youth homicides in West Philadelphia showed that gang wars were becoming a "way of death" in the city. In streetcorner conversations with teenagers, he found remarks about killing common and casual. "When you're warring some guy and you go up there and body on 'em, it makes you feel good," commented an eighteen year old. "Body" on them, asked the reporter? "Yeah," responded a fourteen year old with a broad smile, "body on 'em! That means go up and hurt 'em." "No," shot back two younger gang members, "it means kill 'em."[12]

This lightheaded commentary suggests not only the gang members' indifference toward serious injury but also their alacrity to go into battle for very trivial reasons. Group standoffs often explode from a bad look, a nasty remark, an argument over a girl, or an intrusion into another gang's "turf" (territory). Sometimes violence develops out of a search for adventure or a desire for "kicks" to relieve a night's boredom.[13] While adult residents occasionally become prime targets or find themselves innocent bystanders caught between volleys, they are not the big game gangs usually hunt. Bloodshed from gang activity occurs most frequently when youth groups confront other gangs over affairs of "honor." It is this emotional, chauvinistic, and territory-obsessed quality in youth violence that has led many observers to liken gang fights to wars between xenophobic nations. If gangs operate like irrational, war-hungry nations, they ask, might the same procedures used in modern diplomacy—negotiations—help to prevent the bloodshed?

Peace negotiations between battle-ready youth groups can help, but usually offer only superficial, short-term solutions. Nonetheless, the bold individuals who attempt these negotiations (often former gang members themselves) deserve great credit for their efforts. Many cities now have agents working in this capacity through community youth services, and some of them have lost their lives while trying to avert flareups and arrange peace treaties. On other occasions gang members sabotage negotiations by striking at each other. Sometimes a minor incident can lead to chaos when nervous gun-toting young warriors meet each other to work out a settlement. In Philadelphia, for example, one conference between warring parties appeared to be making progress until an argument between two girls over ways to operate a new "peace council" provoked a shootout. Three youngsters were wounded in the melee.[14]

Some social workers have tried to find more fundamental

ways to avert gang warfare through improving employment
opportunities for inner-city youths and creating better recreational facilities. Many are very optimistic about the potential of
job programs. Ted Gross, New York City commissioner of Youth
Services, was pleased with the Neighborhood Youth Corps' 1972
program. "It helped a lot," said Gross, noting that the jobs kept
more than half a million young people busy in the summer,
providing them with honestly earned spending money and giving
them some dignity. [15] In addition to public campaigns to help city
youths, many individuals make their own personal contributions.
In Philadelphia, for instance, the owner of an inner-city variety
store employed three neighborhood youths in a voluntary effort
to alleviate the gang problem, and to avoid intimidation from
local gangs. His young workers performed well. "A kid needs a
dollar in his pocket," commented the merchant, briefly summing
up his philosophy about the importance of jobs in trimming down
gang violence.[16] Kids also need something to do with their time,
add other observers of the gang problem, who show disgust over
the lack of recreational facilities in urban areas. The few available
facilities are grossly inadequate for the huge concentration of
young people, they note. This absence of good opportunities for
adolescents to congregate in a healthy social environment makes
the gang's headquarters a favorite center for passing away leisure
hours, meeting friends, and achieving a sense of belonging and
personal worth.

If alternative opportunities were made available to urban
teenagers in a broad-scale effort, creating something akin to a
New Deal for Youth program, the changes would, no doubt, do
much to alleviate the problem of violent gangs. Youth service
agencies can improve communications between gangs as well as
understanding between gangs and community residents. Job
opportunities give youths a stake in the economy and the social
system, and provide a monetary basis for personal dignity.
Recreational programs can direct leisure-time energies into safe
channels. While all of these opportunities can improve the situation, they still fall far short of tackling directly one of the most
important causes of trouble. The difficulties do not pertain simply to economic deprivation, lack of recreational facilities, or the

like. Many youths in other cultures around the world (as well as in certain sections of the United States) live in much more squalid conditions than those in Chicago, New York, Philadelphia, or Los Angeles, yet they do not resort to the gratuitous forms of violence popular with so many teenage gang members in America's large cities. There is something more to this chemistry of youths hunting for battle and blood than solely a question of inequality.[17] That special factor is the cult of violence itself, the value system popular with many American youths that associates toughness, maturity, manliness, courage, and prestige with a willingness to bring injury to others. No doubt many underprivileged youths can be expected to show interest in violent behavior as an alternate source of status, but the exaggerated infatuation with violence in today's youth culture well exceeds the unfortunate but likely byproducts of living in a low-income environment. Youth's interest in violence for violence's sake has become unusually harmful for themselves and for the residents around them. Now that these machismo-obsessed youngsters have abundant firearms in their hands, they are a much more serious menace than ever before.

7

ASSASSINATIONS

In the summer of 1972, one of the many serious assassination scares in modern times took place . . . and most people hardly took notice. The incident occurred during the Democratic National Convention in Miami Beach at the plush Doral Hotel, George McGovern's campaign headquarters. It was the second day of the convention, the apogee of McGovern's fight for the presidency. During the previous night his political soldiers finished a successful floor battle over the seating of California delegates, a victory that assured McGovern's nomination. By the next morning excited McGovernites gathered around the Doral entrance and in the lobby, waiting for their hero to appear for a brief speech. Suddenly there was commotion near the hotel portico, as FBI agents grabbed a man sitting in a car parked in front. The man's comrade dashed away, rushing into the hotel lobby before agents caught up with him.

Why such drama over the appearance of two men? Because the FBI had received a tip that these two black "liberationists," presumed to be dangerous, were on a suspicious mission. After following the suspects for a few days, the FBI decided the moment for action had come when the men parked their car in front of McGovern headquarters. Agents found two loaded revolvers on the suspects. Whether the two men had any intention of making an attempt on the presidential candidate's life could not be fully determined, but the circumstantial evidence was enough to give cause for worry. While McGovern's associates immediately canceled the candidate's planned appearance, an army of young campaign workers walked around the lobby confused and dazed, their euphoria abruptly punctured. A brief act of violence, they realized, could end what they had worked toward over several years. They suddenly recognized, at least for the moment, the fragility of the American political system and its vulnerability to the venom of just one angry person.[1]

For the many citizens who are less emotionally attached to a presidential candidate, news of assassination threats is tranquilly accepted as an unfortunate fact of political life. Reports on the Doral Hotel incident attracted little attention. A day after it occurred, many people had no knowledge of the event. Even the news media gave it little coverage. Reports appeared in short articles on the inside pages of newspapers, and some TV news programs gave the incident brief coverage. On that summer day in 1972 baseball scores took precedence over reports that the likely Democratic presidential candidate might have been targeted for an assassin's bullet.

Assassination hoaxes as well as serious threats are so commonplace in American life that few people react intensely to reports of *alleged* plans for an attack. It is only when a major figure actually falls from bullet wounds that the public dialogue turns to penetrating questions about the problem of violence. In addition to the Doral incident, several other threats or suspicions of assassination occurred during the 1972 campaign, yet they too aroused little notice. In one situation police, responding to a tipoff, arrested a young man with a live grenade in his pocket. Authorities learned that the man intended to drive to the Coast Guard Academy, where Vice-President Spiro Agnew was scheduled to speak. Although additional information on the case released a few days later suggested the suspect had been engaged in a prank rather than a true threat, public indifference to initial reports exemplified the nonchalant response to potential assassinations.[2] In another case during the 1972 campaign, a man purportedly offered to pay an agent $1,000 to assassinate President Nixon. To the alleged plotter's misfortune, the agent he accosted happened to work for the FBI. This news item, too, tended to receive back-page, short-column newspaper coverage, and only a small minority of Americans knew about it the day after it happened. Finally, news that George Wallace's attacker had earlier stalked President Nixon before changing targets also failed to stir much interest. Just a few weeks after Arthur Bremer's arrest for shooting Wallace, the Canadian police reported that the attacker had been only ten to twelve feet from Nixon during the President's diplomatic visit to Ottawa. An entry in Bremer's diary confirmed the report. "He passed me six times and he's still alive!," wrote Bremer, apparently angry about losing his opportunity.[3]

Behind these examples of scares from the 1972 presidential campaign are several unsuccessful attempts, some of them little known, against other Presidents or Presidents-elect. Lee Harvey Oswald's infamous deed of November 22, 1963, is well known, but few remember that John F. Kennedy had been targeted for murder a few years earlier. In 1960, when he was President-elect, a demented Kennedy-hater planned an attack with seven sticks of dynamite, but the Secret Service acted on a tip and succeeded in aborting the plot.[4] Harry Truman narrowly escaped death when White House policemen engaged in a shootout to prevent two Puerto Rican nationalists from completing their mission. The armed attackers were stopped on the lawn, outside Blair House where President Truman was sleeping.[5] Franklin D. Roosevelt also was nearly assassinated. In February 1933, an angry immigrant with a general hatred for capitalists aimed at Roosevelt but missed, killing the mayor of Chicago instead.[6] Such attempts on U.S. national leaders date back into the nineteenth century. Most people with a general knowledge of American history know that Abraham Lincoln was the first United States President to be assassinated, but few know that Andrew Jackson was the first President to be fired at by someone who intended assassination. Good fortune saved Jackson in the 1835 incident, as both of his assailant's pistols misfired.[7] These are the quirks of history. Jackson, Roosevelt, Truman, and Kennedy. Might American history have been different had the foiled attempts against them been more successful? Undoubtedly so, but we need not indulge in speculation about the variety of possible consequences. It is enough to recognize that the acts of determined assassins can prove to be accidents of very great significance in the course of American history.

When a prominent figure does get assassinated, many people search to find rational meaning in the "accidents" of violence. Often the public responds immediately with jeremiads about the evils society has brought upon itself. These chest-thumping expressions of guilt vary in accordance with the prejudices of each individual. Many of these wailings about violence fail to pinpoint primary causes, as did the commentary of Governor Ronald Reagan in 1968. He responded to Robert Kennedy's assassination by warning that "this nation can no longer tolerate the spirit of permissiveness that pervades our courts and other institutions."[8] His analysis was about as irrelevant to the situation as the foreign observation of *Izvestia,* the Soviet government's official newspaper. *Izvestia* believed the Kennedy assassination showed violence to be "an organism of capitalistic society" and that "violence is innate to imperialism."[9] Perhaps equally off the mark was Richard Drinnon's view that assassinations point up the basic injustices in American life. Drinnon said Americans should not be surprised if assassins who seem paranoid are really cruel images of society's rulers. Those who insist that assassinations are only manifestations of irrationality are people who want to forget the oppression against Mexican-Americans, Indians, and blacks and believe America is a free and just society, claimed Drinnon.[10]

Although it would be interesting to find some rational pattern to support an ideological explanation for assassinations, the list of potential victims precludes such a possibility. Consider the diverse backgrounds and political viewpoints of leading figures targeted in the 1960s and 1970s. What did John F. Kennedy, Martin Luther King, Jr., George Wallace, Malcolm X, George Lincoln Rockwell, Medgar Evers, and Robert Kennedy hold in common? Even their postures on militancy differed from one another. Malcolm X once appropriately speculated about who would be assassinated first— Martin Luther King, Jr., the advocate of nonviolence, or himself, the spokesman for violence.[11] Conservative, liberal, or radical, ultraright or ultra-left—representatives of all major positions in the political spectrum can qualify for liquidation by an angry assassin.

Actually, it is the assassins who have much more in common than the assassinated. The Violence Commission's study of assassins shows a group of men desperately in search of ways to demonstrate their machismo. This study found that they are usually below average in stature, unsuccessful in employment or in pursuit of employment, withdrawn, and lacking in both male and female companionship. They are profoundly unhappy people, haunted by a lack of respect for themselves. Such persons are usually anxious to find personal redemption, to "prove themselves" in one dramatic act that can change them suddenly from unknown failures to "great men" in history. Aching for martyrdom, assassins believe their act of violence will serve some noble, transcendent purpose.[12]

Many of these characteristics certainly apply to Lee Harvey Oswald, Sirhan Sirhan, and Arthur Bremer. They also relate to the personality profiles of men who went after presidents or Presidents-elect earlier in American history. Of all those who attacked American Presidents or Presidents elect, only the Puerto Rican nationalists who sought Harry Truman's life showed clear political goals (they wanted to draw attention to Puerto Rico's independence cause) and did not demonstrate highly unusual personality characteristics which could be associated with serious mental disturbances. Richard Lawrence, who attacked Andrew Jackson, suffered delusions, imagining himself to be Richard III of England. John Wilkes Booth became hypersensitive about the Southern cause, to the point of nearly strangling his own brother-in-law for slighting the President of the Confederacy. Booth believed Lincoln intended to make himself a king and saw himself, in the assassin's role, as an agent of God. Charles J. Guiteau, who murdered James Garfield, thought God had called on him to save the country by killing its President. Leon F. Czolgosz, assassin of William McKinley, was so appalled by cruelty that he refused to kill insects, but his fascination with the murder of a European monarch figured in his decision to gun down the President. Giuseppe Zangara, who failed in an assassination attempt against Franklin D. Roosevelt, had sought out President Herbert Hoover in the winter of 1932-1933, but could not bring himself to commit assassination in a cold climate. His attack on Roosevelt occurred in Miami, Florida. Lee Harvey Oswald, the man responsible for John F. Kennedy's death, had undergone psychiatric treatment by a specialist who noted his "schizoid features" and "passive-aggressive tendencies."

If assassinations of Presidents are usually committed by highly insecure, irrational people, what can be done to prevent repeated incidents of this kind? There will always be sick individuals in the national population who experience extraordinary frustrations in their search for self-gratification and recognition. Must national leaders wait through this psychological Russian Roulette, hoping that madness will not strike during their term of office? Some enthusiasts for psychiatry think they have a partial answer. Serious danger could be prevented, they say, if social scientists could develop sophisticated techniques for identifying potential assassins.

Relying on psychiatric predictions as a defense against assassinations is itself so farfetched that it is surprising so many can seriously discuss the prospect. Just how does one begin picking out potential assassins? The idea can convert "presumptive danger" into political repression. It is one thing to speculate that a man's personality profile resembles that of typical assassins but quite another to begin limiting his freedom on the basis of that resemblance. Many thousands of people would probably meet the criteria established by social scientists. To incarcerate them because they fit the profile of dangerous personalities would not only be illegal but morally outrageous. Furthermore, reliance on personality profiles assumes a great deal of reliability and validity in the assessments of psychiatrists. It suggests that psychiatry will soon be able to predict the behavior of individuals almost as accurately as physical scientists predict the behavior of electrons and protons. Psychiatrists cannot claim such accuracy in their present predictions, and there is no reason to believe that their record will improve substantially.

Evidence of the uncertainty of psychiatric analysts often appears in the contrasting courtroom testimony of "experts." Psychiatrists frequently diverge greatly in assessing the mental condition of assassins up for trial and proffer very different criteria of sanity. Defense and prosecuting attorneys for Jack Ruby, Sirhan Sirhan, and Arthur Bremer easily produced expert testimony both for sanity and insanity. As expected, psychiatrists called by the defense tended to speak of the accused as insane, while psychiatrists called by the prosecution emphasized the defendant's control over his mental faculties at the time of the crime, suggesting that he was responsible for the acts he committed. Trial lawyers know that they usually can find social scientists who will testify for the desired point of view. Recognizing this fact does not negate the value of psychiatry. It simply acknowledges that conflicting assessments have their place, since there is no clear, generally acceptable dividing line between sanity and insanity. These labels are subjective categories representing the serious but speculative efforts of trained psychiatrists to weigh diverse data and to identify subjects' conditions. Psychiatry cannot offer preventive medicine against assassinations and it certainly cannot predict precisely which people in a population of millions will, in the future, attempt to murder a national leader.

If it is not possible to remove assassins from the political scene, argue some, it is still possible through protective devices to diminish the potential killer's access to national leaders. Some of the defensive measures advocated have already gone into effect. Among those used to protect Presidents are increased numbers of Secret Service agents, armor-plated cars with bullet-proof glass, and helicopters to survey crowds from above when the President makes open-air public appearances. Some of the new ideas considered for ultraprotection by innovative scientists sound more comical than helpful. For example, the Rand Corporation concluded a special study on the problems of presidential protection in 1964 by recommending body armor, shielding and evasive techniques, armored speakers' platforms, blast-containment chambers, and even an electroacoustic device to detect a gunshot and immediately activate a protective shield around the public figure.[13] Any leader availing himself of such gadgets would lose more than he would gain through public appearances. He would do better delivering an address on TV than appearing before a crowd as an armored knight.

Short of using a futuresque invisible protective shield similar to those featured in science fiction films and toothpaste advertisements, there is no guaranteed protection for the politician determined to meet the public against the assassin determined to bag his target. The Alabama state trooper who was wounded while protecting George Wallace from Arthur Bremer commented on the problem perceptively, saying, "In looking back, I don't see that we could have changed any security arrangements that would have made anything better."[14] Once George Wallace took off his coat and walked into the crowd, he subjected himself to very substantial dangers against which even three times as many security guards could not have protected him. This reality was obvious in the attack on Robert Kennedy. When Sirhan Sirhan pumped bullets into Kennedy, the presidential candidate was standing between two professional football players and an Olympic decathlon champ. In Martin Luther King, Jr.'s case, more than thirty Memphis police were on assignment to guard the civil rights leader and his entourage, yet James Earl Ray escaped after firing a single deadly shot. Could elaborate preparations have prevented these occurrences? John F. Kennedy spoke candidly and prophetically on the matter, commenting, "If anybody really wanted to shoot the president of the United States, it was not a very difficult job—all one had to do was get on a high building some day with a telescopic rifle, and there was nothing anybody could do to defend against such an attempt."[15] J. Edgar Hoover apparently agreed. The FBI chief dismissed complaints that his agency did not provide strict safety precautions for the President, considering such post-facto recommendations as proposals for "totalitarian security."

If elaborate security measures can offer only limited protection, what should the President do: avoid public appearances or take his chances by venturing into crowds? Whatever his choice, democracy suffers from the outcome. If the President chooses to remain at a safe distance, the precious opportunity for personal contact between leaders and constituents is lost. A democracy thrives on these contacts. Many Americans know the dynamics of standing amidst an enthusiastic crowd, waiting for the appearance of a political favorite. On a purely rational level the entire situation may appear ludicrous, a time-consuming, emotional exercise in hero-worship. Thousands of people stand pressed against each other for hours awaiting a brief opportunity to see their favorite in the flesh and, perhaps, to hear him make a few trite statements. A lucky minority, benefited by good position and motivated by the desire for physical contact, push to the front for a momentary closeup of the leader and a coveted handshake. As the politician moves through the crowd, exhuberant admirers exclaim like children, "I touched him!" "I shook his hand!" Or, "Doesn't he look great? He's much more handsome in person than on television!" Despite all the corny appearances of emotional hoopla, it is fundamental to the effective workings of a democracy. Politics must offer more than cool assessment of the issues. It must provide drama, excitement, and personal "experiences." It should give the people a sense of involvement and a circus of events featuring live performers. Politics must have schmaltz. Yet with the new assassination contagion, this person-to-person style in politics is very risky.

Democracy suffers when one bullet is mightier than millions of votes. This is a major current difficulty that has significantly weakened the American political system. As the editors of the *Philadelphia Inquirer* commented after the Wallace shooting: "When violence becomes a substitute for the ballot box, or threatens to, democracy is in deep trouble."[16] In recent years just a few men with a few guns have denied the public its choices for leadership. Given the current assassination fever, other national leaders could fall victim in the decades ahead. This discomforting possibility should prompt more serious concern for the quality of vice-presidential candidates, but this, clearly, is not a solution to the problem. Presidential assassinations tear large holes in the democratic fabric which substitute leaders, even capable ones, cannot mend.

Assassinations shake the people's confidence in the stability and legitimacy of the political system, especially when they affect the life of a popular leader. The depth of impact is reflected, for example, in the way Americans remember John F. Kennedy's death. Few who were adults in 1963 have forgotten precisely where they were and what they were doing when they first heard the news report. What explains this extraordinary span of detailed memory in millions of Americans who often have trouble enough just remembering their social security number? The record of that day stays in their minds because it profoundly shook their own personal lives. News of Kennedy's death signified more than just the loss of a President; to many it represented the loss of order and direction in the world around them. Psychologists have likened public reaction to assassination of a popular President to family reaction to patricide. A popular President serves as a father figure to the national family; his murder leaves members shocked, disoriented, and insecure—like a family suddenly forced to face life's challenges without their patriarchal leader.[17] In this sense political assassinations weaken the stability and legitimacy of political institutions, producing sudden turnovers in government and raising questions about the rightful authority of new leaders to govern. If the shocks occur repeatedly at short intervals, they can seriously wear away faith in the overall political system.

In an environment of frequent assassinations and assassination attempts against diverse prominent figures, the American public is growing increasingly pessimistic about the prospects for enjoying a future leadership not threatened by assassins. Many Americans have come to *expect* several more attempts on the lives of national leaders in the near future. Speculation about Senator Edward Kennedy's political prospects following McGovern's 1972 defeat is a case in point. In almost every extended conversation on the subject at that time, people expressed serious concern that Kennedy would be marked for assassination either while campaigning or, if elected, while in office. Many said they did not believe Kennedy should ever run as a presidential candidate precisely because of the high probability of an assassination attempt. Such was the tenor of conversation about America's future presidential leadership. The potential for assassination was weighed as if it were just one more unchangeable reality among the many in national politics.

8
PROTEST

Before moving on to a discussion of the sources of the problem of violence in American civilization, it is appropriate to devote some attention to an aspect which dominated public interest just a short time ago: the issue of violent civil disobedience. Ironically, the problem which probably most alerted Americans to violence in the 1960s and provoked angry cries for Law and Order almost disappeared as a significant public issue by the early 1970s. Collective violence, a wave of upheaval and destruction developing out of protest from large groups of discontented Americans, set off harsh reactions and inflamed the populace against each other in a way that deeply shocked contemporaries. For a short time, especially between 1967 and 1970, America's confidence was knocked off-balance by growing tensions and conflicts, and the populace appeared seriously worried about the nation's future. Violent demonstrations, riots, and other large-scale incidents prompted many to ask very general, sweeping questions which they had not asked before, namely: Why all the violent protest? What caused it? Was America becoming a violent nation? Looking in retrospect we may add some relevant questions: Why did the protest movements eventually wane? What did the period of upheaval demonstrate about the effectiveness of violence in forging social change?

Richard Hofstadter, perhaps America's finest modern-day historian, devoted much of his professional time to these questions before his death from cancer in 1970. In a major essay published posthumously in 1970, Hofstadter explained his special interest in ideological and political characteristics of the problems. "Our new concern about violence today is, among other things, a response to a sharp increase in its volume," wrote Hofstadter, "but it is also a response to its shifting *role*. Violence has become, to a degree unprecedented in the United States, the outgrowth of forcible acts by dissidents and radicals who are expressing hostility to middle-class ways and to established power." Hofstadter saw antecedents to the contemporary challenge in historical examples of riots, industrial violence, lynching, vigilantism, and slave revolts and their suppression, or, as he described them, "some of the most costly and symptomatic varieties" of violence in the annals of national life. He acknowledged that many other aspects of the problem deserved attention—criminal violence, gangster shootouts, feuds, assassinations—but, because of limited space, Hofstadter decided to confine his discussion to historical cases most relevant to the social conflagration around him.[1] In the aftermath of collective turmoil in the late 1960s and early 1970s, problems which concerned Hofstadter and millions of other Americans still seem relevant to an understanding of the national malaise, but they do not appear to identify the central challenge. *Individual* violence represents the greater and more persistent threat to American civilization. Yet it would be unfortunate, indeed, if the waning of dramatic, collective clashes should create a false confidence about America's dealings with the threat of violence in modern times.

Although a rising crime rate, assassinations of public figures, and other problems worried Americans by the mid-1960s, the emergence of widespread protest action and collective confrontations made violence a matter of prime concern. Newsmaking clashes over ideological and political differences shattered America's self-assurance that it could progress in an environment of domestic tranquility. All the hosannas to national traditions of consensus, compromise, practical good sense, flexible institutions, effective politics, and a workable system began to appear embarrassingly inappropriate. In urban ghettoes thousands of young blacks angrily rushed into the streets, leaving a path of great destruction. In Detroit, Newark, Washington, Chicago, and elsewhere, rampages produced memorable scenes of looting, fighting, shooting, and arson in shocking newspaper and television pictures. Millions who lived in large cities as well as smaller urban centers worried that the upheaval would eventually affect them. In these nervewracking conditions some believed they were witnessing the collapse of a great national myth—the idea that America finally had made significant progress in civil rights, providing new opportunities for the black community, and, consequently, giving blacks feelings of respect for the American political system. Riots showed the melting-pot approach had not worked, they said. Rather than producing satisfaction, civil rights gains of the period only stirred greater anger over the many promises still not fulfilled.

Nervousness about domestic turmoil intensified when belligerent college students began protesting en masse, turning campuses into areas of noisy protests and dangerous confrontations. Student complaints which seemed only minor at first quickly mushroomed into "nonnegotiable" demands. Sons and daughters of "fine" families besieged deans in their offices, took control of campus buildings, and disrupted classes. When police tried to evict them, some resisted with force. The mere presence of police on the campuses escalated tensions immensely, creating new clashes and complaints. The crescendo of protest looked still more ominous when buildings went up in flames, and, in some places, excited students and nonstudent protestors spilled out into the city streets to join in more destructive forays. Bloodshed resulting from the clashes of Chicago, Kent State, and Washington showed the highly explosive potential in rising antagonism between the student protestors and the law enforcement representatives sent out to control them. These occurrences seemed to explode another favorite American myth—the idea that the country's middle classes could be expected to resolve their differences nonviolently because of their economic and social stake in the system. Youth's confidence in the Establishment now weakened measurably, and interest in radical ideologies appeared from the most unexpected sectors of society's comfortable classes. Rather than producing satisfaction, the age of affluence saw its children of abundance tramping off in anger and disgust.

As many citizens struggled to understand the confusing events, spokesmen for two schools of political thought gained considerable attention. They stood at opposite poles, trying to make sense of the upheaval in simple, uncomplicated terms. Each school's interpretation of events contained some measure of fact, but like most blanket judgments they also offered much fiction and oversimplification.

Many spokesmen from the left side of the political and ideological spectrum saw violent developments as evidence for their most pessimistic impressions about America. Society was corrupt, decadent, exploitative, and imperialistic, they said. Now the country would receive its just deserts. News of violent clashes might shock the naive, they explained, but those who recognized America's true condition could only shake their heads with sad understanding. Why be shocked by the violence, they asked, when anyone familiar with American history should know that it had long been part of national life? Indians, blacks, abolitionists, trade-union organizers, socialists, and civil rights workers had long experienced terrible repression. The latest examples of violence only indicated the continuity of history. As in the past, defenders of the status quo and protectors of special interests were crying out again for repression of groups that raised legitimate grievances. Now the aggrieved would act on the lessons of history. If fighting and destruction had been used to maintain injustices in the past, fighting and destruction could also be used to win justice in the present. Turning to a strategy of fighting fire with fire, society's angry critics sanctioned violence as a legitimate tool of protest. Violence was an effective weapon, they asserted, and, in the light of history, an appropriate means of confronting problems in America. As H. Rap Brown put it, "Violence is as American as cherry pie."

From the other side of the political and ideological spectrum came angry protestations of equal intensity. Many citizens responded to the growing turmoil by rallying around the flag and ostentatiously announcing their faith in America. The country was not a land of exploitation and repression, they insisted. It was a proud nation with a long heritage of democracy and freedom. The new breed of punks did not appreciate these traditions. They mocked freedom, refused to work in the system, and, in a contemptuous, un-American manner, tried to destroy the ideals of law and order. Rather than speaking of cooperation and construction, youthful troublemakers talked of dissension and destruction. Though they mouthed such words as justice, peace, and brotherhood, their actions belied their speech. Demonstrators tried to turn minor disagreements into dramatic confrontations. Their frequent lapses into violence revealed their lack of respect for the system. They had become radicals. Viewing demonstrators against the Vietnam War as advocates of internal revolution and appeasers of foreign enemies, many citizens left them a harsh message on their automobile bumper stickers: "America: Love it or Leave it." Violent demonstrations had no place in American society, they insisted. If violence was the only language these troublemakers could understand, they would have to face an instructive spanking of counterviolence in the name of law and order.

In this search for easy answers to the very complex causes of America's violent outbursts, the two sides made simplistic assumptions which failed to recognize many other factors in the volatile situation. Without resorting to party-line explanations, let us examine some of the major reasons for the 1967-1970 upheaval under two principal categories: underlying causes and general causes.

Underlying Causes:

Although the protestors of 1967-1970 often showed emotionalism, hysteria, and paranoia, it would be a grievous error to dismiss their complaints as fabricated or insignificant. Their placards and screams often identified some of the major contemporary problems in American life, serious problems that required urgent attention. They pointed out many shameful blots on the national record and courageously demanded change in the face of both widespread public indifference and resistance. Among the many problems which attracted their attention and aroused their protest, two stand out particularly: dissatisfaction with the treatment of black Americans and disillusionment over the Vietnam War. Although the story behind these cries of discontent has been related many times, a review of its main outlines may clarify the validity of the protestors' complaints. Whether violence is an effective challenge to the problems is an issue we shall take up in the next chapter.

Regarding black Americans, the historical reasons for discontent should be obvious. In the aftermath of the ghetto riots, the Kerner Commission concluded that "the events of the summer of 1967 are in large part the culmination of 300 years of racial prejudice."[2] Certainly no assessment of the sources of turmoil can overlook that significant historical pattern. Except for the American Indian, no American minority group has been so consistently victimized by foul play as the blacks. They were most peculiar newcomers in a "Nation of Immigrants," to use John F. Kennedy's title. Virtually all came as slaves, and through their first 250 years of activity in America, most of them continued to serve as bondsmen. The Civil War brought them only fettered freedom. Society set blacks loose without capital, property, education, and skills and told them, in essence: "Compete, and good luck." In this situation alone their condition was roughly parallel to that of America's most desperate new immigrants. But the deeply imbedded color prejudice in national attitudes made their situation more difficult than the condition of immigrant groups. America was to be a "white man's country," insisted the majority, and every black aspiring for a better life had to face the painful reality of this persistent view. After decades of eking out a living as sharecroppers and tenant farmers in the South, some new hope appeared during World War I. Since America needed manpower in its highly mobilized wartime economy, thousands of Southern blacks left the farms to take new jobs in Northern cities. A major new era in the Afro-American experience began, offering both exciting prospects and new problems.

In the decades following World War I, a large sector of the Southern black population moved to Northern urban centers to find better opportunities. Their per capita income improved, but employment in the cities remained insecure and downward spins in the economy painfully demonstrated the relevance of an old saying: "Last to be hired, first to be fired." Moreover, the quality of life in urban ghettoes posed many new difficulties. Tenement houses evacuated by ethnic groups leaving the center-city were already dilapidated. Development investments poured into the suburbs where many of the best new jobs could be found. "Dark Ghettoes" became virtual colonies within a developing nation—separated sectors where heavily concentrated poor blacks looked jealously at a society of increasing affluence. Very slowly, the blacks made economic gains, and civil rights legislation made inroads against some of the most blatant institutions of racial discrimination. Nevertheless, blacks could not forget their persistent poverty, the contempt many whites held for them, and their distances from equality of opportunity. In the 1960s their pent-up frustrations burst into ghetto riots. No matter how shocked a white man might be by the mayhem and destruction, he could hardly ask, "Now what are those people so angry about?"

In many respects, the Vietnam War protest was analogous to the black unrest. In both cases intense emotional outbursts developed out of frustrated efforts to change the course of events. The antiwar movement gained increasing numbers of converts as the public became indignant over American escalation of what appeared to be senseless and immoral destruction in Southeast Asia. They watched the world's mightiest nation intervene in a small country's civil war, employing sophisticated and highly lethal weaponry against people vaguely described as the enemy. They saw the nation's leaders define policy issues in Cold War terms, talking about the contest in Vietnam as an example for the world to see, a demonstration of America's determination to stand firm against international Communist aggression. To the war critics, it appeared that the country's policy-makers were prepared to use millions of the Indochinese people as cannon fodder with the Domino Theory as their justification. America seemed ready to apply to all of South Vietnam the infamous logic of a United States marine officer, the idea that it was necessary to destroy a Vietnamese village in order to save it. Napalm, anti-personnel bombs, B-52 strikes, defoliation—a frightening variety of weapons and tactics went into the supposedly noble effort to "save" South Vietnam.

Protests against the Vietnam conflict began peacefully. College groups helped the movement when they first attracted attention from the news media in early 1965 with the "teach-in" concept. Then groups moved out from the campuses to manifest their complaints through marches and demonstrations in city streets and squares. These activities helped win some new supporters to the cause, but they also drew tremendous abuse from citizens who considered demonstrators disruptive and un-patriotic. Meanwhile, the Asian conflict continued to escalate and the fear of draft notices increasingly plagued the young war critics. Why should they go off to fight in an immoral battle, they asked. Others saw the question in more pragmatic terms. The war seemed senseless; why should they risk their lives for a cause they could not understand?

The protestors' situation became extremely frustrating. Some who faced draft notices had to choose between two extremes: accepting the call without question or fleeing from their own country. Others worked on new strategies of protest. What approaches could be effective, they wondered. Peaceful demonstrations apparently failed to change policy; they occurred simultaneously with the war's greatest escalation. A temporary rush into the political arena in 1968 produced little satisfaction. Eugene McCarthy's strength at the polls petered out, and Robert Kennedy died of an assassin's bullet just as his campaign looked like it had a chance for success. Unable to bring discernible change, many protestors began to focus their anger in other directions. They heckled prowar speakers, attacked university administrations, and burned down ROTC buildings. Some even plotted to set off bombs in business, university, and government buildings. As reprehensible as these activities were, we should remember that they occurred during America's most prolonged and most unpopular war, a time when proponents of peace found frustration at almost every turn. It is not surprising that, over the years, some of the most desperate and impatient protestors began to reject peaceful strategies of protest. They thirsted for opportunities to give supporters of violence in Vietnam something to worry about on the home front.

These "underlying causes" for the social disorders of the late 1960s and early 1970s suggest that the protestors had many valid reasons for complaint. Their collective acts of violence were not mere examples of "psychic crises," for they had good reasons to complain. As we broaden the scope of analysis now to consideration of general causes—the social, psychological, and political phenomena at work in collective violence—we should keep in mind that neither broad category should be considered to the exclusion of the other. To acknowledge that general causes played a role in the turmoil does not negate the relevance and validity of underlying causes.

General Causes

The civil disorders involved a crisis of legitimacy. America's apprehensive years of mass violence occurred when much of the population began to lose respect for society's basic institutions. Perhaps most strikingly reflective of this feeling was the prevalent disrespect protestors showed for law enforcement officers. To recall Mark Twain's words on this problem: "No country can be well governed, unless its citizens as a body keep religiously before their minds that they are the guardians of the law, that the law officers are only the machinery for its execution."[3]

The contempt many protestors showed for the law, as personified by police officers, illustrates this breakdown of legitimacy. In the ghetto riots, for example, many angry blacks stoned, kicked, stomped on, or shot at policemen. Quite clearly these angry people did not view uniformed officers as protectors of their community. Instead, they attacked policemen as convenient symbols for many of the problems irritating them. Certainly some of the ghetto community's complaints involved police abuses; but in the emotion of a riot situation, this anger made even innocent officers (including black policemen) targets of indiscriminate attack. Similarly, the shouting college students who confronted police and National Guardsmen viewed uniformed men as unwanted intruders, as symbols of the most repressive forces in the state's institutionalized machinery of violence. These protestors, too, had cause for complaint against some treatment by uniformed forces (e.g., actions of "the law" in Chicago in 1968 and at Kent State in 1970). But many of the confrontations involved indiscriminate verbal and physical abuse of any uniformed figures in sight—gestures of defiance against those whom the protestors perceived as representing many of their troubles.[4]

Why the breakdown of legitimacy as evidenced by attacks on police officers and others as symbols of oppression? Popular expressions of scorn for uniformed officials by masses of youthful protestors occurred concurrently with the height of American involvement in the Vietnam conflict, a parallel that suggests the force of war in eroding legitimacy. As Richard Hofstadter notes, "Any liberal democratic state is in danger of wearing away its legitimacy if it repeatedly uses violence at home or abroad when the necessity of that violence is wholly unpersuasive to a substantial number of its people."[5] In the Vietnam affair, the rationale for violence abroad seemed most unpersuasive to a large segment of the citizenry. Discontent compounded when predicted victories turned into embarrassing setbacks. As hopes for a quick settlement faded, the public prepared for a protracted conflict in Southeast Asia. The public's growing discontent as shown in opinion polls buoyed the confidence of young protestors. They could operate with a tacit understanding that many onlookers approved the reasons for their demonstrations, if not the form of protest itself. Middle-aged, "established" citizens were less likely to manifest their disgust through marches (demonstrations might be judged puerile or radical by neighbors, business clients, or managers at the office). Yet they could support the spirit of protest through casual conversations with youths or display of the "V" sign to marchers (symbolic of support for the peace movement). These small, informal manifestations of sympathy from the older generation inspired protesting youths with further confidence and determination. Their cause was far less lonely than the cause of protestors in "popular" American wars like World War II. Moreover, they had much more time to build the momentum of their movement than had critics of America's other "small wars." Although significant pockets of discontent developed during the War of 1812, the Mexican War, and American fighting in the Philippines after the Spanish-American War, each of these conflicts terminated before public discontent could wear down institutional legitimacy and protest groups could develop formidable strength.[6] The long, frustrating contest in Vietnam enabled the critics' minority sentiment to turn into majority opinion.

The development of something akin to domestic warfare at home concurrent with foreign war in Vietnam is not surprising in the context of popular wartime rhetoric. Long ago Clarence Darrow recognized the consequences on the home front of psychological mobilization for war. "War means the breaking up of old habits, the destruction of many inhibitions, which in the strongest civilizations are only skin deep," Darrow explained. War meant teaching people to hate and offering the highest honors for those who thought of new and more efficient ways to kill. It forced society's leaders to counsel rejection of the Biblical commandment "Thou shalt not kill," and required them to substitute lessons on the value of killing. Society could not expect to nurture and reward these attitudes toward supposedly expendable foreign peoples without seeing some product of it at home, thought Darrow. Once a nation officially sanctions one form of violence, many among the masses begin pondering the relevance of violence to their own particular grievances.[7] A statement in the SDS newspaper, *Handwriting on the Wall,* illustrates this desire to feed the Establishment a taste of its own medicine during the Vietnam conflict. "Don't let violence hang you up," the newspaper told its readers. "Most of us have been living off violence for a long time; living off a system that does violence to most of the world."[8]

The pattern of unrest should be familiar to historians, for American history again and again reveals correlations between incidents of foreign violence and incidents of domestic violence. A disproportionate number of major examples of collective violence and rioting occurred during or shortly following the nation's major wars. The most disruptive period in terms of collective violence occurred in the years following the Civil War. Precisely because that war was a *civil* conflict, dividing citizens against each other, its hostilities engendered hatred that continued to trouble society long after the formal conclusion of hostilities. During Reconstruction, the South experienced numerous violent episodes, as federal troops, ex-Confederates, carpetbaggers, blacks, and others scrambled to gain dominance in a new social order. As a consequence, respect for law became extremely fragile.[9]

Regarding long-term correlations, the concurrence of wars and race riots in American history is particularly instructive. During the Civil War, Irishmen attacked blacks in one of New York City's worst civil disruptions. The conflict involved both the Irishmen's resistance against the draft (which could send them into an unwanted battle against slavery) and competition with blacks for the most menial jobs. Hundreds died from the riots and many buildings were destroyed. Mobilization in World War I set the fuse for more racial riots as blacks began moving northward to work in defense-related industries or fill the job vacancies left by drafted whites. One major outbreak began in East St. Louis in 1917 when a group of whites drove through the black district, shooting into homes. According to police estimates, the riots caused the deaths of more than a hundred blacks and the destruction of more than 300 buildings. Another major disturbance developed in Chicago in 1919 when a black youth swimming in Lake Michigan went past an imaginary boundary line separating the "white" and "black" beaches. Seven days of destructive activity left twenty-three blacks and fifteen whites dead, over 500 injured and about 1,000 homeless. In 1943, during World War II, another major race riot occurred, again developing out of competition for jobs in the defense-related industries. Thirty-four people died, twenty-five of them blacks. The years of the Vietnam War corresponded with the great conflagration of Watts, Detroit, Newark, Washington, and many other cities. There were multiple causes for these outbursts, no doubt, but it is difficult to reject the hypothesis that war mobilization often legitimizes and fosters concomitant violence at home. Wartime emphasis on hate and killing weakens sanctions against domestic violence, encouraging angry groups to unleash their rage.[10]

Protest movements and riots such as those of the United States in the late 1960s and early 1970s also corresponded with "rising expectations." They were times of rapid economic and social change and growth, periods when people's hopes soared. For example, in the early 1960s many blacks applauded the successes of the civil rights movement and the promises of new government legislation. Many white college students enjoyed a brief era of optimism and enthusiastic patriotism during the Kennedy era. But developments in the middle and late 1960s destroyed this euphoria. Blacks in the ghettoes realized they were still far from a Promised Land, while idealistic students saw their nation slipping into the madness of war in Vietnam. The once excited and expectant people became frustrated and disillusioned. When this condition combined with other distressing setbacks in the late 1960s, it helped produce reaction similar to what political scientist James C. Davies calls the J-Curve. According to Davies' thesis:

> Revolution is most likely to take place when a prolonged period of rising expectations and rising gratifications is followed by a short period of sharp reversal, during which the gap between expectations and gratifications quickly widens and becomes intolerable. The frustration that develops, when it is intense and widespread in the society, seeks outlets in violent action.[11]

The existence of protest movements in other countries broke down the protestor's sense of isolation and promoted an environment conducive to civil disorders. Student outbreaks in America in the late 1960s were not peculiar to this country; they were part of an almost contagious movement of young people from universities to the streets in many parts of the world. In 1968 in particular, the problem appeared to be a global epidemic.

In Paris, Mexico City, Prague, Rio de Janeiro, and numerous other urban centers, students organized mass demonstrations for political purposes. Like their counterparts in the United States, young people opened up a barrage of criticism against university administrations and the Establishment outside. Some of their complaints reflected anger over issues blown out of proportion. Yet at base were substantial problems that student protests properly brought into the open: inequality of the working classes, abridgement of freedom, control over national affairs by foreign power blocs. These were issues of long concern; it was the students' comforting knowledge that their counterparts elsewhere were engaged in similar activity that helped bring protest into the open.

A similar revolutionary contagion took place across the United States. Between 1968 and 1970 many college students on campuses that had been relatively quiescent even worried how this serenity might reflect on the quality of their schools. "Why are we so lethargic?" they asked. "Look what's happened at Columbia and Berkeley; then look at the *indifference,* the *passivity* of our bunch, " they commented with bitter envy. Happily or unhappily, many of them eventually did experience campus upheaval on their home grounds. Many college faculty members also distrusted campus quiescence when it appeared that so many serious issues deserved angry protest. Silence on the issues could be construed as indifference, they thought, which, in turn, could be interpreted as a form of guilt.

Although college faculty and other adult intellectuals were less likely to indulge in *acts* of violence, some did contribute significantly to the milieu of protest by frequently using the *language* of violence. Comments from those respected for their expertise and academic titles seriously undermined the legitimacy of institutions and policies in the eyes of the young. Historian Crane Brinton comments on this phenomenon in a classic study of revolutions, noting that "the desertion of intellectuals" from support for the Establishment constitutes one of the major prerequisites for revolutionary violence.[12]

Many college professors, writers, and journalists found the language of violence increasingly attractive as their frustration over the war and civil rights grew. For some, tough language served therapeutic purposes: if they could not bring change through action, at least they could find psychological satisfaction through blunt vocalization of their anger. For others, violence appeared to be the only instrument to bring effective change when other approaches proved futile. The white intellectuals' use of violent rhetoric in reference to racial problems is a case in point. Deeply aware of the nation's tragic history of racial injustices, these intellectuals were plagued by remorse. How could they respond to the impassioned cries of their militant black friends? By mouthing the rhetoric of confrontation, at least they received rewarding nods of approval from blacks. Many white intellectuals arrived at their advocacy of violence honestly. They did not know what to tell disheartened blacks, and they, too, wondered if militancy might be an answer. The more they pondered the difficulties, the more their disapproval of violence began to fade. The intellectual's growing tolerance for violence in the late 1960s signaled a new, intense preoccupation with effective protest. How should discontented Americans press for change? Which strategies would be most successful? Could violence work when other approaches failed? These were some of the painful questions many troubled Americans asked themselves as they searched for effective modes of action in a dramatic period of confrontation, emotion, and bewilderment.

9

SANCTIONS

During the height of intellectual ferment and civil protest in the late 1960s and early 1970s, many disenchanted Americans viewed violence as a necessary and effective means for dramatizing grievances and effecting changes. Their perspective seemed sensible on both moral and practical grounds. Because their criticisms of war, racism, and many diseases of American life touched on humane concerns, they considered violence a justified device for furthering good causes. In this period of great excitation, the disaffected did not labor long with important "ifs" about the effectiveness of violent tactics. They found ready arguments for its productiveness in the lessons of current events and American history. But as public reaction set in against violent civil protest and as militant approaches began to fail miserably in producing the radicals' desired effects, many in the protest movements reexamined fashionable arguments about justification and effectiveness. In time, militancy lost favor and protestors themselves came to recognize glaring moral and practical shortcomings in the once attractive arguments for violence. The lessons learned in this period are worth recalling by future generations.

During the late 1960s, sanctions for violence appeared in numerous assessments of America's contemporary crisis. For example, Andrew Kopkind offered a variation of Mao tse-Tung's famous maxim that "Power comes out of the barrel of a gun" with a suggestion that morality comes out of the gun's muzzle.[1] Black Panther leader Huey Newton liked to read and quote from Che Guevara and Fidel Castro. Above all, popular quotations from H. Rap Brown and Frantz Fanon conveyed the new perspective. Brown's belief that "violence is as American as cherry pie" became a popular expression. On a more sophisticated level, the thoughts of Frantz Fanon, a black psychiatrist from the West Indies, excited both black and white dissidents for their moving justifications of violence. In a best-selling book entitled *The Wretched of the Earth,* Fanon sounded the trumpets of revolution, using the Algerian revolution as a keynote. When people have very little else to free them from the yoke of colonial oppression, said Fanon, violence can be a precious end in itself. Glorifying violence in one of the book's most famous passages, Fanon argued: "Violence is a cleansing force. It frees the native from his inferiority complex, and from his despair and inaction; it makes him fearless and restores self-respect."[2]

Basic to Fanon's analysis was a criticism of the dominant class's hypocrisy in condemning violence. How had the ruling groups achieved and maintained power in the first place, he asked. Through violent oppression of the masses, he answered. Many writers in the United States worked variations on this theme, pointing out that revolutionaries were essentially engaged in counterviolence rather than initially provoking violence. A sweeping interpretation of violence in America, written by Alfonso Pinkney, represents this approach. Because of its broad scope and relevant biases, his book, *The American Way of Violence,* is an appropriate subject for detailed attention.[3]

In eight chapters on a variety of topics Pinkney punched away at the history of American oppression against blacks, Indians, Vietnamese, and others. He also explored the seamier activities of America's uniformed agents—the police and the military—offering some hard-hitting evaluations of the prevalence of violence in the American value structure. Summing up his interpretation, Pinkney argued that violence is institutionalized in America.

In cataloging a long list of horrors committed by the American Establishment, Pinkney described contemporary violent groups as innocent victims of maligned forces. In some passages Pinkney's stark contrasts between supposedly good and bad forces in confrontations made militant protest groups look like innocent soda-pop kids who are constantly hunted down by vicious exploitative political officials. In places the analysis smacked of interpretative paranoia. For example, Pinkney described the Black Panthers as "a logical target of official America."[4] Why were the Panthers being chased? Because they espoused an ideology opposed to U.S. economic doctrine and because they armed themselves to protect their brothers against violence. Pinkney's explanations did not acknowledge that a militant's turn to firearms could create a multifaceted tragedy resulting in death of confused young "revolutionaries" as well as innocent policemen and other public officials. The myopia was strikingly evident in Pinkney's treatment of the shootout outside California's Marin County Courthouse, which led to the death of four convicts, an armed intruder, and a judge. Pinkney assessed the behavior of the seventeen-year old youth who smuggled weapons to the prisoners by saying, "The action of this youth indicates a loss of faith in the possibility of securing justice for black people in America."[5]

In line with his simplistic approach, Pinkney portrayed the police in stereotypes. They are the enemy, guilty of unspeakable oppression and violence against the population they are charged to protect, he argued. Moreover, the police are guilty by association. After all, as everyone knew: "Police are often members of the Birch Society, the Ku Klux Klan, the Minute Men, and other right-wing groups. Furthermore, they frequently support the most conservative candidates for political office, such as George Wallace of Alabama and Barry Goldwater of Arizona."[6]

How, then, should society react to the outbreaks of collective violence? By recognizing that violence has a place, suggested Pinkney. We should understand that the problem of violence has been chronic in American history, he explained, and most cases involve oppressors employing violence against the oppressed. Pinkney saw an important lesson in this pattern, a message for all the troubled and angry victims of injustice in America. Perhaps it was time to give the Establishment some of its own potent medicine, he hinted. Can the counterstrategy work? "It is often claimed that violence is an ineffective means of resolving conflict," he explained, "but the history of the United States demonstrates that in fact many social disputes have been settled by violent means."[7] If violence has been effective in protecting the oppressors, insisted Pinkney, it can also be effective in protecting the interests of the oppressed.

Similar arguments justifying violence appeared in numerous books and magazine articles of the period. The authors of these works emphasized that the violence of protest groups was principally a reaction to society's institutionalized violence and that it was unfair to concentrate on the domestic violence of disaffected groups while excusing official violence. For example, Thomas Rose tried to place violence "in perspective" by showing that two sides could play the same game. Exposing the irony of public complaint, Rose commented, "We are horrified when a teenager tosses a brick, but not when a corporation steals millions of dollars." Rose reminded readers that if the underprivileged turn to violence, they should recall that "the rich—for example, mine owners and grape growers— have had their private police or armies at their disposal plus the local police, the militia, the national guard, and other coercive instruments of the state."[8] Relating a similar perspective on violence to the problem of criticizing the Vietnam war, Kingsley Widmer stressed the need to fight the official violence of America's political, military, and industrial warmaking Establishment with something more potent than peaceful dissent. In a hard-hitting article in *The Nation,* Widmer argued that peaceful dissent can be "irrelevant" and that it is violent dissent "that stirs public interest and helps to initiate dialogue about significant issues that need attention." Widmer showed his disgust for straitlaced moderates who wanted to shout against the Vietnam War but veered back with embarrassment when protestors exhibited bad manners, used offensive tactics, or, most horrid of all, employed a little violence to show the true dimensions of their rage.[9]

Was violence the answer? Could militants change the disturbing direction American society seemed to be taking? Were conditions in America propitious for revolutionary activity? Historian Barrington Moore, Jr., rejected this idea flatly. The situation in America was unlikely to produce the revolution angry radicals so keenly awaited, declared Moore, but their predilection for violent language boded human tragedy nevertheless. All the "talk about revolution is pure talk," insisted Moore, but laden "with potentially dangerous consequences." It would be tragic if radicals should misread the realities of their own society, he thought, and fail in a senseless effort at great cost in property and human lives. [10]

Moore's thinking reflected that of many intellectuals in the United States who became increasingly intolerant of blithe remarks justifying tough tactics. Their reaction against the rhetoric of violence gathered force in what might be called "The Spring and Summer Offensive of 1970." In this period many college faculty members, journalists, free-lance writers, and others decided that the prevalence of destructive activity compelled them to voice their doubts about certain current attitudes. A spate of campus takeovers, confrontations, threats, bombings, and shootouts added new force and determination to their criticisms of the "violence is justified" philosophy. As their attack strengthened, others joined in to reveal concerns that had troubled them all along. Momentum grew, and within a short time the enthusiasm for violence fell under sharp attack from many quarters. In books, newspapers, and magazine articles, in public addresses, at professional meetings, and on college campuses, efforts to refute the intellectual sanctions for violence reached a loud crescendo.

Many spokesmen for change and reform, people with strong credentials as progressive and humane intellectuals, began condemning the New Left, militant blacks, and others who supported violent strategies. Hannah Arendt offered a particularly strong indictment in her incisive book *On Violence*. Arendt made a major distinction between power and force, explaining that true power rested on attitudinal support from the people, not just rule by coercion. A government's dominant classes could not expect to rest their strength on control by force, and neither could the revolutionaries in challenging the power of the dominant classes. In this context the idea that "power grows out of the barrel of a gun" appeared ludicrous.[11] Others raised serious questions about the brutal language used in the appeals of self-styled revolutionaries. In an article on "The Rhetoric of Violence," Eugene Goodheart asked if all the fashionable tough harangues might commit angry speakers to go further in their protests than they intended. Militants could not continue forever just talking about throwing bombs. To maintain credibility, in time they would have to practice what they preached.[12] Marie Syrkin warned that the popular rhetoric of the Black Panthers could not be dismissed as innocent talk. Comments like "Burn, baby, burn!," "Get honkey!," and children's rhymes like "Kill the Pig Upon the Hill; If You Don't, the Panthers Will" might condition youngsters to destructive behavior. "Our time has witnessed the fearful power of words for good or ill," lamented Syrkin. Clearly, language had the potential for stirring much mischief of its own.[13]

During this period, some writers offered scurrilous, sweeping indictments of militant activity without showing much appreciation for the roots of protest. S. I. Hayakawa, then president of San Francisco State College, represented the viewpoint of those Americans who were intolerant of dissident protestors. Hayakawa's angry and contemptuous opinions of rebel youths appeared in syndicated newspaper columns. He also carried his message across the country in public appearances. He grossly simplified issues, repeatedly discussing the dangers of violent ideas and actions while giving very little attention to the root causes of the upheaval. Hayakawa was quick to condemn young blacks and white radicals, yet overlooked the relationship of racism and war to their protest. He harped on the irony that the New Left adopted tactics often associated with ultra right-wing groups or neo-McCarthyism as a device to evade penetrating evaluation of the protestors' grievances. Hayakawa's short-term experience as a star in the press and at the podium is significant, for it reflects the fast-growing "hard line" against violent protest of mainstream America in 1970-1971.

It was not writers like Hayakawa, of course, who finally persuaded radicals to change their strategy. Rather, it was the *consequences* of tragic events and emotional reactions to them (including the reactions of radicals themselves), in combination with the intellectual offensive, that contributed significantly to bringing about the change. One of the most telling events involved a bomb explosion at the University of Wisconsin. It killed a graduate student who had been working in the targeted building during the early morning hours. Public indignation over what seemed to be cruel insensitivity to the human consequences of radical violence was intense. In a rather typical response, an article in the *Wisconsin State Journal* laid the blame not just on the extremists but on all who had employed revolutionary rhetoric glibly:

> It isn't just the radicals who set the bomb in a lighted, occupied building who are guilty. The blood is on the hands of anyone who encouraged them, anyone who has talked recklessly of "revolution," anyone who has chided with mild disparagement the violence of extremists while hinting that the cause is right all the same.[14]

Even earlier, Irving Howe gave eloquent expression to the growing disgust with dynamite-oriented protest. Howe showed appreciation for some of the radicals' aims but seriously questioned the persuasive power of their means:

> True, some of the New Left young have by now devoted as much as five or six years to politics and appear shocked that the centuries-long struggle for social justice did not come to instant triumph in 1969. It is not callous, it is merely humane, to suggest that the struggle seems likely to continue a while longer, and that among the requirements for it are the maturity needed for speaking with patience and decency to the unconverted. No one has ever been convinced by a bomb.[15]

Evidence regarding the Wisconsin explosion and other bomb incidents suggests that accidental bloodshed could prompt radicals to rethink some of their major assumptions about strategy. This was particularly true in the case of a March 1970 explosion in a Greenwich Village townhouse that killed three radicals. The location had been a secret "bomb factory." Nine months later a suggestive announcement appeared in underground newspapers. Sources in the radical movement attributed the statement to Bernadette Dorn, a fugitive "Weatherman," friend of the dead Greenwich Village radicals, and an earlier advocate of violent strategy. Now, in an apparent change of tactics, she called for revised planning. Violence had not proven a panacea. "This tendency to consider only bombings or picking up the gun as revolutionary, with the glorification of heavier the better, we've called the military error," she said.[16]

The tragic events at Kent State also affected a change in attitude. When President Nixon announced expansion of American fighting into Cambodia in April 1970, students at Kent State University first reacted with explosive anger. Many threw bottles at police cars, smashed store windows, firebombed the ROTC building, and hurled rocks at the Ohio National Guard. On Monday, May 4, a day of tense confrontations, nervous and irritated guardsmen fired volleys into a large crowd. Four students fell dead—none of them radicals—and eleven were left wounded. Across the country college campuses became scenes of turmoil as students attacked the offices of deans and presidents, set fire to buildings, and forced universities to close down. President William J. McGill of Columbia University evaluated the situation as "the most disastrous month of May in the history of American higher education."

After the disaster at Kent State and its destructive aftermath, both sides in the internal fight over America's Vietnam War policy began to draw back from violent confrontation. Kent State became a symbol of the dangerous level of divisiveness which the nation had reached. While defenders of the war continued to show contempt for student protestors, they worried about future accidents involving the deaths of more innocent youngsters. Even President Nixon tried to assuage feelings through awkward but politically calculated efforts to improve communications with the university community. He ventured out into a crowd of Washington demonstrators in the early morning hours to talk about football and surfing and conferred with presidents of major colleges. Students returned to calmer campuses in the fall of 1970 and, while demonstrations against the war continued, the crowds grew smaller. By spring of 1972, when Nixon made the dramatic announcement that U.S. planes were mining Haiphong harbor, campus outbursts were relatively peaceful compared to previous years and only a small contingent of demonstrators turned up in Washington. Instead of producing a new and prolonged era of campus violence, reactions to Kent State eventually moved most college students in the opposite direction.

In the early 1970s a swarm of doubts swept many who before had confidently cited the rhetoric of violence. The new questions being raised were not easy to answer. For example, might militants be corrupting their own "noble cause" by sanctioning the most extreme tactics of force? After crying out constantly against America's callousness toward humanity and readiness to wage violence against innocent people in Vietnam, it appeared that the New Left might be exercising a double standard. How could they condemn the opposition's violence while glorifying their own? In *The Politics of Protest* Jerome Skolnik noted that "nonviolence . . . has been making some unexpected converts within the peace movement, not because of the rising tide of pacifism, but because activists have begun to understand that their first target must be the psychology that acquiesces and delights in war."[17]

In addition, in assessing violent tactics, radicals had to confront one of Mahatma Gandhi's principal contributions to the debate on violent tactics, namely, the idea that means are ends in the making. Even if radical tactics began to work, would consequent successes be worth celebrating? Victories won by coercion and fear might not offer much. Indeed, they would be very fragile victories if popular attitudes toward radical ideas remained hostile. Goals attained through violence could leave a post-revolutionary society still relying on force to resolve its differences. As sociologist-historian Feliks Gross noted, "terror, even in the name of the highest ideals, has created, in the end, political habits that have moved into patterns of political life, and have continued even after conditions were changed."[18]

Along with these painful questions, militant radicals had to face another serious possibility—the prospect that violence would only beget more violence. The familiar boomerang effect might apply to their own activities. According to the scenario, once destruction gains momentum, protest movements have great difficulty containing it. Sporadic, spontaneous acts of violence by various participants in a movement force it to depart from carefully organized, strategic plans. In time, the movement loses its direction. Factions within it begin to pull in different directions. Then someone commits an error, opting for a dramatic act of violence that excites intense public reactions. As the public expresses indignation over the act, the movement loses popular sympathy. In time, the decline in moral support emboldens those in society who want to employ counterviolence, both official and unofficial. Society's security forces regain control, treating the revolutionaries more repressively; vigilante-type groups appear to deal with the challenge extralegally—all to the applause of many frustrated and angry citizens.

Was there substance to these doubts? Was violence a less efficacious tactic than radicals were first inclined to believe? Could militant approaches backfire? Indeed, the record of recent developments began to point up dramatic shortcomings in violent strategy.

Transformations in the Black Power movement through the late 1960s and early 1970s provide a good example. At the time of Martin Luther King's death, the movement was near its zenith both in strength and in popularity. Many of its leaders and supporters viewed the assassination of King as proof of their prophecy that nonviolence could not work. Julius W. Hobson, an economist and chairman of a Washington civil rights group, reacted to the news of King's death by pronouncing an obituary for nonviolent resistance. "The Martin Luther King concept of nonviolence died with him," said Hobson. "It was a foreign ideology anyway—as foreign to this country as speaking Russian."[19] Stokely Carmichael, who coined the words "Black Power," responded to the news of assassination angrily, warning, "A lot of people who were afraid to pick up guns will now pick up guns."[20] Others talked about the need to "get whitey" and "kill ten whites for every Negro killed."

But the years following King's death witnessed neither continued momentum for the civil rights movement nor accumulated proof of the superiority of violent tactics. Instead, the civil rights crusade suffered severe setbacks. Social justice legislation stalled in Congress, and voters manifested their fear of militancy in the polling booths. Blacks made some gains in the Establishment in the years following—increased minority enrollment in universities, election of more black mayors in large cities, and more frequent, better portrayals of blacks in television shows. But, generally, the public assumed a tougher posture against demands couched in threatening or violent language. Moreover, in the wake of ghetto riots and sniper activity, a spate of law and order statements appeared from diverse political camps, showing little tolerance for demonstrations of anger by urban blacks. Many who normally could have been counted on to support minority claims backed away, revealing their displeasure over the direction of events. For example, when the governor of New Jersey temporarily suspended the Bill of Rights during rioting in Plainfield, many moderate citizens viewed this suspension as necessary under the circumstances. Mayor Daley of Chicago won accolades from the more intransigent groups by asking his policemen to shoot looters and maim children who participated in rioting. By the end of 1968 it was becoming painfully clear to members of the black community that rioting had created not only a political backlash, but many more black than white casualties as well.

As for the militant heroes of the 1960s, by the early 1970s most were under indictment, in jail, dead, in exile, writing books, or working within the Establishment. H. Rap Brown received a sentence of five to fifteen years for armed robbery. Zaybmalik Shakur was killed in a shootout with the police on a New Jersey turnpike. Stokely Carmichael was living in Algeria. Huey Newton lectured across the country to promote his new book *Revolutionary*

Suicide, and Bobby Seale was actively campaigning for the mayor-ship of Oakland, California.[21]

A few groups of extremely militant blacks remained, but their appalling butchery in the name of freedom alienated even many members of revolutionary black organizations. The venomous hatred and wanton acts of extremist groups now seemed repulsive examples of reverse racism. For example, numerous press reports associated the bloody deaths of policemen and citizens across the country with snipers who called themselves the Black Liberation Army. A series of deaths in the San Francisco area became known as the Zebra killings. Furthermore, members of a Chicago-based terrorist organization known as De Mau Mau were accused of killing nine whites in a series of bizarre, indiscriminate murders. The only thing all the victims seemed to have in common was their whiteness. Accord-ing to one report, De Mau Mau members were roaming the countryside looking for whites to kill. The black president of Malcolm X College, who had known some of the accused when they were students, dismissed explanations that would identify their acts with high ideological purpose. "It is not a political group," he explained. "It's just a group of very bitter young men. Most are drug users. They have no way of living, and no saleable skills."[22] In another case, one of the most brutal examples of violent militancy, tragedy resulted from intense competition be-tween Muslim sects. The revolting deaths of several blacks in the home of basketball star Karem Abul-Jabbar (formerly Lewis Alcindor, Jr.) was apparently related to this rivalry. Abul-Jabbar and his friends were reportedly opposed to violence. While he was away, a group of blacks raided his home and murdered five children (four by drowning) and two adults.[23] Violent militancy now seemed far from the noble statements of the 1960s. It appeared to be leading to wanton acts of murder and even, as far as Black Power was concerned, to self-destruction.

The failures of violent radical groups outside the United States also sapped the American militants' confidence in the efficacy of violence. Through the late 1960s, radical groups fre-quently referred to foreign examples to buttress their arguments that revolutionary guerrilla tactics could work. By the early 1970s, these examples were less impressive.

Guerrilla activity in Latin America served as one of the most popular models for revolutionary violence. Many North American radicals revered the names of Fidel Castro and Che Guevara, displaying their pictures on posters, quoting from their writings, and following he Latin American movements inspired by their examples. Che Guevara was especially appealing for his fighting exhortation to create "one, two, many Vietnams" in the Third World and for practicing what he preached by carrying out a daring guerrilla campaign in the jungles of Bolivia. Che's efforts to "liberate" Bolivia ended in his capture and execution in 1967, and he became a world-renowned martyr after his death. When a new spurt of guerrilla activity challenged the Establishment in several Latin American countries following Che's abortive adventure, U.S. radicals read the news with great interest. They learned of dramatic successes by left-wing terrorists in Latin America's sprawling cities, where guerrillas were able to catch governments off guard. In Brazil underground movements shocked the military regime with surprise kidnappings of foreign diplomats. Guerrillas ransomed their hostages for the release of political prisoners, cash, and government commitments to broadcast radical manifestos through the communications media.[24] Dramatic terrorist activities followed in Argentina, Guatemala, and elsewhere. One of the most theatrical of urban guerrilla groups, the Tupamaros of Uruguay, pulled off several extraordinary escapades calculated to humiliate the government. One adventure included the successful escape of 106 of their imprisoned colleagues through an underground tunnel connected to a jailhouse.[25]

Latin American guerrilla campaigns looked like strikingly successful models for U.S. radicals to follow until a wave of repression pushed out the terrorists in almost all the Latin American countries where they had been active. In Brazil a counterrevolution implemented brutally oppressive measures, as the military regime cracked down severely on civil liberties, sent "death squads" to wipe out guerrilla leaders, and used torture to extract confessions. By 1972 the underground movement's major leaders were dead or noticeably silent. Extreme governmental oppression followed guerrilla tactics in several other countries too. In Guatemala the situation got wildly out of hand as many right-wing extremists supplemented their "law and order" president's campaign with a widespread bloodbath against both leftists and moderate-leftist leaders. After a wave of *la violencia,* guerrilla activity waned and a strong-armed general tightened his grip on the country. A backlash of oppression also developed in Uruguay. By 1973 the Tupamaros had suffered painful reversals, and the military men who led the campaign against them gained enough power to leave Uruguay's long-standing democratic government in a shambles. Thus, instead of opening a new era of freedom in Latin America, violent revolutionary activities seemed mostly to provoke more repression, more violence, and more power for the military in Latin American society.

As would be expected, a historical reassessment of the role of Che Guevera followed these developments. Upon closer scrutiny, many began to view Che's strategies as more foolish than brilliant. Guevara enjoyed tearing down society, they said, but he was not a builder. Unsuccessful in Cuba once the revolutionaries were in power, he left on an absurd mission to liberate other peoples according to his own prescription. He was an intruder in Bolivia, being Argentine by nationality and unversed in the native Indian languages. He was contemptuous of Bolivian peasants who were ignorant of the outside world, and he refused to cooperate with the Communist movement in Bolivian cities. If Che's Bolivian revolution was doomed from its inception, they said, why should radical young Americans copy his strategy of failure? This decline of Che's legend signaled the explosion of a myth which earlier had served as an inspiration for American radicals.[26]

Myths about the efficacy of militant, radical, and even terrorist violence exploded in other areas of the world as well. In Canada, for example, an underground movement of French-speaking secessionists was apparently very successful when it temporarily upset the Ottawa government. But public sentiment turned against it as its violence backfired. After a wave of robberies and bombings, the *Front de Libération du Québec* (FLQ) dramatically kidnapped two high government officials. Terrorists demanded release of twenty-three political prisoners and half a million dollars in gold bullion. After Prime Minister Pierre Trudeau turned down the offer and invoked emergency police powers, the guerrillas responded by strangling Canada's labor minister. The impatient citizenry now demanded a quick end to the terrorism. With more than 2,000 people gathered on Parliament Hill to sing *O Canada* (the Canadian national anthem), the House of Commons approved use of the power-bestowing War-Measures Act by a vote of 190 to 16. Within a short time, underground members were on the run, and the terrorist movement dissipated. Though these events did not mark the end for French-speaking secessionists in Canada, their terrorist approach had clearly failed.[27]

America's violence-prone radicals were also instructed during these years by the fast-moving, eye-for-an-eye game played by the very serious contestants representing Palestinian guerrillas and the Israeli government. During the 1960s, Palestinian guerrillas attempted numerous raids on settlements in Israel from neighboring lands until Israeli counterattacks and pressure on various Middle East governments made conventional military attacks difficult. Extremist Arab groups then utilized more unconventional and dramatic terrorist activities. They planted bombs in airplanes, plotted a massacre at Tel Aviv Airport, hijacked jetliners, assassinated diplomats, mailed letters containing explosives, and gunned down Israeli athletes at the Olympic Games in Munich. But terrorism only made the Israeli government more belligerent. Israelis replied with bold commando raids, air attacks on guerrilla camps, and "reprisal strikes" against countries that permitted terrorists to operate within their boundaries (such as two attacks on Beirut—one involving the destruction of jetliners at the city airport and the second involving a surprise assassination raid on underground leaders).

Overall, the violent strategy proved counterproductive for both Palestinians and Israelis. Palestinians did not make gains in the demands they had made of Israel; instead, the terrorism only made Israel more inflexible. Moreover, terrorist raids produced cries of outrage from the world community. Nor did the Israelis' counterterrorism, which they judged necessary as a deterrent, bring security. It contributed to the tensions leading to the October 1973 war. It also made Israel look more like a garrison state, raised defense budgets, brought worldwide criticism of Israel, and moved Israeli society further away from the peaceful and humanitarian values which had motivated many survivors from World War II to establish the new land. Instead of producing victories, violence waged by both sides in these confrontations only intensified the pain and misery as each group escalated the destruction in efforts to avenge previous atrocities. Violence begot violence, and everyone seemed to come out a loser.

Reevaluation of the radicals' confidence in violent tactics involved assessment of historical as well as current events. Throughout the period of popular debates over the role of violence in protest movements, many young Americans argued that American history showed violence to be an extremely effective weapon in forcing reforms when more peaceful efforts failed. At first this interpretation seemed very plausible, gaining many adherents even from discontented people who would not participate in radical protest themselves. A "violence works" theory of history was much in vogue and seemed difficult to dispute. In time, however, as society gave the issue more careful attention, very different lessons from history appeared.

Of the many examples from American history that radicals often cited to show the efficacy of violence, two of the most popular concerned the trade-union movement and campaigns to guarantee the rights of blacks. According to popular descriptions, the American labor movement made its inroads into the power structure largely through pressure, force, and coercion. When facing the hard fronts put up by companies, complete with secret agents and private police forces, friendly persuasion was not effective for organized workers. Only by forcing companies to knuckle under could the unions win their case, for force was the only language fierce anti-unionist managers could understand. Through pitched battles with Pinkerton Cops, roughing up "scabs" hired to replace workers on strike, and other forms of pressure, laborers wore down company resistance. Finally, they made major gains in some of the mass production industries by supplementing their activities with another form of violence: taking physical control of the factories. The sitdown strike in automobile plants in the 1930s broke employer resistance in major mass production industries and enabled further gains in other plants. Hence, the lesson from labor-movement history, argued the radicals, was that "violence pays." Contemporary groups struggling for power could profit from this example.

Careful scrutiny of the details of labor history, however, revealed that in most cases labor-initiated violence had been counterproductive. Instead of strengthening the union position, violent tactics seriously undermined their chances for success. Efforts to organize unions in the steel factories provide a relevant example. Workers struck Andrew Carnegie's Homestead plant in 1892 in an attempt to establish collective bargaining procedures. As the strike dragged on, public pressure built up against Carnegie's factory manager and negotiator, Henry Clay Frick, urging him to accede to union demands and return his plant to the production of much needed material. But an attempt on Frick's life by an anarchist changed the situation dramatically. Public sentiment, frightened by portents of radical labor violence, moved away from the workers. In time the steel laborers capitulated and returned to their jobs without the right of collective bargaining.[28]

Another major effort to organize steel unions, which came close to success, occurred in 1919. The workers' basic demands seemed reasonable, including the right of collective bargaining, one day's rest in seven, an eight-hour day, abolition of the twenty-four-hour shift, a decent wage, and extra pay for overtime. To press for their cause, workers again went on strike, and again they received much public support. And again incidents of violence helped to drive a wedge between labor and the public. Riots broke out in Gary, Indiana, and some radicals involved in the upheaval called upon workers to arm themselves and to kill police and soldiers. Opponents of the unionists seized upon these examples, circulating them in major publicity campaigns that labeled the union movement "red" and "Bolshevist." Public opinion shifted quickly, and again the workers capitulated, this time at a loss of approximately 112 million dollars in strike wages.[29]

Finally, in the 1930s, workers in the mass-production industries made very significant gains. Yet the oft-cited case of labor's success in the auto plants does not support the thesis that violent tactics really worked. In the first place, sit-down strikes were efforts to find a peaceful option rather than a violent one. Second, once the workers learned that their mode of protest could cost them reinstatement rights according to law, most called a halt to the takeover. Third, much of the real violence that occurred during these confrontations emanated from management—violence which cost the companies dearly in public support. Finally, and perhaps most important for labor's success, was the presence of friendly leaders in government. In previous decades, the 1930s-style labor protest would have been enough for governors or the chief executive to declare a national emergency and call in troops to oust the workers. Because of the Great Depression and the political ascendancy of the New Deal, however, a different response came in the 1930s. Many government leaders now showed sympathy for labor's cause. Through the National Labor Relations Act, Congress gave workers the right to bargain collectively and prohibited employers from interfering with union organizational activities in their factories. The companies had to obey the law. With institutionalized machinery to establish collective bargaining, the problem which had so long aroused violent contention —unionization—could be settled through relatively peaceful means.[30] As the prominent labor historians Philip Taft and Philip Ross summarize these lessons from the history of the labor movement, violent behavior by unionists "seldom changed the course of events." After reviewing union victories in the 1930s, they concluded: "It appears highly probable that the advocacy or the practice of organized and systematic violence on the union side would have prevented the enactment of the New Deal legislation."[31] Thus, while the threat and use of violence helped to secure worker demands in some instances, far more often the strategy backfired, prolonging the suffering of working people.

Even when toughness did bring immediate successes in the labor movement, history shows the unfortunate legacies which all sides could inherit from the tradition of violence. The United

Mine Workers Union, for example, rose to power during the years when mining interests committed a variety of atrocities against their workers. The Ludlow Massacre of 1914, in which many men, women, and children associated with the union lost their lives, is just one infamous case of the violence perpetrated against the miners and their political supporters. Over the years, of course, miners, too, developed power and did not hesitate to use its own dirty tricks against management. Mineworkers developed an "eye for an eye" philosophy during their rough and tumble organizational battles. Eventually, the United Mine Workers' power became more secure under the brilliant leadership of union president John L. Lewis. But violence did not fade from Appalachian coal country in modern times within the union itself. When Lewis passed away, union affairs fell into the hands of Tony Boyle, whose integrity in managing union funds seemed much more questionable than Lewis's, and whose reaction to competition within the union took an extreme form. In a shocking development Joseph (Jock) Jablonski, a union reformer who challenged Boyle's leadership, was assassinated in his Pennsylvania home along with his wife and daughter. Eventually the murderers were convicted, and Boyle went to prison for his involvement in the crime. In light of the long and sorry record of violence associated with labor and management in the mining industry, as described in Joseph E. Finley's study, *The Corrupt Kingdom,* these new chapters in labor history were not surprising. Violence had become a way of life in mining and Appalachia; relationships in Appalachia remained tense, raising serious questions about the price of bloody victories achieved by all sides. With painful precision, labor history validated the warning that violence can beget violence.[32]

The history of blacks in America also took a different turn as emotions began to calm and as the historical shortcomings in the "violence works" idea became known. During the height of the militant black movement, ghetto rioting, and national interest in the causes of black protest, several new books were aimed at readers eager for historical justifications for violence. Many authors seemed anxious to present histories that would satisfy the desires of white readers for self-flagellation and of black readers to be stirred into rage. These studies emphasized the violent aspects of black-white relations. They focused on brutal injustices, slave whippings, activities of the KKK, attacks on urban blacks by white policemen, and other wrongs, as well as the dramatic cases of black resistance: slave uprisings, the history of ghetto riots, and the rise of strong-minded militants, like Malcolm X and Eldridge Cleaver. Out of this emphasis came a strong suggestion that white exploitation of the black community was first and foremost a matter of force and that history indicated violent rebellion was the blacks' best means of counteracting this force.[33]

After books on Afro-American history glutted the market, readers began to look more discriminately upon simple assessments of the problem and easy nostrums for changing power relationships. During the height of interest in the "violence works" persuasion, the name of Nat Turner loomed large in the list of heroes from Afro-American history. When novelist William Styron treated Turner as distinctly human in a work of fiction—portraying him as emotional and indecisive as well as clever and cunning—protest arose from many angry readers. An anthology of highly critical essays, entitled *Ten Black Writers Respond,* expressed the disgust of many who insisted on seeing Nat Turner as a hero. When the furor died down after a few years, however, the assessment of Turner's place in history once again seemed perplexingly difficult. Turner's desperation in a condition of bondage could be well appreciated, but what had his abortive rebellion wrought? Actually, it produced the death of about fifty-five whites and well over a hundred blacks, including many innocent blacks executed in the hysterical aftermath of rebellion. Moreover, instead of bringing down slavery, Turner's violence set off a wave of repression in the South which made the peculiar institution more inflexible and repressive than before. As enthusiasm for violent tactics began to wane in modern America, Frederick Douglass once again eclipsed Turner as the favorite black hero from the nineteenth century. Douglass, a slave and later a brilliant abolitionist, also considered violent resistance, but he appreciated other means to bring about change. His very significant contributions to the antislavery cause through nonviolent methods could not be disputed. Douglass' career was more a story of successes than setbacks and of constructive achievement rather than abortive, destructive forays.

Reviews of the gains and losses of the civil rights movement also revealed that accomplishments often glibly attributed to violent tactics were really the outcome of nonviolent resistance. Though opponents of the civil rights movement called Martin Luther King, Jr., a destructive, trouble-making radical, students of American history knew that this was far from King's own view of his role. During his successful Montgomery, Alabama, bus boycott, King stressed that his supporters "must not succumb to the temptation of becoming bitter or indulging in hate campaigns. To retaliate in kind would do nothing but intensify the existence of hate in the universe," said King. "All along the way of life, someone must have sense enough and morality enough to cut off the chain of hate. This can only be done by projecting the ethic of love to the center of our lives."[34] Later, in King's last major address before his assassination, he left a group of followers with a memorable comment on one of the principal issues in question. "It is no longer a question of violence or nonviolence in this day and age," said King. "It is nonviolence or nonexistence."[35]

Careful assessment of the civil rights record of the last twenty years shows that it was the violence of the *opposition* which helped the movement secure its most important gains. When extremist forces for segregation resorted to dangerous threats and even murder, public reaction was one of greater sympathy for civil rights workers. Ironically, among the major contributors to human rights legislation of the 1960s were Bull Conner, who (in front of TV cameras) set his police guards on peaceful demonstrators; the murderers of Medgar Evers and three civil rights workers in Philadelphia, Mississippi; and those responsible for the killing of four black girls in a bomb explosion at a Birmingham, Alabama, church. These were the violent people who helped move Congress from lethargy into a flurry of legislative activity that produced several new measures to protect the liberties of minorities.

King's wisdom could have been better appreciated in the 1970s than during the volatile period of his assassination. On college campuses, for example, just half a decade after King's death, the student majority moved away from the belligerent sanctioning of violence that characterized student attitudes during the 1960s. What had happened? First, the violent protest movements petered out because it is in the nature of things that highly emotional campaigns lose their momentum following a limited period of high enthusiasm. Second, the Vietnam War passed as a major issue, thus ending the most bitterly divisive controversy in domestic politics. Third, public events showed that violence-oriented protest was more counterproductive than successful. Harsh public reaction to violent protest and the consequences of this reaction also did much to undermine arguments about the efficacy of violence. Protestors began to realize that Richard Nixon's election as president in 1968, an electoral squeaker, was made possible by voters disgusted with rioting and by Nixon's association with that part of the electorate which sought to check the youth rebellion. Certainly the melee at the Democratic National Convention, described by the Walker Commission as a "police riot," worked in Nixon's favor.

Other developments in the late 1960s attested to backlash effects. The tough governor (like Ronald Reagan) and the tough college president (like S. I. Hayakawa) won greater power and support in troubled states and on troubled college campuses. The civil rights movement lost its force, suffering from new lethargy in all three branches of government and new worries of many white moderates troubled by increasing violence. "Law and Order" became more prominent in the American vernacular as an expression of indignation over violent protest and a desire to see society's leaders crack down on it. In those years America's political and social environment became severely inhospitable to people of announced radical and militant sentiments.

Part II
Sources

10
AGGRESSION

Sigmund Freud once suggested that the greatest *obstacle* to civilization was "the constitutional tendency in men to aggression against one another" and perhaps the greatest *challenge* to civilization was to discover how to dislodge this obstacle. What was this "constitutional tendency?" In Freud's estimation, man's long, soiled record of violence could be explained in terms of his innate, instinctual qualities.[1] Freud presented a fascinating analysis of this problem in *Civilization and Its Discontents*. Therein he spoke of a menacing instinctual drive toward aggression which constantly threatened civilized societies with disintegration. It became a classic probe into man's potential to make trouble for himself.

At times Freud seemed resigned to a gloomy assessment of his subjects. The senseless tragedies of World War I, which stimulated him to write *Civilization and Its Discontents*, dimmed prospects for reforming mass behavior. "Why do we, you and I and many others, protest so vehemently against war, instead of just accepting it as another of life's odious opportunities?" he asked, claiming that war "seems a natural thing enough, biologically sound and practically unavoidable." Freud thought man had accomplished much in containing the destructive forces of his natural environment, but he was far from controlling the destructive forces within himself. Giant strides in technology only made the threat from inner forces all the more dangerous, since they gave man's violence more devastating potential.[2]

Despite these depressing signs, however, Freud also detected some areas of hope. He questioned the familiar pessimistic predictions about mankind's fate. An extremist view of inevitable tragedy was unsatisfactory to Freud, though he had no precise answer to the monumental problems. Complete laissez-faire seemed a foolish reaction. What was the wisdom of saying nothing about violence, refusing to act, or pretending the difficulty did not exist? On the other hand, a policy of total control did not look attractive. Freud believed there were some aspects of man's behavior that society could not manipulate for its own satisfaction. Seeing contrary impulses within the human mind, Freud could not predict confidently the outcome of a struggle between man's inner destructive instincts and society's civilizing forces. Working toward a most inconclusive conclusion, near the end of his book Freud left readers with a flicker of hope, assuring them that "whatever makes for cultural development is working also against war."[3]

Well before Freud's time and well beyond his death, people have argued heatedly about whether man possesses destructive tendencies. It is an old concern. Biblical interpreters mulled over the idea (e.g., why did Cain slay his brother Abel?). Thomas Hobbes conjectured about it when he spoke of man as a naturally selfish animal, constantly at war with other men, and man's life as "nasty, brutish, and short." In the nineteenth century, Guy de Maupassant had the matter on his mind when he watched French soldiers in drill practice. Maupassant looked on woefully, thinking

> Alas! we shall never be free from oppression of hateful, hideous customs, the criminal prejudice, and the ferocious impulses of our barbarous ancestors, for we are beasts; and beasts

we shall remain, moved by our instincts and susceptible of no improvement.[4]

A similar thought troubled Glen Gray, author of *The Warriors,* a moving volume on war in the twentieth century. Commenting on the soldiers' readiness to kill, Gray wrote, "Thousands of youths, who never suspected the presence of such an impulse in themselves, have learned in military life the mad excitement of destroying."[5] In recent times, noted scientists have been concerned about this impulse. Niko Tinbergen, a student of animal behavior, cited some of the brain's problematic contributions to man. The brain is the finest life-preserving device to develop out of nature, observed Tinbergen, yet it has been so successful in fighting off nature's threats to preservation that now this instinctive combativeness is left to turn against itself. To Tinbergen, examples of man's war upon himself show that "the brain finds itself seriously threatened by an enemy of its own making."[6]

Americans show much interest in current theories associating violence with human nature. Their fascination parallels a growing disillusionment since World War II over prospects for peace both at home and abroad. Episodes of domestic violence and entanglements in Korea and Southeast Asia shattered American dreams of a postwar era of civilized tranquility. News of mass violence from other places in the world provoked larger questions about the course of mankind. How could one explain the massive slaughters in diverse places like Indonesia, Nigeria, or Bangladesh? Though viable disputes contributed to each confrontation, the differences between contending parties were not so irreconcilable as to require wholesale destruction. An up-to-date version of old theories on human behavior began to crystallize. According to this explanation, when people settle their differences with force disproportionate to the issues at stake, it shows that man's ability to master his own actions is getting out of control. Sometimes economic, political, religious, and ethnic controversies serve as catalysts that spark the most destructive impulses in man's nature. That such wanton violence can deeply trouble American civilization as well as less developed nations shows the universality in the human condition. It suggests that no civilization is ever far from barbarism, because the savage is ever within man. No panoply of cultural or technological ornaments can hide that reality.[7]

Popular interest in this persistence of violence in some of the world's most civilized societies has given rise to an abundance of new "scientific" studies of the idea of man's innate aggressiveness. Research on aggression is now quite sophisticated, and specialists in the field recognize that the term has multiple meanings. People may manifest aggressiveness in such diverse ways as exerting great energy in the pursuit of success in sports or business, saying something that one knows will be psychologically painful to the person listening, or expressing disapproval by maintaining stony silence after hearing an appeal. But the form of aggression that particularly concerns us here involves action that leads to physical injury. We are speaking of violence meted out by people against *other* people. In this sense violence is a specific category under the rubric of a more general subject often identified as aggression. Since traditional philosophical debates as well as recent scientific disputes couch theories about the problems of man's violence under the broader heading of aggression, we shall use both terms in the discussion which follows. We do so with the understanding that both aggression and violence are multidimensional concepts and can deal with many more phenomena than are treated here.[8]

The new scientific interest in the issue of man's innate aggressiveness, which attracted considerable attention in the 1960s and 1970s, found expression especially from prominent ethologists and their admirers. Generally defined, ethology is the study of innate behavioral patterns in animals. Since man is an animal too, a researcher's discovery of patterns in mice or dogs may help us to understand ourselves better. Ethologists view with amusement the angry reactions of some people against these comparisons of human behavior with the impulse patterns of the household pooch or the banana-chomping chimp. Zoologist Desmond Morris enjoys toying with the ramifications of an ethological approach in his stimulating book, *The Naked Ape*. Morris graciously acknowledges that man is highest on the scale of life on earth, but reminds us that the scale in question is that of the animal kingdom. Man is the hairless ape and an aggressive ape at that.[9]

Another stimulating popularizer of ethological interpretations, Robert Ardrey, relates evidence on animal behavior to man's problem of violence. In two very influential books, *African Genesis* and *The Territorial Imperative,* Ardrey eloquently and quite partisanly weaves together a case for innate aggressiveness.[10] In *The Territorial Imperative,* Ardrey extrapolates from findings on instinctual pressures in animals for control of territory to interpret man's ferocity in defending property and national boundaries. He has a poignant message for historians and political scientists who are troubled by man's sorry record of highly emotional violence: "If we defend the title to our land or the sovereignty of our country, we do it for reasons no different, no less innate, no less irradicable, than do the lower animals."[11]

Ardrey, Morris, and other popularizers of ethological ideas owe much to the groundwork laid by Austrian ethologist Konrad Lorenz. Lorenz is unquestionably one of the most respected fathers of the modern Instinct School of interpreting human behavior. In his now famous study, *On Aggression,* Lorenz begins with an analysis of animal behavior, then broadens his scope to consider its implications for human behavior. The lessons Lorenz picks up from these investigations appear to be Neo Darwinism, since he stresses the survival function of aggression in animals. Lorenz sees fighting spirit and fighting skill as beneficial to animals. They can serve the defensive needs of the group, allow stronger animals to mark out territorial rights vital to feeding needs, or establish a pecking order where more skilled animals can provide their group with leadership, discipline, organization, and stability.[12]

When Lorenz moves beyond descriptions of the behavior of fish, geese, and the like in his final chapters to generalize about the lessons for man, the argument becomes especially titillating. Humans, too, possess biologically inherited aggressive drives, says Lorenz, drives which, through evolution, proved helpful for survival. Until a short time ago, man also needed fighting and hunting instincts for survival—the skills necessary to gain and protect his possessions and to defend himself. In modern civilization this kind of aggression no longer has functional importance. We need not track down our breakfast in the woods each morning, fight off predatory animals at the front door, or wrestle with fellow men over scarce food. It seems, then, that man's instincts have not caught up with the milder requisites of sophisticated community living. When people turn violent in modern situations, therefore, often it is *not* in direct response to serious provocation from the environment. Internal aggressive drive functions within man independent of environmental stimuli. If this biologically inherited drive does not get sufficient opportunities for release, it can build up to explosive proportions and discharge violently from the mildest of stimuli.

Lorenz's impressions about man's prospects for avoiding violence would be extremely pessimistic were he to stop at this point. Lorenz does see hope, however, in the idea of channeling aggressive behavior into safe outlets. If even animals can avoid violence by acting out ritualistic patterns of attack instead of actually drawing blood, why can't man safely cope with his instincts? Lorenz recommends athletic competition as a good, safe way to release pent-up aggressive instincts. If people must become aggressive and put their physical power to a test, let them have fun doing so and profit from its cathartic effect while leaving others around them free from danger.[13]

Obviously, Lorenz did not singlehandedly discover the concept of channeling. The idea has been with us for a long time, partly as a common sense notion, partly as a thought for inquiry by philosophers and scientists. William James helped circulate the idea through his famous essay, "The Moral Equivalent of War." James urged pacifists to recognize the "inwardness" of bellicosity. He thought society needed to provide the martial type with some mode of expressing his warrior impulse that would not drag other people into destruction.[14] Sigmund Freud made a similar observation. When Albert Einstein wrote to him, asking for his views on the persistence of war, Freud replied, "Complete suppression of man's aggressive tendencies is not in issue; what we may try is to direct it into a channel other than warfare."[15]

In recent years, various scientists have offered their own

recommendations for safe channeling, expanding on Lorenz's theories about the value of sports. Ethologist Niko Tinbergen recommends competition through scientific investigations. This activity not only releases tensions, notes Tinbergen; it also helps improve the lot of mankind.[16] Psychiatrist Anthony Storr views nonviolent forms of international competition as a way to play out aggressive pressures safely. He sees the space race as a healthy relief of Cold War tensions.[17] Psychiatrist Bruno Bettelheim recalls that, in his native Austria, woodcutting or the slaughtering of a pig provided safe means for releasing energy. Bettelheim urges Americans to find their own ways to drain off pressures that can otherwise induce destructive behavior.[18] All of these diverse suggestions for channeling instinctual aggression are potentially relevant.

The idea of channeling, redirecting, or sublimating aggressive impulses is especially enticing to students of the Instinct School, because it provides them with an escape from an otherwise sadly pessimistic assessment of entrapped man. Complete emphasis on the innate aspects of violence carries discomforting implications. If destructive, intra-species aggression is a natural part of man's makeup, how can we hope to eradicate it? We cannot remove the aggressive impulse, say the instinct theorists. It is real, it is in all of us to some degree. We will not go far by trying to teach people not to be violent or by constantly reprimanding them when they are. History shows the utter failure of massive cultural efforts to inhibit man's aggressive impulses. The task is not to prevent shows of aggression but to provide safe and legitimate forms for its expression. Ironically, then, say the instinct theorists, aggression can best be handled by accepting it, not denying it.[19]

This interpretation, stressing the potential of channeling behavior, looks so relevant to a world troubled by violence that, understandably, the Instinct School has won many admirers. The theory both explains violence, and offers a remedy for it. Its simplicity is attractive at a time when the task of understanding the causes of aggression is so complex. Instinct theory relieves confusion about how to confront twentieth-century violence, much like Henry George's single tax theory relieved confusion about how to confront nineteenth-century economic inequality. Both answers, however, fall short when carefully scrutinized.

First, there is cause to resist the temptation to identify behavioral phenomena simply on the basis of first appearances. Take the sports fetish, for instance. Why do so many Americans feel compelled to sprint around a track to near exhaustion, rush off on all-day hiking and camping expeditions, or engage friends in heated competition on the tennis courts? Ask the man who sprints, hikes, or swings the racquet. He will usually interpret his activities as a desire to release pent up aggressive impulses. This common explanation may reveal more about attitudes in our culture than the true motivation for athletic endeavors. Clearly, there are other possible, and more probable, answers. An interest in sports can reflect a desire to exercise one's limbs, to get away from the sedentary life of home and office. It can also show a desire for personal achievement, a quest for the satisfaction that comes with taking on a physical challenge or succeeding in competition. These or many other purposes may motivate the sports enthusiast. Yet in a culture preoccupied with matters of violence, Americans seem especially anxious to assume pent-up aggression is a prime cause for sports enthusiasm.

We are left with the uncomfortable feeling that the thesis about channeling instincts diagnoses violence incorrectly and prescribes medicine that does not affect the true problem. In short, the remedy cannot work. For example, if juvenile hoods make the streets unsafe for pedestrians, their antisocial behavior may be due to unemployment, boredom, a desire for peer group status, or a host of other factors. To say that youngsters are exploding from pent-up instincts tells us little about the difficulty or its possible solutions. Instinct channeling theorists might respond that community workshops, country camps, job training programs, and social centers are safe outlets for aggression. But to which stimuli would such programs respond? The link between antisocial actions and social or economic frustrations is patent in these examples. By contrast, relationships to an instinctive aggressive drive seem much more remote. For a more direct application of the instinct channeling theory, we might provide each delinquent with his own personal punching bag. Would that effectively solve the problem of criminal violence among juveniles?

Instinct channeling theorists may have placed their fingers on the *symptoms* of trouble rather than the trouble itself. As psychologist Abraham Maslow explains, aggressiveness and destructiveness are not necessarily primary instincts; rather, they seem to be the end-products of other personal problems. Maslow does not tolerate simplistic interpretations which posit a single impulse toward destructiveness. When a subject turns to violence, Maslow explains, he may well be manifesting (a) his reaction to a real threat, (b) insecure feelings which create perceptions of a threat, (c) behavior developing out of an "authoritarian personality," or (d) incidental behavior that takes place in working toward a particular goal. In short, the goals and perceptions of an individual represent the dog in this situation; an outburst of aggression is only the tail.[20]

Robert Ardrey's description of a territorial imperative is vulnerable to similar criticism. Ardrey stretches the concept to cover everything from man's protection of his hunting grounds to violent defense of towns, cities, and nations. But doesn't much domestic fighting arise from economic grievances, social status frustrations, dissatisfaction with political decisions, ethnic, racial, and religious hostility, and other problems? Did Irish Americans riot in New York in 1863 to release their pent-up aggressive instincts, or because they did not want to be drafted for the war front and lose their jobs to blacks? Furthermore, Ardrey's territorial theory does not explain imperialism. If people march beyond their homelands in violent forays, need we assume that territorial instincts propel them when it appears that they are actually motivated by economic booty or quests for power and security in international affairs? The case for instinctual territorial drive may really be a description of symptoms manifested from other, more direct causes. If this is the case, efforts to treat violence through channeling will be misguided, since the basic causes of violence are misinterpreted in the first place.

A channeling approach, moreover, may not only be ineffective, but might also *stimulate* violent behavior. We can question the belief that violence is best treated by encouraging subjects to be violent and that releasing aggression in safe situations will reduce the probability of its explosion in dangerous situations. As psychologist Roger N. Johnson points out, if this hypothesis really worked, "we should require all children to be maximally exposed to violence and bloodshed in an effort to *reduce* crime and delinquency. In the same vein, we should be able to reduce sexual desire by exposure to erotic stimuli; perhaps a starving man would feel less hungry if he were teased with filet mignon and caviar."[21] The relevant difficulty is obvious in the first part of Johnson's statement: we should not expect to reduce crime and delinquency by giving children maximum exposure to violence and bloodshed. Through several important experiments, psychologist Leonard Berkowitz shows that channeling techniques can bring results opposite from those claimed by instinct theorists. When Berkowitz's subjects were exposed to violence or were given opportunities to act out violent behavior in supposedly safe ways, they became more rather than less inclined toward aggression.[22] Extrapolating from this thesis to comment on behavior outside the laboratory, political scientist James Channing Davies reminds us that urban riots did not provide a healthy release of tensions. Instead of satisfying a few people, isolated acts of aggression sparked neighborhood-wide explosions. Mayhem can feed on its own momentum, and once it gets started it can escalate into more serious destruction. Attempts to remedy these violent outbreaks by subjecting people to alternative forms of violence can be highly dangerous.[23]

Of all the questions raised about the instinct channeling thesis, the most fundamental focus on the very idea of instincts. Why assume aggression is instinctive when so much evidence shows that it is learned, many critics ask? Why attribute violence to man's nature when his environment obviously has much to do with his problem?

The nature versus nurture argument has been around for a long time, and we can confidently assert that it will remain for generations to come. The authors of a special commission report note that this debate "has occupied philosophy, religion, and political theory for some millennia, and the absence of convincing data will probably continue to outlast contemporary theories."[24] Though the debate never closes, over the years each side has enjoyed modest ascendance. Until the recent pall of gloom over increasing violence, the nurture side of the argument predominated in American thinking. For many years, an extreme form of this argument remained highly influential—the "frustration-aggression" hypothesis of John Dollard and his followers. Essentially, this school believed that aggression is *always* a consequence of frustration.[25] Many other scholars refined the thesis, validating the importance of other factors. Yet all along, their evidence and interpretation supported the fundamental thesis that aggression is learned. Then, with new disillusionment over man's deteriorating condition and the revolution in ethology, laymen found scientific theories to firm up their impressions on the persistence of violence.

Throughout this recent revival of the nature school of aggression, spokesmen for the nurture school continued to protest the public's sudden infatuation with "instincts." Environmentalists (supporters of the nurture theory) thought they had already beaten the term instinct to death, at least as a general idea that could be tossed about glibly as an explanation for human violence. Learning was the principal causal factor in problems of human violence, they insisted. Through all the ethological excitement, environmentalists continued to remind the public that there is a very sizable difference between the learning capacity of human beings and any other member of the animal kingdom. To recognize this basic contrast does not require a philosophic or religious commitment to glorification of Man the Unique. Nor does it call for rejection of Darwinian theory. As nurture theorists have pointed out for so long, the idea rests on a simple comparison of the learning potential of animals and man. Man far surpasses any animal in tests of ability to cope with his environment and manipulate it according to his needs. Even the genius of the nonhuman animal kingdom, the chimpanzee, quickly drops behind the human youngster in an I.Q. test after the first few years.[26]

Interestingly enough, even animals deserve some compliments in this discussion since they, too, show capacities for nonviolence. Obviously, not all animals are vicious aggressors, and some who score highest in the passivity scale are also among the brightest on the animal list. For example, the orangutang, the chimpanzee, and the gorilla are noticeably nonviolent.[27] Moreover, animals, too, show the mental capacity to learn to be either violent or nonviolent. Psychologist Jerome Frank observes that "members of the same biological strain of mice can be taught to be vicious fighters or absolute pacifists."[28] Even wolves can be tamed considerably, especially if their learning process begins very early. Little wonder, then, that environmentalists are exasperated when they must constantly remind their fellow humans that they are neither mice nor wolves and that *their* capacity to learn makes comparisons with animals positively invidious.

We should remember, though, that the influence of learning on violence is double-edged. Learning can be as harmful as it can be helpful to man: people can easily learn to be violent. The early years of life are particularly crucial in this regard. Once violence is learned, it is "unlearned" with great difficulty. We can submerge a child in violent stimuli and create an aggressive little monster. Beyond that point efforts to reform and redirect his behavior are often ineffectual and frustrating. This is the disturbing lesson of learning theory: a society that does not carefully evaluate the value system it teaches its young will eventually find itself victim of its own negligence.

The most crucial period in the development of potentially violent behavioral patterns occurs between childhood and adolescence. It is during this stage that a youngster picks up multifarious cues from others that can direct his own life. Some of the important lessons come from parents or teachers through forms of reward or punishment for behavior and expressions of approval or disapproval in response to specific attitudes. But most learning about violence occurs more subtly. It does not develop out of formal instruction in the do's and don't's; rather, it emanates from experimental learning. The youngster sees how others behave. He listens to the way they talk. From casual experiences he picks up values and attitudes that will influence his life significantly—the streetside conversations with peers, the programs that he views on television, the informal comments he hears from his elders. If violence sounds like a norm, a regular and accepted part of life, this impression may sink in deeply and affect his actions in later years.

It appears that the problems of violence in modern American society have much more to do with the consequences of learning than with instinctive drives. As Marvin Wolfgang, one of the foremost students of violent crime, notes, violence is not a spontaneous need among normal persons. The prediliction for criminal violence comes from outside, from learning, from environmental stimuli, says Wolfgang, who describes the small worlds of tough youths as "subcultures of violence."[29] It is from this point of view that psychologist Alberta Spiegel gives an extreme example to highlight the potentially dangerous impact of the environment. "Any civilization is only 50 years away from barbarism," she comments, referring to the amount of time it takes to teach a new generation to be savages.[30]

Hence, the more frightening problem to ponder is not the instinct theorists' hypothesis that an innately aggressive impulse can spring forth from any of us, but the environmentalist's hypothesis that almost any normal child can become a vicious danger to society and to himself. Many years ago Clarence Darrow stated the case pointedly:

> If [a person] lives unwisely, if he is defective, if he is antisocial, it is not because he chose it; but it is due to a thousand conditions over which he has not the slightest control. And the wise society seeks to change his environment, to place him in harmony with life. They know that they can only change the man by changing the conditions under which he lives.[31]

Darrow blamed society as the most likely culprit when men exploded into violence. Since society was only a body of individuals, he said, its members might begin a study of violence by asking how much they themselves unknowingly had contributed to the problem.

It seems, then, that the essential difficulty is not the "beast" in man but man himself. An old adage claims that man is distinguishable from other animals primarily in his capacity to make trouble for himself. To recognize that man has engendered violence by his own doing is not an easy task, for it implies a strong sense of accountability. Blaming instincts for our violence is a monumental copout. By admitting the problems are of our own making, we acknowledge that we can change them by our own efforts. This is not an easy idea to accept unless one is ready to take on the responsibility of action.[32]

It would not be proper to close discussion of the nature versus nurture debate without referring to some new research that points to other sources of understanding and action. In light of recent discoveries, we should be cautious about attributing *all* aggressive behavior to learning. There is weighty scientific evidence that some aspects of violence are inherent in man. The most sophisticated research in this area avoids simplistic generalizations such as references to instincts. Instead, some of the most promising findings link aggression to neurological conditions and genetic inheritance. In a sense, this scholarship establishes a middle ground in the nature versus nurture argument, making a case for interaction between the two.[33] As physiologist K. E. Moyer explains, "We would be misguided to try to control aggression with a scheme derived solely from either group's premises." Moyer believes research into the "physiology of violence" gives a more satisfactory basis for understanding behavioral problems and remedying them.[34]

Moyer stresses the importance of the nervous system in activating violence. Physiological research shows that the brain contains inborn neural systems which activate in the presence of particular stimuli, resulting in violent behavior. We also have abundant evidence indicating that experimenters can induce both verbal and physical aggression in human beings through stimulation of particular areas of the brain. Impressive evidence of the importance of neural conditions can also be found outside the laboratory, apparent in some memorable news stories of sensational murder cases. For example, in 1966 Charles Whitman, a usually mild-mannered young man, coolly slaughtered members of his family, then went to a tower at the University of Texas and picked off unsuspecting people with his rifles.

Whitman shot 38 people and killed 14 of them before police gunned him down. Doctors later discovered a tumor the size of a walnut in his brain. Apparently, the tumor affected his neural condition and, hence, his behavior. In another much publicized slaughter Richard Speck killed eight student nurses. Psychiatrists later attributed much of Speck's problem to severe brain damage from childhood injuries and illnesses.[35]

The most important and controversial implications of such physiological studies concern their potential for correcting dangerously aggressive behavior. K. E. Moyer notes that experiments in which scientists implant electrodes in a human brain and hook people up to radio receivers are not dreams of science fiction. They are presently being carried out in scientific laboratories across the country. Furthermore, former president of the American Psychological Association, Kenneth B. Clark, reminds us of the numerous effective pharmacological agents available for taming violent individuals. Clark speculates on the value of administering these drugs to world leaders to make them less aggressive and less likely to lead their nations into war.[36]

The controversial aspects of these experiments are glaring. Most obviously, they represent frighteningly direct attempts to control human behavior. Scientists like Moyer and Clark acknowledge the problem; they admit to raising highly controversial issues that cannot be resolved easily. Then, too, electrodes or drugs may stimulate unknown byproducts of behavior and create a new series of problems for subject-patients. Man is still in the very early stages of understanding the complex neural system.[37] As we have already learned from the use of many highly celebrated drugs, some medical panaceas turn out to have dangerous side-effects not initially suspected by the developers. Moreover, heavy dependence on a drug can produce other personality patterns that are also undesirable.

A genetic approach to human violence and its possible remedies also shows serious shortcomings. There is good evidence that we can breed animals or humans to be less aggressive, but what society will do with that information remains problematic. We understand that fox terriers are more aggressive than cocker spaniels, and we know that the genetic constitution of

Jim Savage may give him a more explosive personality than Roger Milktoast. Does that understanding suggest a blueprint for improving the human condition? It is easy to speculate on the prospects of a Brave New World in which society can, indeed, try to breed out aggressive qualities. Disregarding the morality of such a society for a moment, we might toy for a moment with some of the widest implications of this prospect. What would happen if it were played out to its fullest potential? In time the experiment could prove frustrating even to the most benevolent experimenters. Without any reduction in violent environmental stimuli, the newly bred population could hardly take giant strides toward peace and harmony. Many of the genetically sweetest would still gun down their fellow Alphas.

Though physiological and genetic approaches to violence look attractive for basic research, they do not offer much in the way of effective solutions to the problem. Most individuals who harm society with their aggressive acts do not qualify as "pathologically hostile patients" in terms of genetic inheritance, chromosomal abnormalities, brain damage, chemical imbalances, or the like. Instead, they are individuals born potentially noncriminal and nonhomicidal. They are people who have fallen into violence through life experiences. Even if we can try to counteract these violence-producing life experiences with drugs or electrodes, we cannot start dosing and wiring up all potentially violent criminals. To do so would be to provide neural treatment for a very sizable proportion of our total population. In short, although physiological and genetic studies offer more sophisticated explanations of violent behavior than do theories based on nebulous ideas about human instincts, these investigations, too, fail to provide practical ways to improve the human condition.

If the American public continues to court schools of thought that emphasize aspects of violence inherent in man's makeup, we should not expect to see much compensatory action by society. Frequently, a profound sense of fatalism accompanies acceptance of theories about inherent problems in man. Such fatalism was evident in religious doctrines of centuries past, when many were obsessed with the idea of man's natural sinfulness. It was evident in the late nineteenth century when people often explained away inequality and violence as part of an evolutionary struggle, as a brutal but necessary battle for survival of the fittest.[38] This thinking also accompanies contemporary interpretations of man's biological makeup. As Sally Carrighar warns, "Nothing could more effectively prolong man's fighting behavior than a belief that aggression is in our genes."[39]

Why the persistence of this belief? One answer is that acceptance of war and violence as emanations of man's natural endowment absolves people of moral responsibility. Hence, the problems are inevitable, they are the way "things have to be." The new dependence on "science" to explain away difficulties is analogous to an earlier twisting of Charles Darwin's biological concepts into desired social theories. Indeed, much popular discussion of the new theories leaves students more adrift than even the leading ethologist would imagine. For example, Samuel Feinberg essayed the importance of Lorenz's and Tinbergen's work in *Women's Wear Daily* with the conclusion: "Pending 'effective therapy', it seems, man must continue to live—or exist—in a 'malfunctioning' personal and outside world. If you can grin and bear it, so much the better! If you can't, what's your alternative?"[40] Leo Tolstoy's reaction to this kind of resignation carries a poignant message for today. Tolstoy did not believe in the inevitability of fighting and war, denouncing the idea as a way in which "the educated classes . . . deaden their conscience." He lamented the way "sensitive men of genius" could recognize all the horror, folly, and cruelty of violence, yet, instead of looking for means of escape, "take a morbid delight in realizing to the utmost the desperate condition of mankind."[41]

This "morbid delight" in resigning to violence as part of man's nature is a noticeable part of American popular culture. It appears not only in purportedly scientific commentary, but also in barroom conversations, TV talk shows, and discussions about the movies. We can find rather specific endorsements of the ethological point of view in some highly popular films. Sam Peckinpah, director of controversial films like *The Wild Bunch* and *Straw Dogs,* defended his treatment of violent themes by arguing: "Everybody seems to deny that we're human. We're violent by nature . . . I would like to understand the nature of violence. Is there a way to channel it, to use it positively? . . . But don't say to me we're not violent. Because we are. It's one of the greatest brainwashes of all times to say we're not."[42] Director-producer Stanley Kubrick also found a chance to play with the nature versus nurture debate in his film *A Clockwork Orange,* based on the book by Anthony Burgess. When asked about the philosophical implications of his film, Kubrick responded with the Instinct School's party line. "Man isn't a noble savage, he's an ignoble savage," Kubrick asserted. "He is irrational, brutal, weak, silly, unable to be objective about anything where his own interests are involved—that about sums it up. I'm interested in the brutal and violent nature of man because it's a true picture of him. And any attempt to create social institutions on a false view of the nature of man is probably doomed to failure."[43] A prophet of pessimism would find Kubrick's comment a difficult act to follow. Yet Malcolm McDowell, the actor Kubrick selected to play the lead role in *A Clockwork Orange,* gives us an even gloomier picture. "People are basically bad, corrupt," McDowell explains. "I always sensed that. Man has not progressed one inch, morally, since the Greeks. Liberals, they hate 'Clockwork' because they're dreamers and it shows them the realities, shows 'em not tomorrow but *now.* Cringe, don't they, when faced with the bloody truth?"[44]

Contempt for man's nature seemed to be in season when films like *A Clockwork Orange* reached neighborhood theaters. The original refined and compassionate message of Konrad Lorenz, dramatized and coarsely popularized by Robert Ardrey, appeared in crudely simplistic form at the local cinema. It is amusing to listen to movie buffs intellectualize the themes of such motion pictures when they walk out of the theater and struggle to define the supposed brilliance of media symbolism. What was the director trying to tell us, they ask? What insights can be gained from the philosophic as well as artistic masterpiece? For films like *A Clockwork Orange,* discussions tend to settle on lessons about violence and the nature of man. Yet the statements of directors and actors referred to above show this unrefined philosophy in naked form, stripped of its artistic embellishment. As simplistic as the thesis may be, it clearly has become a popular part of our intellectual baggage.

Endorsements of the instinct thesis may be an amusing exercise in chatter about movies, but it is not very funny when people apply the idea to serious problems. Espousal of the "depraved man" or "man is a bastard" doctrine can be frightening when this doctrine touches on human tragedy. Should we laugh at American psychoanalyst Gregory Zilboorg's approval of the channeling approach, evident in his 1940 comment, "We should do nothing about the Nazis, because they have to live out their aggressions?"[45] And what is amusing about German philosopher Karl Jasper's description of "the pleasure of violence" and the impulse "to sacrifice oneself to such violence, to die or to be victorious" as feelings which reveal "fundamental instincts?" The subject of his lecture was "The Atomic Bomb and the Future of Man."[46]

Considering the many extremes and absurdities in interpretations of the Instinct School of human aggression, we might wonder how such a theory has remained consistently popular, in various forms, in American life. Its popularity in other cultures notwithstanding, the extraordinarily favorable reception given to instinct theories in the United States prompts several questions. How do these attitudes about violence jive with the American people's belief that their society is a paragon of civilization? Why do so many Americans continue to place credence in a variety of explanations of violence that smack of fatalism in interpreting man's potential to control his own destiny? Why are Americans ready to accept violence, so tolerant of its subtle and pervasive presence, so ready to resign to it (and, sometimes, praise it) as an inevitable and necessary condition of mankind? Perhaps the idea of violence is so strongly integrated into the culture that Americans cannot step outside of it to see that things could be otherwise. Perhaps violence has become an integral part of the American's world-view, a fundamental element in the national ethos.

11
ETHOS

When we talk about murders, assassinations, police brutality, riots, vigilante activity, or any other example of violence, it is very easy to isolate these acts as extreme forms of behavior, seemingly unrelated to what happens in mainstream America. Yet we can err egregiously in singling out violent people who appear in newspaper stories as odd, despicable types while commending as nonviolent the many who never score a criminal or antisocial record. To dump all responsibility for violence on the individual who commits an overt, dramatic act is unfair when the entire society contributes to the problem. The menace is not concentrated in the behavior of a few criminals or hyperaggressive people; it exists within the entire population. Mainstream Americans are not anxious to recognize their own involvement in a value system that condones violence, yet they are indirect contributors in thousands of subtle ways. They are, in a sense, accessories to the very crimes that shock and disgust them. The proverbial man in the street, the law-abiding, upstanding citizen, and the pillar of the community are all deeply immersed in an ethos of violence.

Ethos, a very general concept, relates closely to the problematic contributions of mainstream Americans. It is one of the most sweeping terms used to characterize a society, a word that broadly identifies a combination of national sentiments, beliefs, customs, ideals, standards, and practices. In short, ethos is a people's world-view, their attitude toward life. If most Americans were asked whether violence is an important element in their outlook on life, they would quickly answer in the negative. By phrasing the question differently, however, we may discover a wide resignation toward or acceptance of violence. For example, popular expression of the instinct theory of aggression receives much public endorsement in the United States. One poll taken in the 1960s found 58 percent agreeing with the statement, "Human nature being what it is, there must always be war and conflict."[1] Many speak of violence as a fact of life and look incredulously at proposals for change, commenting, "What the hell. That's the way people are. You can't change human nature."

Many Americans view violence so casually as part of life that often they do not ponder the implications of their commonplace attitudes, speech, and behavior. A brief, variegated list of news items is suggestive:

—A woman civil defense aide shows exhilaration after watching an atomic explosion at Yucca Flat, excitedly calling the experience the greatest "thrill" of her life.[2]
—Children in a Dallas school break into applause when they hear that President Kennedy has been shot.[3]
—The director of a publishing house featuring books on guerrilla warfare, snipers, and assassins responds to criticism that his products may be contributing to violence with the comment, "I feel I should be no more concerned about that than the auto dealer who sells a car that runs somebody down."[4]
—The Secretary of Defense dedicates a new chapel room in the Pentagon in 1970, saying, "After all, peace is the business of this building."[5]
—Millions praise Lt. William Calley as a "hero" after an army court judges him guilty of murdering twenty-two Vietnamese men, women, and children.

Violence is so prevalent and subtle in everyday attitudes that Americans become oblivious to it. Some popular patriotic songs and sayings, for example, are pregnant with violent connotations yet raise few questions from the populace. Consider the National Anthem. Children learn its words in their early school years and recite it from memory through the rest of their lives. At football games, club meetings, and political rallies citizens sing out its message. But do they stop to think about the message? To review that most familiar stanza:

O say, can you see, by the dawn's early light
What so proudly we hailed at the twilight's last gleaming—
Whose broad stripes and bright stars, through the perilous night
O'er the ramparts we watched were so gallantly streaming!
And the rockets' red glare, the bombs bursting in air
Gave proof through the night that our flag was still there;
O say, does the star-spangled banner yet wave
O'er the land of the free, and the home of the brave?[6]

Rockets' red glare? Bombs bursting in air? Americans have a battle song for their national anthem! While glorifying the flag, it also gives a blood and guts story, a poetic description of an event in the War of 1812 that cost many American and British lives. Over the years some have suggested that *America the Beautiful* would make a better national anthem because of its more inspiring melody. Perhaps, *America the Beautiful* should be substituted—first because of its more inspiring words, second because of its more spirited tune. Americans can do much better advertising their "good with brotherhood" than "bombs bursting in air."

Specific references to violence, generally unrecognized, also appear in popular patriotic sayings. For example, when one small Ohio town (Granville) decided to make "Quotations for Freedom" the theme for its Fourth of July float parade, townsfolk found their first thoughts gravitating toward fighting words. Before turning to reference books, a few basic sayings seemed to be on the tips of most people's tongues. "Give me liberty or give me death," Patrick Henry's immortal warning from his 1775 "Call to Arms" speech, was most popular. Following closely behind were two other war chants: "Don't fire until you see the whites of their eyes" and "I have not yet begun to fight." Ultimately, the good folk of Granville recognized the propriety of more pacific themes, and after a bit of research, adopted more peaceful and positive messages for their "Quotations for Freedom."

Americans also frequently reveal a preoccupation with violence in their discussions on history. In this context, too, they give little critical thought to the fact that violent themes have a very conspicuous place in their thinking. Many professional historians know this syndrome well from casual acquaintances made in airports, bus terminals, and the like. As strangers meet, introduce, and indicate their occupations, the historian often finds his new friend excitedly reporting on an abiding interest in history. Pleased with the show of enthusiasm, the historian asks: What are your favorite topics from history? The Civil War, World War I, and World War II, replies the layman. Then, proud to show his familiarity with major historical works, the layman reveals in depth knowledge of several of Bruce Catton's books on Civil War battles. Moving on to discuss favorite "ifs" of history, he conjectures on fascinating possibilities of the great wars. What would have happened if Lee had taken Gettysburg? Suppose Hitler had not declared war on the Soviet Union? Wide-eyed speculation about warmaking strategy typically predominates over consideration of great economic, social, and political issues from history. Laymen scrutinize the decisions and options of generals or admirals with the care usually displayed in an actuary's study of longevity tables. These typical displays of military interest in conversations with historians often reveal the casual and leisurely way many people evaluate great crises in the human record. They view the history of wars like a chess game where men move around as pawns, and the loss of several pieces means little if gambits lead to a glorious checkmate. Battle tales become great adventure stories, connoting challenges of planning and strategy rather than blood and pain and death.

This antiseptic approach to the history of warfare sometimes makes subtle appearances in school and college classrooms when students discuss controversial decisions of national policy. It is often evident in the familiar debate about whether the United States should have dropped atomic bombs on Hiroshima and Nagasaki in World War II. In such a discussion one student usually condemns the action as moral outrage. The critic explains that nuclear attacks are too complete, too indiscriminate in destroying the civilian population, and inhumane in their legacy of radioactivity. At this point the informed skeptic intervenes to note that many more people died in one night of firebombing over Dresden than in the atomic attacks on either Hiroshima or Nagasaki. Outnumbered in a battle of body-counts, the moralist critic of nuclear warfare typically sulks. He allows the statistical game to throw him off balance, forgetting, for a moment, historical and diplomatic distinctions between the two examples as well as serious moral implications.

The impersonal body-count approach to assessing military and foreign policy events is familiar to Americans who watched day-by-day television reports about the Vietnam War. Through the long years of hostilities, officials such as General William Westmoreland and Secretary of Defense Melvin Laird tried to stir hatred for the enemy by fostering a we/they mentality and announcing enemy casualty figures with the pride one would expect from analysis of points scored in a shooting contest. Military leaders would point out the low Allied deaths and the high body-counts of the enemy. Even media language added force to the buildup of we/they enmity. Television newsmen referred to Allies killed versus Communists killed. The comparison was not complementary, of course. "Allies" connotes a position in a conflict, while "Communists" refers to an ideology. If newsmen had compared "communist" dead with "capitalist" dead, they would, at least, have maintained some consistency and compatibility in their use of terms. By comparing unlike categories in their reporting, newsmen helped to confuse the issues and intensify contempt for the enemy. Their language contributed to the growth of hatred for Southeast Asian "Communists" and an impersonal attitude toward their deaths.[7]

Depersonalization of the enemy became evident most graphically in reaction to Lt. William Calley, Jr.'s trial. Despite the tremendous weight of evidence which associated Calley with heinous crimes, millions of Americans defended his acts and hailed him as a hero. Calley faced indictment for the murder of 102 persons, yet cries of public wrath went up when the Army brought him to trial. Significantly, most of the protestors did not doubt Calley committed murder. They accepted this charge unabashedly and defended the lieutenant for his actions. "We make [our boys] go into the armed forces and teach them to kill, then we punish them," complained one woman in a typical statement.[8] As popular arguments explained the affair, the military sent a young officer into Vietnam's jungles to "do a job." His first obligations were to lick the enemy and protect his own men, whatever the cost. If Calley shot down children, women, and old men, that was excusable, they said, because all civilians were dangerous in an all-out conflict like the war in Vietnam. Even five-year-old youngsters were known to surprise G.I.s with grenade attacks, they said—a danger that justified slaughtering children in an "enemy" village. President Nixon tried to make political capital of the sentimental outburst by expressing his own sympathies for Calley's plight. Some businessmen tried to make economic returns out of the new *cause célèbre* of Vietnam War advocates. One firm scored with a hit album called *The Battle Hymn of Lieutenant Calley,* set to the tune of *The Battle Hymn of the Republic.* In Vietnam new signs appeared on the walls of army camps: "Kill a gook for Calley."[9]

Through all the excitement, Calley enjoyed sudden glory without apparent anxiety about facing a lifetime of incarceration. Following the trial he remained under light house arrest at Fort Benning, Georgia, while an Army panel reviewed his case. After five months, the panel decided to reduce his life sentence to forty-five years, but the Third Army Commander reduced it further to a twenty-year term. Appeals continued to yet higher levels in the hope that the sentence would be reduced further, particularly through a generous decision from the President. In 1974 a federal Circuit Court of Appeals ordered Calley's release.

Psychologist Stanley Milgram raises poignant questions about Vietnam War atrocities in his controversial book, *Obedience to Authority.* Milgram does not accept the popular notion that Americans are incapable of the gross forms of inhumanity that were practiced in Nazi Germany. While many emphasize the differences between democracy and a totalitarian state, Milgram finds a common denominator. Authority is a key factor in such malevolent behavior, he argues. Even in a democracy, once men are elected and installed in office or achieve authority through appointment within the military, people react with expected obedience. The typical response of the common man is to obey orders—as in the My Lai massacre. Extrapolating from his psychology studies, Milgram concludes:

> The results, as seen and felt in the laboratory, are to this author disturbing. They raise the possibility that human nature, or—more specifically—the kind of character produced in American democratic society, cannot be counted on to insulate its citizens from brutality and inhumane treatment at the direction of malevolent authority. A substantial proportion of people do what they are told to do, irrespective of the content of the act and without limitations of conscience, so long as they perceive that the command comes from a legitimate authority.[10]

The depersonalized killings of "the enemy" in the Vietnam War, shown in a highly visible and shocking form in the Calley case, more typically occurred in ways that gave attackers a sense of distance from their victims. Massive destruction and killing took place in unemotional ways through the use of highly sophisticated technology. Most American servicemen killed without seeing their individual victims. Many of the fighters were decent young men who had no great personal hatred for the people who were their targets, and they did not think of themselves as killers. They went about their tasks routinely, engaging in highly impersonal warfare, destroying from a distance through use of F-104 jets, B-52 bombers, or Navy cruisers as their bases for attack. Button pushers could comfort themselves with the belief that they were only targeting trucks, gun implacements, or ammunition supplies. Even if they did conjure up images of bombarding people, usually these targets seemed to be no more than an anonymous group of enemy forces. Reports on the war at battle stations distant from enemy lines testify to the antiseptic nature of this activity. For instance, the destruction seemed remote and unreal to a seaman who pulled a brass trigger for the cruiser *Newport News* from several floors below deck. His flick of the finger unleashed computer-aimed missiles to soar many miles over sea and land to fall on enemy positions, but he had little emotional sense of the devastating consequences. "You just can't tell much from down here, so I try not to think about it," he commented from his air conditioned firing station.[11] The Vietnam conflict seemed similarly unreal to a group of American fliers after they dropped thirty tons of explosives from 30,000 feet. "That was a good run, fellows," a controller beamed out on the microphone as the fliers prepared to eat their TV dinners. "Have a nice ride home and see you another day."[12]

These trigger pullers and button-pushers were highly destructive killers, but they did not view themselves as such. Probably most had no taste for cold-blooded killing. Thinking about the consequences of their actions abstractly rather than from personal observation, they had ample opportunity to believe they were attacking war supplies, not harming people. As an F-4 pilot told an interviewer, "I do enjoy the challenge of seeing if I can hit something on the ground. Not people. I don't enjoy the idea of killing people. It happens sometimes. But that's not our primary purpose."[13] As in the saying "Out of sight, out of mind," these gunners from the air, sea, and land found that the distance between themselves and their targets relieved feelings of guilt or responsibility. Niko Tinbergen sympathizes with pilots who are emotionally confused or indifferent in these situations, noting, "Very few aircrews who are willing, indeed eager, to drop their bombs 'on target' would be willing to strangle, stab, or burn children (or for that matter, adults) with their own hands; they would stop short of killing, in response to the appeasement and distress signals of their opponents."[14]

During the Vietnam War, on the domestic battle front the American public responded with similar coolness to warfare conducted from a distance. Night after night many television viewers numbly watched evening news anchormen tell of the latest air strikes or ground clashes. War reports seemed routine and unmoving, except occasionally when newsmen dramatized the human consequences of destruction on the Vietnamese people. Sometimes eagle-eyed cameramen focused on memorable events, or accidents occurred which put scenes of typically unrecorded tragedies in the living rooms of American families. Viewers reacted strongly to destruction they could see. Film clippings of a U.S. marine burning a suspected Viet Cong village, and the filming of a South Vietnamese soldier knifing an enemy soldier to death fired public indignation. In one case of accidental destruction, television cameramen got an opportunity to offer, closeup, the results of U.S. bombing. During the siege of Anloc, pilots mistakenly dropped napalm on innocent civilians, and newsmen on the scene filmed the agony of a little Vietnamese girl with unforgettable detail. The film clipping quickly became a famous historical document of the war. A sickened American public reacted intensely to the incident, stirring up enough interest to send a team of doctors to give the girl exclusive treatment in plastic surgery. The thousands of other war victims like her would never become the center of emotional attention; they remained anonymous numbers, victims of distant, technological warfare.

The antiseptic style also appears in discussions of foreign policy issues that speak to even more devastating possibilities of warfare. In the 1969 Senate debates, for instance, some particularly callous remarks came out in arguments over the wisdom of deploying an expensive new Anti-Ballistic Missile System (ABM). Many senators thought that even if America did hold superiority in both offensive and defensive atomic weapons, actual deployment would bring disaster. If the United States and Russia unleashed missiles and anti-missile missiles at each other, some bombs would surely go through the defenses. Would an American victory be worth anything if it left only a fraction of the U.S. population alive in smouldering ruins after devastating the Russians? Senator Richard Russell answered unblinkingly in the affirmative, winning the dubious distinction of giving the most Strangelovian defense of an ABM system in the entire floor fight. Russell supported continued escalation of America's nuclear arsenal, even if, eventually, both sides decided to use their weapons, saying, "If we have to start all over again with another Adam and Eve, I want them to be Americans; and I want them on this continent and not in Europe."[15] Outside the Senate, J. William Fulbright, reflecting on the cool nature of argument he had heard in committee hearings, commented:

It's not that we have become insensate monsters. It's more as though we didn't really believe our own words. We are talking about these things—these fifty million deaths—as if they were unreal; we are talking about them in the abstract, and in the abstract they are unreal. We are acknowledging possibilities that we do not really feel to be possibilities because they are so far outside anything we have ever experienced. Even a word like "megadeath" has an antiseptic sound. It doesn't sound like blood and pains and burns and mutilation.[16]

Most of the senators who voted to begin the Nixon Administration's new ABM program explained their decision in terms less coldly bellicose than those of Senator Russell. Their support for ABM would help *prevent* war, they argued. By maintaining U.S. weapons superiority and a threat of devastating retaliation, America could discourage others from the folly of nuclear attack. Sophisticated advancement of U.S. nuclear weaponry helped to guarantee peace, not war, they insisted. These defensive arguments were strangely reminiscent of the reasoning of Alfred Nobel, a Swede, creator of the famous Peace Prize and the inventor of dynamite. When criticized for his dynamic enterprise, Nobel responded: My factories are perhaps more likely to make an end to war than . . . [peace] congresses. On the day when two army corps can annihilate each other in a second, all civilized nations will probably shudder back from a war and dismiss their troops.[17] Hopefully, history will not show the proponents of nuclear arms escalation to be so deadly wrong as Nobel in their confidence about military deterrents.

If Americans seem coldly indifferent about death in these examples, it is not because they are an unusually cruel and inhumane people. However, many Americans have become oblivious to the sanctity of human life. Many have allowed their thinking and language to become insensitive to the point where human suffering has lost much of its meaning.[18] It is an unbecoming coolness for a modern, highly developed civilization. It leaves an unflattering impression of the national ethos. Insensitivity toward people exhibited in foreign policy can easily rub off on attitudes in domestic life. If much of mainstream America is indifferent about violence and the preciousness of human life, what kind of behavior can be expected from those who do not care to be part of a mainstream—those whose foremost concern is to show their anger, despair, and desperation to gratify immediate needs? Americans in the mainstream have not been model citizens in their attitudes toward violence. They should not then be surprised to see the brutal ethos of society's troublemakers.

12
MACHISMO

Just as disturbing as callousness toward violence is the glorification of it. The problem of attitudes is not just one of indifference: it often develops out of genuine respect for aggressive behavior, indeed, out of a positive sanction for displays of violence. Americans applaud toughness, associating demonstrations of bravado with virility and manliness. They cheer the man who "puts people in their places," one who does not back down when faced with a challenge and is ever ready to defend his honor. This popular interest reflects an image of the way men ought to think and act. It offers a set of reactions identifying ways to attain respect among peers. For a young male seeking confidence and security, it looks like an unwritten code for success, a cult that shows how to win admirers and influence people. It is machismo, American-style.

The term *machismo* derives from the Latin American word *macho*, meaning a manly spirit or style. To be *macho* in Latin America is to be "very much a man." By adding *ismo*, an equivalent of "ism," Hispanic-Americans convey a belief system developing out of this concept, a doctrine that values sexual prowess, virility, and power.[1] People in the United States are generally aware of the popular connotations of the term in Latin America, but they limit the images it evokes to *hombres* south of the border. To Americans (the North Americans, that is), machismo suggests the egotism of male behavior in a less civilized culture where people are more given to uncontrolled emotional outbursts. The North Americans' smug, holier-than-thou attitude in applying the word only to foreigners masks the close resemblance of their own thinking to the macho mentality.

Attitudes related to the machismo ethic can be found in most cultures. We see it in Winston Churchill's ideal of the British soldier during the sunset of England's empire;[2] it is also noticeable in Yukio Mishima's description of the samurai cult in Japan.[3] This is not to say that machismo is a universal feature of human cultures. Anthropologists' findings on highly pacific cultures and on cultures where women are more aggressive and dominant than men make such an assertion problematic. It is clear, however, that a machismo ethic is prevalent in many societies, carrying greater force in some than in others. Although Latin American countries have long been recognized as the home of machismo, it is time to recognize that the United States also scores high in macho spirit—perhaps, in some ways, even higher in its obsession with the idea.

The tendency to associate machismo much more with Latin than with North American culture reflects, to a large degree, differences in the way the two peoples address the issue. Latin Americans use the word machismo frequently, openly admitting its great relevance to their way of life. They even joke about it. North Americans view the matter more seriously. They prefer not to admit its prevalence, at least not in terms of national character. Although Americans often point out the symptoms of machismo in individuals—egotism, pride in aggressiveness, and the like—they resist identifying what they see with a broadly descriptive term that characterizes many popular attitudes in their culture. Neither the man in the street nor the leader in the White House finds the concept of machismo compatible with his ideal of advanced civilization, and neither can admit its pervasive influence.

In examining machismo in the United States, we can profit

by keeping in mind some of the major characteristics of the phenomenon as noted by observers of Latin American culture. Although there is no officially accepted, systematic blueprint for describing the macho ethic in Latin American life, a few aspects seem especially salient. To simplify this discussion, we shall refer to these aspects broadly as mentioned earlier, that is, as (a) a cult of sexual prowess, (b) a cult of virility, and (c) a cult of power. Each is closely related to the problem of violence in the United States.

The Latin American cult of sexual prowess is familiar to North Americans. Through television, the cinema, books, and travel they are acquainted with Latin American veneration for the male's sexual conquests. Latin American men enjoy boasting about their success in bedding down women, often during early adolescence. They continue to brag about their relationships into the later years of life. Marriage does not necessarily foreclose sensual adventures; many Latin American husbands maintain a mistress or enjoy rendezvous with a variety of *amigas*. They expect these extramarital affairs to be one-way streets, insisting on the double standard. Wives often suspect or know of their husbands' escapades, yet, in obedience to social customs, refrain from comment. The reverse is considered intolerable, however. If a husband discovers his wife to be adulterous, tradition gives him maximum opportunity to redeem his honor.[4] Although modernization has begun to weaken the customary acceptance of extralegal "settlement," in many areas an aggrieved male still obtains the traditional vengeance without great hindrance. According to expectations, he shoots his disloyal spouse and, perhaps, her lover as well. Instead of calling in the police, community members applaud him for doing what they believe is the only manly thing a male with wounded honor can do. Law enforcement officials frequently excuse the killer for his behavior, interpreting it as an act of passion that is understandable and forgivable.

Jorge Amado, one of Brazil's greatest story tellers, gives a suggestive twist to the ending of one of his novels about this kind of machismo. In *Gabriela*, Amado shows the transition of a small backward Brazilian town, Ilheus, into a more modern way of life. The community has a long tradition of violent reprisals for wayward wives; in a period of new developments, however, the central male character of the story, Nacib, cannot bring himself to handle his problem in the traditional manner. He continues to feel sparks of love for his wife, the beautiful Gabriela, who could not be tamed to reserve her lust for one man. His friends urge him to pick up a gun as did another betrayed husband in the town shortly before. Nacib decides against violence and, instead, turns to a lawyer and obtains an annulment. When a court surprisingly condemns the man who settled his problem with traditional violence, some observant citizens interpret the two events as signs of change. Civilization is finally coming to Ilheus![5]

While violent enforcement of the double standard is passing to more refined ways of settling disputes of passion in modernized Latin American communities, a tougher machismo prevails in Latin America's poverty areas. In these environments, quarrels often involve love associations rather than legal marriage. Anthropologist Oscar Lewis describes numerous incidents of this sort in his studies of Mexico's cultures of poverty.[6] The ugly pattern also appears in the memorable anecdotes of Carolina Maria de Jesus, a Brazilian slum dweller whose diary is a moving document of life in shanty towns. She speaks of several bloody confrontations that arise from petty disputes over women. Men in the *favela* (shanty town) advertise their readiness for violence especially when they think a woman's inattention or preference for other men might make them look foolish in public. Maria de Jesus describes one example of explosive male egotism that occurred when a *Pernambucano* (a man from the state of Pernambuco) asked a girl to dance at a party:

She didn't want to dance. She looked him over carefully and then said she didn't want to dance with him. The *Pernambucano*, when he saw he was refused, got furious. He pulled a knife out of his belt and went for Cho's woman. The only thing I've seen move fast were rats, rabbits, and lightning. But Cho's woman, when she saw that knife coming in her direction, even outdid lightning. The people snatched the knife from him. The *Pernambucano* ran out snorting and shouting:
"Today I kill! Today blood will run in the favela."[7]

Such violent egotism exists in the United States too, of course. Among the upper and middle classes in the United States, angry males usually bolster their wounded pride by other tactics. Among the lower classes, however, violent reprisals are quite common. Social scientist Jackson Toby gives evidence of this cult of sexual prerogatives from an interview with a twenty-five-year-old reformatory inmate. When Toby talked about extramarital affairs, the inmate, identified as "Jimmy," commented, "As far as her going out with another guy, I'll tell you one thing and you can believe this or not. If she shacked up with some guy, she'll be dead—even if they give me the chair—that you can believe." When Toby probed his subject's logic, pointing out the double standard, Jimmy replied, "If a man fools around, some people will admire him. They'll say he knows how to bullshit a broad. Let a woman do it? She's a fuckin' whore." Toby appropriately titled his study "Violence and the Masculine Ideal."[8]

Statistics suggest that the cult of sexual prowess figures in America's strikingly high homicide rate. For example, cases involving "Domestic Triangle and Lovers' Quarrel" and "Spouse Killing Spouse" accounted for almost one-fifth of homicides officially recorded for the 1960-1970 period—situations in which, in many cases, a machismo complex can violently emerge.[9] Whether the new interest in women's liberation can effect changes regarding which lover metes out the violence remains to be seen. Fragmentary evidence suggests the potential for change. In 1974 Inez Garcia became an instant heroine to liberation militants when she went on trial for murdering a man she accused of holding her down during a rape. Garcia angrily expressed regret for having missed her principal shooting target—the man she identified as the rapist. Even in Latin America there was evidence that greater aggression from women might be in the offing. Venezuelan women demanded "equal shooting rights" in cases of wayward husbands.

The second major aspect of machismo, the virility cult, sometimes becomes intertwined with the cult of sexual prowess. The virility cult is evident in both societies, yet pronounced emphasis on sexual prowess in Latin America often mitigates pressures for virility. For example, North American visitors to Latin America are surprised to find many of the most popular and confident Don Juans small in stature and unconcerned about their athletic abilities. A Latin American male who has a way with women, who demonstrates an ability to conquer the *señoritas,* can find considerable ego fulfillment without needing to advertise complementary physical toughness. Men in the United States, on the other hand, often associate the tough, muscle-hardened physique with impressing the girls and achieving manliness. They labor diligently at getting their bodies in shape, for women, they reason, do not respect the weakling. The North American male suffers nightmares about being caught in Charles Atlas' preconditioning position, where the now-proverbial bully kicks sand in his face and marches off with his impressed girl.

Along with a muscular physique, the virility cult emphasizes toughness of character and a fighting spirit. It values "courage" and gives prestige to males who plunge into risky situations without qualms of getting hurt. Above all, virility comes out in the fight itself: participation in violence can redeem the manliness of one who may have appeared chicken-hearted before.

Sam Peckinpah's popular motion picture, *Straw Dogs,* a subject of much controversy when it appeared in 1971-1972, illustrates a North American idealization of virility combined with sexual prowess. The story involves an American college professor on sabbatical in Scotland with his attractive wife. The bespectacled academician seeks refuge from the tense confrontations on his campus, hoping to find serenity in his study at a country home. His wife shows declining respect for his mousy, escapist behavior and does her voluptuous best to attract some roughnecked townsmen. She watches her husband bungle through one extreme display of weakness and cowardice after another, then succumbs half-unwillingly, half-desirously to rape, suggesting her subtle hunger to be bedded by an aggressive man. Eventually the mild-mannered scholar reacts violently to the bullying and discovers, we are told, a part of himself he never knew before. When the ruffians attack his country home, he bursts out in superman style. Finding manhood through violence, he defends his home like an animal hellbent on protecting its territory. Not only does the suddenly combative professor liquidate several intruders in various interesting and bloody ways, but he also cures his wife of her apparently weaker-sex fits of hysteria in crisis by thrashing her around like a caveman putting his woman in her place. As we would expect, she seems to like the treatment; it gives her new respect for her husband.

Literary critic Joseph Morgenstern assessed the message of *Straw Dogs* pointedly when he said it gives us a sense of our machismo, picturing the true male winning merit badges through combat and murder. As Morgenstern observed, the film "puts you promptly on the defensive. You can't be much of a man if you don't dig it, or at least concede its underlying wisdom."[10] Numerous theater-goers seemed afraid to offer anything but praise for the show, revealing reluctance to challenge the machismo of their own culture.

Often the virility cult in American society refers only indirectly to sexual prowess, placing greater stress on bravery and courage in the eyes of other men. These appeals play on the "chicken complex" of American males—the fear of being branded weak or cowardly by peers. The military has traditionally capitalized on this concern for many years in its efforts to attract young men. Army life will make a *man* out of you, the posters promise. This is no small service to an insecure adolescent who would enjoy wearing a uniform as a badge of virility for all of society to admire. More importantly, politicians have exploited the virility cult to silence critics of military policy.

During the Vietnam War, President Lyndon Johnson got much political mileage out of appeals to the virility cult. He blasted opponents of the war as "Nervous Nellies" and asked his countrymen to show they had the guts to fight. The brave soldiers abroad should not be undermined by weak-willed doubters at home, he insisted. Johnson defended America's involvement in Indochina as a case of "valor" and "individual acts of heroism" on the part of U.S. soldiers in a noble effort in the cause of little people who were being pushed around. "The bravery of young American patriots on the battlefield, the steadfast determination of our people at home, will in time bring an end to this trial of aggression," he asserted. "And if valor alone were required, there would be no cause for concern for the future." With characteristic bravado, he warned North Vietnam, "You cannot drive us out of South Vietnam by force."[11] In 1967 General Wallace M. Greene, Jr., Commander of the Marine Corps, expanded on the President's call for national courage (or was it machismo?). He claimed that the tough determination of his young marines destroyed popular assumptions about the "softness" of American youth. Speaking of wounded marines who asked for a chance to go back to their units and fight again, Greene said proudly: "These are teenage Americans I'm talking about. Boys who were in the classroom this time last year . . . Boys who have earned every right to be known as men."[12] Since going off to war supposedly demonstrated manliness, it is not surprising that many Americans proudly displayed a bumper sticker showing the peace symbol with the identification: "Footprint of an American Chicken."

The virility cult also seems to have troubled many of the most prominent men in government during the Vietnam War—men who worried about becoming stereotyped as weak-willed, spineless eggheads. "They wanted to show they were men of action," explains David Halberstam, author of *The Best and the Brightest*. "You know, 'we're intellectuals, but we're tough too'—eggheads with balls."[13] The incisive Halberstam study leaves readers wondering how much a machismo complex may have influenced American foreign policy in other crises—the Bay of Pigs invasion, the Cuban Missile Crisis, and intervention in the Dominican Republic.[14]

Although men of all ages are influenced by a machismo ethic, teenagers are probably most susceptible to its social pressures. Adolescence is a particularly difficult and sensitive period, a time when they must struggle for identity as men and confront their own strengths and weaknesses. Someone who is bothered by a "chicken complex" during these insecure years can unwittingly be a menace to society and to himself. Such a one was Raymond A. (Sonny) Kuchenmeister, whose struggle for machismo status ended in disaster. Sonny, an unusually tall and portly boy, wanted desperately to be treated as an adult. After fantasizing about leaving his Ohio home to become a cowboy in the West, "where they treat you like a man," Sonny (age fifteen) and his twelve-year-old brother decided to stow away on a plane at Cleveland's airport. At first he planned to go to Montana but later changed his mind in favor of Mexico, noting, "we can get tortillas down there." In 1954 Sonny became the first person to attempt a hijacking of an American commercial airliner. When he made his demand with a broken, unloaded revolver, the pilot shot him dead.[15]

Research into the personal problems of adolescents reveals that the virility cult is often an important influence on their behavior. Many youngsters who develop early bouts with alcoholism begin indulging heavily because they learn from peers that the ability to hold one's liquor is a virile accomplishment.[16] Similarly, many specialists on drug addiction believe that the greatest influence on an individual who experiments with drugs is not a rebellion against poverty, boredom, or disgust with the Establishment. It is the peer group pressure he feels, the need to show he's not afraid to try something different. According to the researchers, the comment that can most frequently push a youth into experimentation is, "If you don't try it, you're chicken!"[17]

This aspect of the virility cult relates directly to the problem of violent street gangs. Adolescents from urban slums join such gangs for much-needed social gratification. Many of these youngsters cannot meet mainstream America's criteria for status. Family background, low-quality education, habits picked up from the inner-city environment, and unemployment frustrate their efforts to lift themselves up in traditional ways. They begin to seek other satisfactions. The gangs offer not only security but status as well. Gang members can raise their esteem within the membership through acts of violence. Lewis Yablonski, one of the foremost students of violent gangs, found the most coveted "rep" (reputation) in these groups was that of a "cold killer." Yablonski and others point out that members often "prove themselves" and work out a pecking order of leadership through displays of toughness. Gangs reward the meanest and toughest in the bunch with club officerships. In short, violence becomes a major feature of the gang's operations.[18]

In recent years, the use of gangs for status climbing has become increasingly serious. The proliferation of lethal weapons, especially handguns, makes demonstration of virility through gang violence a dangerous exercise. In the past, members tended to rise to leadership by demonstrating their superiority through sheer physical strength or ability. Fists, knives, sticks, and chains were common weapons. Now revolvers, rifles, and shotguns have changed the rules of the game. Under the new conditions an ironic form of democracy is at work. As one youngster explains, a gun can make you "ten feet high." Firearms serve as the Great Equalizer.[19] Now a gang member of slight build has a better chance of winning respect and power than in days past. By using a gun to risk his own life or threaten someone else's, a little fellow can compete with the big, muscular elites who easily manipulated power in earlier years. As competition intensifies and more youngsters try to obtain status-bestowing weapons for themselves, the interest in firearms becomes contagious among inner-city youth. One newspaper reporter found a fifteen-year-old boy claiming an urgent need for him and his friends to form a gang and obtain weapons. "We got to do it if we want to stop them from ripping off our bikes and our playboys [multicolored high-heeled shoes]," he explained. When asked if he knew of any such problem in his neighborhood, the boy admitted that he did not. The excited talk about gang threats and defensive needs apparently was turning into a self-fulfilling prophecy, with potential for stirring up a bigger inner-city arms race between youthful combatants.[20]

In gang societies as in many other groups in the American population, the virility cult and a form of gun cult are deeply intertwined. This is also the case in Latin America where wielding a gun is viewed as part of machismo. In Venezuela, for example, fathers traditionally give their sons a gun on the eighteenth birthday. This welcome into manhood is something akin to a *bar mitzvah* present, Venezuelan-style. In the United States the pattern usually begins much earlier with the gift of toy guns. It is amusing, or disturbing, depending on one's point of view, to notice the American father's resistance when questioned whether his child might get along better with a different kind of toy. "It's what the little guy likes," he typically responds, noting, "All the other kids have them, and I don't want my boy left out." Many of these fathers also believe gun-play helps Junior learn to be tough and aggressive. They do not seem to accept the development of physical skills and stamina through sports as a less artificial and far healthier exercise in toughness. The connection between handing the youngster a football and handing him a toy gun remains unbroken. Both are viewed with little discrimination as ways to pass the machismo spirit on to another generation.[21]

The popular relationship between brandishing a gun and demonstrating virility is obviously one of the most dangerous aspects of machismo. It prompts some of society's weakest individuals to try to redeem themselves by aiming lethal weapons at others. This is a strange means of attaining manliness, but nonetheless attractive to many. Max Lerner has described this situation:

> We have the wrong picture of most killers. It is not the tough who kill. It is more often the weak who kill, out of fear—yearning to be tough, afraid to face the dismal fact of their weakness, panicking when the moment of test comes. The strong are confident and can live and let others live. They don't have to prove anything.[22]

Lerner's description matches the profile of many assassins of famous national leaders. As mentioned earlier, studies reveal that assassins and would-be assassins typically are weak individuals—below average in stature, introverted, lacking friends, and failing in their occupational pursuits. Through the dramatic destruction of a prominent figure they hope to strengthen their image and find a place as a "great man" in the pages of history. America has paid a heavy price for this form of machismo.[23]

If psychoanalyst Walter C. Langer's secret wartime study of Adolph Hitler's character is accurate, the world, too, paid a heavy price for personal feelings of inadequacy. Langer detected certain weaknesses in Hitler, which, he believed, gave the Führer a grossly exaggerated and distorted concept of masculinity. Hitler may have compensated for a frail body, almost effeminate softness, and sexual inadequacy by trying to create a superman image. "We may assume that in order to quiet his fears, he sometimes imagined himself as a person who far surpasses his enemies in all the 'virile' qualities," wrote Langer.[24] This personality assessment is very familiar to students of assassins in America. Hitlerian psychological disorders probably trouble some of the confused men who threaten American leaders. Psychiatrist Rollo May stresses the need for sensitivity to how feelings of personal inadequacy can lead to violent behavior. In his provocative study, *Power and Innocence,* May underscores the irony that violence arises from powerlessness or impotence rather than from great power and confidence. Such efforts to demonstrate virility aim to fulfill a basic need—to achieve a sense of worth and importance. But May carries the argument rather far, twisting the irony to a point where attempts to understand the causes of violence become efforts to appreciate violent behavior as therapeutic for the individual. May praises the arguments of Frantz Fanon and others who have written on the beauty of violence in redeeming dignity for people troubled by oppression and a consequent lack of confidence. One wonders why May fails to confront adequately the inevitable effects of such personal redemption—the price innocent victims must pay for another's expression of machismo. If people must satisfy basic needs in order to overcome psychic difficulties, we should hope that social scientists will search for nonviolent avenues toward self-confidence and happiness. By subtly or inadvertently indulging the virility cult, we run a very real danger of encouraging a patient to bring greater havoc upon himself and others as well.[25]

The final aspect of machismo, the cult of power, is familiar to students of Latin American society. It should also be recognizable to observers of the U.S. culture. This attitude stresses the importance of holding *complete* power, at least for a man concerned with his macho image. In the Latin American family, for example, the respected father typically rules supreme over his household. All members show deference toward the *padre.* Honoring patriarchal traditions, they indulge him with praise and allow his word to be final in matters of disagreement. Egos run wild in these relationships and, understandably, many pampered Latin males strut about like rulers of small nations.

Their condition is never entirely secure, however. Power-hungry males must ever be on guard for offenses against their "honor." Sometimes the slightest misunderstandings or slips of tongue can lead to violent altercations between two ego-obsessed *señores*. This preoccupation with power extends well beyond private life, influencing political life, especially the personality of the archetypal Latin American dictator. To be truly effective, these national leaders must have complete power. They must indisputably be Number One in their nation. Challengers should be liquidated, exiled, or, if the *jefe máximo* feels magnanimous, sent abroad with ambassadorships. Display of strength from a political adversary can quickly destroy a leader's image of omnipotence, his claim to being the most macho in the land.[26]

Popular attitudes in the American South have probably come closer to this kind of machismo than those in any other section of the United States. Wilbur Cash gives a vivid description of the cult of power in antebellum Dixie in his classic study, *The Mind of the South*. Speaking about the inflated egos of Southern whites from absolute control over slaves and association with the plantation society, Cash says their intense individualism was

far too much concerned with bald, immediate unsupported assertion of ego, which placed too great stress on the inviolability of personal whim, and which was full of the chip-on-shoulder swagger and brag of a boy—one, in brief, of which the essence was boast, voiced or not, on the part of every Southerner, that he could knock hell out of whoever dared to cross him.[27]

Though dueling was by no means limited to the South in antebellum days, there is considerable substance to the popular image of Southern men marking paces after interpreting relatively mild differences as unforgivable offenses against honor. Among the lower classes in the South, these "indignities" to one another's macho image were settled more spontaneously. Barroom brawls and street fights were common. Others avenged family honor in drawn-out feuds similar to the battle between the Grangerfords and Shepardsons in Mark Twain's *Huckleberry Finn*.[28]

The power cult also frequently finds expression in the attitudes and behavior of youth gangs. Like the hypersensitive antebellum Southerner, gang members often resort to violence and sometimes even full-scale gang war over very trivial grievances—a "bad look," a nasty remark, or an argument over a girl. In the Bronx gang members have had face-offs on the street with .22 caliber pearl-handled pistols tucked in their belts —scenes with all the elements of a Hollywood Western showdown.[29] Walter B. Miller, a student of gang behavior, has described this manifestation of the power cult. He says, "Gang members fight to secure and defend the reputation of their local area and the honor of their women; to show that an affront to their pride and dignity demands retaliation."[30]

As in Latin American society, the cult of power extends all the way up to national leadership. It is interesting to examine, for instance, the way U.S. leaders interpreted the Vietnam War in terms of power machismo. General Harold K. Johnson, Lyndon Johnson, and Richard Nixon must have realized the potential impact of emotional words calculated to stimulate macho nerves. They drummed out the rhetoric of "victory" and "honor," warning the people not to speak the horrendous words of defeat. "Please don't . . . talk of despair and defeat," pleaded General Harold K. Johnson, former Army Chief of Staff, in 1965. "Talk instead of steadfastness, loyalty, and of victory—for we must and we can win here."[31] President Johnson insisted that "We are the Number One nation, and we are going to stay the Number One nation." He warned that the enemy had escalated their war effort because they were "encouraged by the belief that the United States lacked the will to continue and that victory was near."[32] Similarly, Richard Nixon asked for support so that the United States would not look "like a pitiful, helpless giant" in its dispatch of the war. "You want peace. I want peace. But you also want honor and not defeat," he insisted, asking: When in future years U.S. Presidents travel around the world, will they receive or deserve respect? The United States would only win respect, Nixon insisted, if it continued "to play the great role we are destined to play of helping to build a new structure of peace in the world."[33] The salient forms of this appeal resemble the concerns of the antebellum Southerner and the modern-day urban gang member, not to mention many others from American history and culture. It rings out the spirit of a power cult, an appeal to glory, to honor, and to victory—attitudes that can lead to much unnecessary bloodshed.

From this brief review of some popular attitudes about manliness, it seems that North Americans have little reason to laugh at Latin Americans for their machismo complex. Though machismo poses as significant a problem here as it has for Latin culture, at least Latin Americans have developed an ability to recognize its existence on a broad scale, something North Americans have great difficulty doing. And for all the violent ways of Latin Americans, we should find it difficult to argue convincingly that North Americans are far less violent. In terms of internal civil wars, Latin America may appear more tumultuous (though we should remember that many of these so-called revolutions are little more than palace coups involving very few people). If we consider individual violence—muggings, murders, assassinations—the United States seems to be in greater trouble than many of its southern neighbors. And, if we make a major criterion the tendency to translate machismo into wars against other nations, the United States looks much more violent.

These comparisons are very general, and conclusions can differ greatly according to the particular countries or regions compared. Yet the principal implication is clear: machismo guides the thinking of many North Americans much as it influences the thinking of Latin Americans. If people in the United States are to begin dealing with their machismo complex, they will first need to recognize its reality.

13

TELEVISION

Whence comes the callousness toward violence in America's ethos and the glorification of aggression that characterizes American machismo? America's values and attitudes have many origins, but certainly the visual media are one of the most controversial of these sources. In an electronic age in which most American homes have televisions and millions seek action-packed entertainment at the cinema, the potential influence of visual media on human behavior prompts intriguing questions. Does today's violence on television affect tomorrow's murderers? Can ultraviolence in the movies direct its audiences toward aggression? Do subtle ideas conveyed through mass media programming influence American attitudes toward violence? Perhaps the answers are more obvious than many Americans are inclined to think.

Just how much impact the media's orgies of blood and death have made on life in the United States can never be measured precisely, but we have good reason to believe that their effect has been significant. "These violent delights have violent ends," said Shakespeare in a message worth heeding today. Yet, media defenders continue to baffle the public with their conclusion that it is impossible to resolve the issue. Strangely, in modern America the idea that media violence has *no* impact—not good, nor bad, nor anything—attracts wide popular support. For years defenders of the media have successfully exercised extraordinary argumentative gymnastics, syllogistic contortions, and theoretical circumlocutions to give complicated and evasive answers to simple questions about media violence. Problems which common sense can master are transformed into insoluble abstract labyrinths and matters only for wild philosophical conjecture. Unfortunately, these confusion tactics work quite effectively, leaving laymen dizzy from a mass of contradictory evidence and inclined to believe that no action is advisable when the problem seems so uncertain.

Before discussing the negative side of potential media influence, some major pro-media arguments deserve review. Since these popular concepts typically apply to disputes about *both* television and movie violence, the following brief summary relates to both media forms. Later in this chapter, when considering the counterarguments, we shall move more specifically to evidence related to television.

Much of the defense for television and movie violence begins with references to the sheer longevity of interest in violent entertainment—a fascination that well predates the age of electronic visual media. Violence has been a common ingredient of drama throughout the history of theater, defenders point out, noting its long-time contribution to suspense and dramatic action. Many of Shakespeare's best plays develop around violent themes (Macbeth is a good example), they remind us. Should we then cast aside the master's works because they stretch dramatic mileage out of murder? To condemn violence in the media outright is to deny its potential value as an instrument of dramatic symbolism and a fascinating perspective on life's problems.[1]

Since fascination with portrayals of violence in diverse media, including live drama and books, has been with us for a long time, we should recognize its relationship to human nature, say the media defenders. The persistent popularity of violent themes develops out of audience interest, not just the author's interest. People *want* to see violence and hear about it. Violence enchants them.[2] This thirst for violent entertainment was evident in the Romans' rush to watch gladiators at the Coliseum; it is evident in modern times in the crowd's excitement at the annual Indianapolis 500 auto race (44 deaths in 42 races) or the roar of an audience as boxers draw blood in a heavyweight championship bout. Youngsters, too, have long shown fascination with violent themes and action. Ever listen carefully to those popular little Mother Goose nursery rhymes?

> Cry, baby, cry
> Put your finger in your eye.
> And tell your mother it wasn't I.
>   or
> There was a little man,
> And he had a little gun,
> And his bullets were made of lead, lead, lead;
> He went to the brook
> And he saw a duck,
> And he shot it right through the head, head, head.

In modern times, children cheer as television cartoon characters smash each other into pancakes or heroes of cowboy sagas gun down the Bad Man on the screen.

Not only has the *interest* in violence been around for a long time, the media defenders point out, but also the *reality* of violence. Television programs and movies should not be made scapegoats for current problems when we know very well that violence troubled Americans long before the electronic age. John Wilkes Booth assassinated Lincoln without ever having cast his eyes on a TV set; Jesse James terrorized bankers without ever experiencing the pleasure of hitching his horse at a drive-in movie theater. If the public remains fascinated with violent shows today, perhaps that interest derives from the fact that violence is a reality in modern America. TV programs and movies mirror life; they reflect attitudes and problems that concern the audience.[3] Movies do not create attitudes but develop out of attitudes that are already present, claims Jack Valenti, president of the Motion

Picture Association of America.[4] "Movies are not beacons but rather mirrors of society," says Valenti. As producer Stanley Kubrick explains, movies may "illuminate something we already feel," but "they don't change us."

Some commentators in this dispute borrow lessons from the instinct channeling theory of human aggression to argue that, if anything, media violence probably has a positive influence because it helps us release pent-up tensions. "Films and television for both young and old permit a safe, passive participation in kinds of action beyond our ken," Norman A. Zinberg and Gordon A. Fellman assure us. Children possess an instinctual destructive drive akin to Freud's idea of the death wish, they explain. Tight "moral standards" that try to close off satisfaction of this instinctive need can bring on psychological difficulties that develop from frustration and inhibition.[5] As psychiatrist Anthony Storr notes, "To forbid a child to watch television or read stories in which violence occurs is a fruitless prohibition more likely to cause anger than prevent it."[6]

When America's problems of violence (rioting, mugging, assassinations, sadistic and senseless murders) swelled rapidly through the 1960s and into the 1970s, criticism of media violence intensified to the point where many of its defenders increasingly tried to bolster their common sense arguments with references to "scientific research." As Anthony Storr commented, "There is no evidence that the mass media are primarily responsible for delinquency or violent crime."[7] Many examples of such arguments came out in the hearings of the National Commission on the Causes and Prevention of Violence. Several witnesses sounded variations of a "no evidence" or "confusing evidence" theme. Commenting on the diverse conclusions of social science researchers, media executive John F. Dille, Jr., asked, "Who is right? Who will give us undeniable and inevitable results of our exposure or non-exposure to violence? We of the media do not possess these divine qualities. We have yet to find who does."[8] Another media spokesman, psychologist Joseph T. Klapper, who directed CBS's Office of Social Research, claimed much of the research already conducted by social scientists had very little practical value. Klapper stressed the relative ease of measuring immediate reactions of subjects in a laboratory contrasted to the great difficulty of studying the influence of media viewing on the behavior of subjects weeks, months, or years later. Researchers have been noticeably unsuccessful in obtaining plausible long-term evidence, said Klapper. When members of the committee asked him to offer some kind of personal, subjective evaluation of the influence of television violence on children, Klapper repeatedly insisted that he did not know but would like to find out. The situation called for much more research, he cautioned.[9] One movie executive stated the case more bluntly. When asked if violent films could influence audiences negatively, Joe Wizan, producer of *Kansas City Prime,* answered, "I don't give it a thought. Psychiatrists don't have the answers, so why should I?"[10]

To investigate further the effects of media violence, giving specific focus to television programming, the U.S. government in 1969 ordered a major new study of the issue, commissioning the Surgeon General to oversee its preparation. Two and one-half years later, when the Surgeon General's office released a nineteen-page summary of its new findings, media defenders rejoiced. A *New York Times* front-page headline on the report read: "TV Violence Held Unharmful to Youth." Later, in a *TV Guide* article, Edith Efron used the report to comment on the presumably confused state of evidence on the influence of television violence. The long title of her essay left little doubt about her interpretation of the report's conclusions: "A Nonsolution to a Nonproved Problem Produced by a Noninvestigation of a Nonresolved Controversy Over A Nonidentified Threat to Nonidentifiable People." Defending television against its critics and strengthened by the Surgeon General's office's cloudy conclusions, Efron asked, "Who might be rendered 'aggressive' by TV violence? How could one test for such a potential response? Might one change programming to diminish the alleged danger? The scientists didn't know."[11]

In time, serious criticism of the Surgeon General's report emerged, highlighting the difficulties of getting accurate summary information to the public when such information stepped on many sensitive toes. Complaints and revelations indicated that preparation of the report had sometimes been moved by political (or, more precisely, economic) considerations, and that its conclusions were less than candid. Many students of the media controversy soon recognized the one-volume final report as another classic example of equivocation in the long history of issue-dodging over violence. The final summary bulged with ambivalent statements, and a reader could quickly become muddled by its contradictory assessments.[12] Interpretations of evidence went bouncing back and forth like ping pong balls. The following list paraphrases some of the point-counterpoint reporting:

On the one hand: Since children spend considerable time in front of their sets each week, what they see may represent an important part of their social learning.

On the other hand: Much of a child's social learning develops from other sources: contact with the family, neighborhood peer groups, the school, etc.

On the one hand: Studies show that people can react aggressively after watching violent films.

On the other hand: The films may only bring out personality characteristics that are one part of the individual's nature anyway; e.g., some people are already predisposed to aggression.

On the one hand: Studies show children may behave more aggressively after watching aggressive acts in the visual media than if they do not witness such acts.

On the other hand: It is improper to generalize from those findings because reactions among children can differ considerably on the basis of their age, sex, and economic status.

On the one hand: Experiments reveal some significant correlations for teenage subjects between watching aggression and tending to act aggressively afterwards.

On the other hand: These are only laboratory experiments. The results cannot be extrapolated to generalize about long-term behavior under normal conditions.

On the one hand: Children often react aggressively to violent shows.

On the other hand: The *way* they react depends on diverse factors such as whether they view the violence as fantasy or reality and whether perpetrators of violence in the story are punished.

The report closed with highly unexciting conclusions. Some mild correlations between viewing and aggression turned up, it noted, but the statistical evidence was not strong enough to warrant confident recommendations for change. The data did not offer any clear suggestions for future programming. "Such tentative and limited conclusions are not very satisfying," its authors admitted, leaving readers with the obvious question: Where do we go from here? The report evaded any answer for that question, too, in its final pages, recommending further research and reminding readers that social scientists still had much to learn.[13]

If parts of the report's equivocal social science jargon sounded familiar to readers versed in other literature on the topic, there was good reason. Much of the writing in the final report, with its abundance of "howevers," came from the pen of CBS media defendant Joseph T. Klapper. Other hard-line spokesmen for the networks' point of view also contributed to the jargon. Within the committee these people, to whom other members angrily referred as the "network five," had considerable influence in preparing the final report. Their inordinate influence did not go unnoticed, however. In the weeks following release of the Surgeon General's report, various other committee members began speaking out against both the means of membership selection and the approach to summarizing research results.

For a committee organized to study problems practically involving investigation of the broadcast industry itself, the means of selecting members was most unusual. The Surgeon General's Office decided first to draw up a list of individuals with good credentials, people recognized and respected by the scientific community, the general public, and, strangely, the broadcast industry. After preparing a list of forty leading figures, the office made a very friendly gesture to the TV industry: it allowed them to veto candidates. CBS declined the invitation, but NBC and ABC chose to blackball seven names, including some of the most prominent scholars of media research. Naturally, the networks were already suspicious of these scholars on the basis of some of their earlier findings. Then pro-network scientists gained strong membership in the high-level, twelve-member advising committee, enabling themselves to turn the final report into a mish-mash of social science verbosity. Hence, members were selected more in the spirit of political compromise than of open-minded study.[14]

When news of political trade-offs reached the press, some frustrated participants in the project revealed their true impressions about the conclusions. "A purposeful fraud" and "a political whitewash" were among the balder comments. Publication of the full five-volume collection of studies helped to clarify reasons for this discontent. Essentially, the nineteen-page summary statement and the 260-page summary report did not accurately reflect the thrust of research findings. Much of the detailed scholarly evidence showed television's potential influence on aggression—including potential long-term influence —to be significant. Moreover, reports about the mood under which committee members prepared the final report gave additional explanation for the discontent. In the last meetings, during preparation of concluding documents, members disputed decisions in a tense atmosphere, which sometimes broke into angry exchanges. Toward the end, representatives of the two points of view became tight-lipped, staring coldly at each other across the table.[15]

These revelations produced some angry public outcries. Congressman John Murphy charged the Surgeon General's office with cowing to television industry interests. Even Dr. Jesse L. Steinfeld, the Surgeon General, admitted he would have preferred a more decisive interpretation of the research results.[16] But first impressions could not easily be wiped away. Two and a half years of investigations by specialists and a million dollars of the taxpayers' money only seemed to produce greater confusion in the public mind. After all the circumlocution, puzzled citizens could have profited more by returning to conclusions reached by the Violence Commission three years before. As the commission reported, "The preponderance of the available research evidence strongly suggests . . . that violence in television programs can and does have adverse effects upon audiences—particularly child audiences."[17]

What is this research evidence? What are the implications of scholarly studies? Although, indeed, many issues remain in dispute, substantial documentation supports the contention that media violence can heighten aggression. Numerous experiments carried out in university laboratories have produced relevant correlations by comparing attitudes and behavior of subjects who viewed aggression before being tested with a control group that had not experienced the violent stimuli. In one of the most frequently cited experiments of this type, Albert Bandura and his associates rated children for aggressiveness, then divided them into three experimental groups of about equal aggressiveness. One group watched adults kick and punch a large inflated doll, the second watched the same activity on a television screen, and the third watched the aggressive activity when the adult was dressed in a cat costume. Control groups did not have an opportunity to see the kicking and punching of the doll in either of the three forms. After all children were subjected to some mild frustration, observers watched as the children went into a playroom, then rated their behavior according to a scale of aggressiveness. The findings showed exposure to aggressive models both through watching personal examples and watching television increased verbal and physical aggressive behavior. The group that had watched an adult dressed as a cat showed more aggression, too, but not as much as in the first two cases.[18]

Leonard Berkowitz and his associates conducted a study which subjected three groups of college students to different arousal treatments. Each was asked to complete a jigsaw puzzle. One group could not complete the puzzle because it actually was insoluble. A second group was insulted by a "confederate" following failure on the puzzle, and a third group was not frustrated or insulted. After the puzzle experiences, each person watched either a prize fight film or a film on an exciting but nonviolent track race. Audiences of the prize fight movie heard an introduction designed to lower inhibitions against aggression. After the films, subjects had an opportunity to shock the "confederate" they had met earlier (through ten buttons which ostensibly administered ten shock levels of increasing intensity). Among witnesses to the track film, those who had been insulted by the "confederate" gave him significantly more intense shocks than nonaroused subjects. Among witnesses to the fight film, however, both the insulted and puzzle-frustrated men administered more intense shocks than did the nonaroused men. Berkowitz concludes from this experiment and other related findings that, rather than releasing pent-up aggression, the experience of witnessing an aggressive movie can lower restraints against frustration-engendered aggression.[19]

After years of experiments with variations of the approaches pioneered by scholars like Albert Bandura and Leonard Berkowitz, most professional psychologists accept the relationship between viewing violence by a visual medium and heightened aggression. Even the ultra-ambivalent Surgeon General's report admitted in one key sentence that "the fact that some children behave more aggressively in experiments after seeing violent films is well established."[20]

Still, we may wonder if the numerous qualifications raised by media defenders may make scholarly evidence less conclusive than we are inclined to believe. Are not various viewers more or less predisposed toward violence, and, therefore, more or less likely to be influenced by what they see on the screen? Aren't there significant differences between the reactions of young and old, rich and poor, male and female, or psychologically well adjusted and psychologically maladjusted? Doesn't it make a difference if the subjects see people punished for their aggression? Isn't it difficult to generalize about heightened aggressiveness displayed immediately after subjects see a film, compared to their attitudes and behavior the next day or the next week? Certainly all of these factors, and others, can affect aggressiveness.[21] Nevertheless, the weight of research information and its relevant implications ought to be suggestive enough about the *potential* impact of television and the movies.

In spite of impressive evidence, those who demand absolute

proof of relationships from social science research can always delay action effectively. It is a harsh, unpalatable fact that social science can *never* deliver positive proof of broad relationships to the most doubting critics. In the final analysis, all evaluation about the effects of media violence becomes "educated guesswork," not truly proven fact. As researcher Percy Tannenbaum explained to the Violence Commission:

> The verdict is not proven. I don't think it will be proved in my lifetime, certainly not in the lifetime of this Commission. And if that is what you are looking for, I think you better stop now. . . . So many of the Government's actions, and even society's actions, are dictated by having to make, because of the exigencies of the situation, a calculated guess on the basis of whatever evidence we have in hand.[22]

Because of these experimental shortcomings, no evaluation of the influence of the media on aggressive behavior should rest on social science research evidence alone. Observations from actual occurrences ought to supplement assessment of experimental findings. The task calls for common sense mixed with scientific rigor, an effort toward subjective interpretation as well as objective reporting.

Let's consider the example of television specifically. Can television programs "teach" viewers to act aggressively? Society is so accustomed to speaking in terms of "book learning" that often it underestimates television's capacity to teach. Drawing an artificial line, many people view the printed word as an important molder of attitudes, but they sharply distinguish the media experience from this kind of influence (at least the fictional media in contrast to news programs). They emphasize that most TV programs in question are "entertainment" programs that give viewers leisurely, vicarious enjoyment but make no significant impact on thinking once the set is turned off. They strongly reject the notion that television violence can *negatively* influence attitudes and behavior. Yet, these same people often admit TV can have a *positive* influence. Many acclaim *Sesame Street* for its clever and subtle ways of improving children's skills with the

A,B,Cs and 1,2,3s. They compliment the networks for giving blacks more prominent and respectable roles in everything from newscasting to drama casting—changes in policy which seem to help break down racial prejudice. And who can forget one of the most controversial of all popular "entertainment" programs, *All in the Family*? When Archie Bunker became a household name, millions commented on the show's loaded political and social connotations. Some complimented the producers for exposing the silliness of bigotry; some criticized the plots for portraying hardhats with condescension; others complained that Bunker's barrage of ethnic slurs offended their groups. These diverse, intense reactions all betrayed the unspoken belief that even television entertainment can have a powerful influence on thought that extends well beyond the viewing hours.[23]

Commercial and political interests for years have recognized the potential influence of television on human behavior. Why then does the public interest have so much difficulty recognizing this relationship? Each year advertisers spend billions of dollars in the belief that television makes a significant impact. They use the medium to convince viewers that life will be unbearable without feminine hygiene sprays or sleeping pills. Political candidates work arduously to attract campaign funds that can help them bombard the public with prime time blurbs, advertising their personal qualities. After election day news viewers are told of many candidates who apparently were successful through effective use of the medium.

To cut off an examination of TV's influence when confronting the topic of violence and claim that fictionalized shootings and destruction make no impact is to show very little respect for the mental capacity of the viewing public. Are we to picture audiences as mindless robots, unmoved by the many subtle messages of program sagas? Are they oblivious to the symbolism and values expressed, intentionally or inadvertently, in television plots? According to the Violence Commission, the television set of the typical middle-income American family is on about six hours a day. The male adult himself watches about two and one-half hours per weekday. Low-income adults watch TV even more: one survey found that they watched an average of five hours each day.[24] That is a lot of time in front of the tube. Are they affected by the experience? As Robert MacNeil, British Broadcasting Company executive, comments: "It is very difficult for me to believe that a generation exposed to thousands upon thousands of hours of violent material from infancy does not bring some residue from it to real life."[25]

What do viewers watch in these many episodes of violence that may carry over into real life? Richard L. Tobin gave a pertinent report, based on eight hours of monitoring the three major networks and six local outlets a week before the assassination of Robert Kennedy. His account:

> We marked down ninety-three specific incidents involving sadistic brutality, murder, cold-blooded killing, sexual cruelty and related sadism. . . . We encountered seven different kinds of pistols and revolvers, three varieties of rifle, three distinct brands of shotgun, half a dozen assorted daggers and stiletos, two types of machete, one butcher's cleaver, a broadaxe, rapiers galore, a posse of sabers, an electric prodder, and a guillotine. Men (and women and even children) were shot by gunpowder, burned at the stake, tortured over live coals, trussed and beaten in relays, dropped into molten sugar, cut to ribbons (in color), repeatedly kneed in the groin, beaten while being held defenseless by other hoodlums, forcibly drowned, whipped with a leather belt.[26]

The commission reporting to the Surgeon General extended examination of program content into a later period. They found that the prevalence of violence on TV had not changed significantly between 1967 and 1969 (the rate of violent episodes remained constant at about eight per hour). Cartoons represented the most violent type of program in these years. Following up these studies with research on Saturday morning programs in 1971, the commission found materials for both children and adults "saturated" with violence in about three out of ten dramatic segments.[27] Taking the long view, an Arizona study calculated that, by age fourteen, a youngster has seen about 18,000 killings on TV.[28]

Audiences are bombarded with so much violence, sadism, and killing on television that it is not surprising that people often seem numb when they hear about actual cases of violence and death. "The best men in the world can become insensitive from habit," said Dostoevsky.[29] Certainly the routine of watching television violence has become a popular habit in America. Extended exposure to media mayhem seems to foster a belief that violence *is* a natural aspect of the human condition, a problem *to be expected* in everyday life. Leonard Berkowitz gives a good example of this attitude as it works in the mind of a young "student" of the medium's perspective on life. "In a family we know, a young child died of illness," reports Berkowitz. "Another child asked the parent, 'Who killed him? Who shot him?' "[30] For this youngster and for many adults, television programming has helped blur the distinction between real and fictional violence. It is little wonder they indignantly reject complaints about program content. They have been victimized by a media environment. After growing up on a regular diet of fictionalized beatings, holdups, assaults, and shootouts, the idea of suddenly changing menus is an upsetting, frightening, and revolutionary proposal.

Beyond criticisms of the sheer quantity of visual beatings and bloodletting on television is another issue—the quality of violent drama. What is the context in which violence occurs? For example, we may ask if it helps somewhat when the "bad guy" receives punishment for his violent crimes at the end of a show. Psychologist Albert Bandura appropriately scoffs at the "justice in the end" approach. It is not a satisfactory means of compensating for the violent stimuli and negating its potential influence, asserts Bandura. He reminds us of a fundamental lesson from psychology: immediate rewards have much more influence in the learning process than delayed punishment. If the "bad guy" succeeds many times in his power grabs and killings through the course of a show but receives punishment only in the final few minutes, viewers lose much of the moral impact.[31] Moreover, the "crime doesn't pay" lesson fails even more miserably when, as in many television shows, violence serves to defeat lawbreakers. In numerous cases the hero makes the villain pay for his crime in the end not by forcing him to court, but by knocking him unconscious or killing him. Showing the defeat of criminal violence through lawful violence has questionable value. Even more discouraging is the fact that, according to the Violence Commission, the question of legality does not come up at all in most television episodes of criminal violence.[32]

To repeat a caveat mentioned earlier, we can never have proof positive that television violence will make some viewers dangerous individuals in real life. But it can provide models of violent behavior and suggest ways of expressing aggression to people who are already predisposed to trouble. In time, these individuals may act on the suggestive powers of television, basing their behavior on models considered impressive. While we may never know for certain *how* influential television viewing is for those who commit or threaten violence, the daily evidence of the potential relationship should be clear enough to everyone except the most obdurate.

Newspapers frequently carry stories suggesting violent criminals model their behavior on television viewing. Psychiatrist Frederick Wertham, a compassionate and prolific pioneer in the scholarship relating television violence to antisocial behavior, has reported on several homicide cases in which youthful murderers were partly influenced by television. In one case an eleven-year-old boy killed a four-year-old girl by strangling her to death with a string and pressing her face into the dirt. The youngster had become fascinated with strangling scenes he saw on television. In another modeling case, an eleven-year-old boy played out an adventure show scene with brutal precision. He raised a mailbox flag to waylay a rural mail carrier, then shot the postman to death, took money from the cashbox, and set the mail vehicle on fire.[33] In addition to Wertham's findings, many other newspaper stories ranging from minor crimes to murder and terrorism suggest the importance of imitating behavior seen on television. In one youth adventure, a gang from the Bronx named itself "Intercrime," after a criminal group in a favorite cartoon show. They terrorized a neighborhood through an ambitious campaign of assaults and purse-snatching until police broke up the "organization." In a more serious example, Susan Atkins, implicated in the multiple-murder case of Charles Manson's "family," described the way a film on TV inspired her with an idea. She said that some murders in the case had been committed primarily to take suspicion off Robert Beausoleil, who was under arrest in connection with a murder which she had actually committed. Atkins hoped the train of new homicides would lead to Beausoleil's release, explaining, "I saw a movie on television like that once. They arrested a man and then there were eight more killings before police realized they had the wrong man."[34] A television movie called *The Fuzz* also became directly associated with serious acts of violence. The movie contained a scene in which a person was doused with gasoline and set aflame. Shortly after the film's airing on Boston television in 1973, six city youths attacked a twenty-four-year-old woman, forced her to pour gasoline over herself, then struck a match to her body. The charred woman died a short time after reporting the incident. A few weeks later another apparently related incident occurred involving four teenage boys who laughingly set a homeless derelict afire.[35]

In other examples, television appears to have stimulated thinking about acts of terrorism that could have turned into major disasters. The checkered history of one TV drama, "The Doomsday Flight," is a case in point. In the show's plot, an anonymous person calls, warning that a bomb will go off when a plane in flight drops to an altitude of 5,000 feet. Within twenty-four hours after the show went on the air for the first time in 1966, airlines received five telephoned bomb hoaxes. Later, NBC considered a rerun of the movie, but the Airline Pilots Association urged cancellation, arguing that "the mentally unstable are highly responsive to, and easily provoked by, suggestion." In 1971 the show finally got on the air again through Montreal television. Within a short time, airline officials, passengers, and relatives went through a nerve-racking ordeal. True to the script, an anonymous caller reported that a bomb would go off when a plane in flight lowered to 5,000 feet. This time the plane in question was a 747 jumbo jet carrying 379 passengers. After a tension-filled emergency landing in Denver (altitude 5,339 feet), the threat turned out to be a hoax.[36]

Although one can comb the newspapers for many other examples of apparent relationships between television violence and human behavior, it would be difficult to uncover a more fascinating example than the case of TV's debut in the South Pacific community of Ili-Ili. Life seemed rather isolated and serene in this section of American Samoa until the tube first appeared in many huts and houses. Suddenly the inhabitants turned avid TV fans, relishing programs about reality and fantasy that seemed delightfully new. "Walt Disney Presents" became a favorite among the youngsters, establishing popular models and ideals. Students frequently signed their lesson sheets "The Swamp Fox" or "King of the Wild Frontier." Trouble began, however, when the local station featured a famous Japanese movie, *The Seven Samurai*. This classic tale relates the experiences of a group of humble farmers who fear a robber band that annually gallops into their village for loot and pillage. In the end, seven warriors lead the farmers in a successful effort to defeat the marauders. Apparently influenced by the TV performance, three youths on the island obtained some horses, shaved their heads, and, in the style of the film, rode into the nearby village of Ili-Ili howling and waving 3-foot bush knives. They helped themselves to some loot (including a TV set, of course) and galloped away. But, much to the brigands' misfortune, the young men of Ili-Ili had also seen *The Seven Samurai*. They hopped on their horses, overtook the raiders, gave them a sound thrashing, and recovered the stolen goods. Ili-Ili seemed to be experiencing America's problems in microcosm.[37]

Assuredly, television is not the single cause of violence. Problems involving family influence, neighborhood environment, poverty, boredom, psychological maladjustment, to name a few, are also important. But the mere possibility that television programming may be a significant casual factor, and not just a *symptom* of real-life violence, should prompt extreme caution. For if human life is at stake, even one significant case of media influence is too much.

14
MOVIES

The fact that *The Seven Samauri, The Doomsday Flight*, and many other controversial television features are really movies hints at the broader problems of media violence. Many of the bloodiest television programs originate from films first shown in the moviehouses. Whether most of the new genre of violent films will appear on TV someday remains to be seen. If they do, the problems posed by television violence could become far more serious than they already are. Modern movies have broken the sadism barrier, giving audiences much more abundant and explicit brutality than films of yesteryear. This new popular style is frequently identified as ultraviolence.

Ultraviolence did a great deal to strengthen the movie industry in the face of television's challenges. In the 1950s and early 1960s, when television sets entered American homes on a wide scale, some predicted the theater-based motion-picture industry would decline. Indeed, the picture industry did suffer in the period, but sectors of it later made impressive comebacks, helped greatly by including ever more violent material. By 1974 a survey even reported that movies were regaining popularity after two decades of setbacks caused largely by the successes of television.[1]

The movie industry's realistic depiction of violence and emphasis on violent plots has been a long time coming. The seed for this concentration appears in the controversial scene from a famous silent, *The Great Train Robbery*, when a figure points a pistol straight at the camera lens and fires away. It expanded in the 1930s and 1940s through the gangster pictures of James Cagney, Humphrey Bogart, George Raft, and others. In the 1950s dramatic beatings in *On the Waterfront* and a lively fight with switchblades in *Rebel Without a Cause* left theater patrons chattering. But the 1960s saw a gigantic leap into fresh, innovative, more colorful, and more realistic portrayals of violence. Films such as *Psycho, Goldfinger, Bonnie and Clyde,* and *The Wild Bunch* showed new sophistication in the treatment of violence and proved that plenty of realistic and dramatic bloodshed can produce lots of profits. Although these films are only a few among the many popular productions of the era, they illustrate some of the major developments.

Alfred Hitchcock contributed significantly to this revolution in 1960 by terrifying theater audiences with *Psycho*, one of his most successful thrillers. Long after audiences forgot the details of *Psycho*'s story, a vivid picture of its shocking shower scene remained in their minds. In this memorable episode, a hand appears on the screen to thrust a knife through a shower curtain. Blood spurts and a woman falls to the floor. Water flowing towards the drain then turns into a whirlpool of blood. Apparently Hitchcock intended to make this shocking and gory portrayal the show's high point. When François Truffaut asked Hitchcock what prompted him to make the novel into a movie, the famous director replied, "I think that the thing that appealed to me and made me decide to do the picture was the suddenness of the murder in the shower, coming, as it were, out of the blue. That was about all."[2] Hitchcock received some virulent criticism, but the lesson for film producers could not be forgotten. Blood pays.

During the mid-1960s James Bond pictures reached their peak of popularity. They combined much of the hard-hitting, knee-in-the-groin action that made Mike Hammer stories successful with the exciting technological modes of destruction developed in Ian Fleming's novels. Bond fans marveled as they watched their hero (played by Sean Connery) drop several opponents with fists flying. They also marveled as, in each new picture, Bond's associates revealed the clever new devices they invented to liquidate the enemy.

Goldfinger, generally viewed as the best in the series, contributed a great deal of humor to movie violence. In the course of the picture Bond and his adversaries dispose of troublemakers in most imaginative ways. During his first encounter, Agent 007 tosses an electric wire into a bathtub where his attacker is conveniently caught while reaching for a gun. Bond destroys his last opponent in similar fashion by electrocuting a muscular, brutal-looking oriental henchman. Between these dramatic episodes, *Goldfinger* offers much more action calculated to whet our sadist appetites.

Bonnie and Clyde, the smash hit of 1967, furthered the cinemagraphic revolution by examining violence in artistic form. Arthur Penn "arrived" as an outstanding film director with his brilliant portrait of the notorious and eccentric gangster team of the 1930s, Bonnie Parker and Clyde Barrow. In a subtle and sophisticated way, the film lures its audience into identifying with the criminals. Their robberies and shootings become exciting adventures, sometimes a sort of search for freedom. Shootouts in the picture are extremely realistic. Both gangsters and lawmen fall with gaping wounds and blood gushing. In the last dramatic scene, when Bonnie and Clyde are finally surrounded and massacred, bullets riddle their bodies and they drop to their deaths in slow-motion, cinematic ballet. Many viewers declared themselves avid fans of the movie while failing to recognize one of its essential messages: what started as a lark for the robber team turned out to be an inescapable nightmare.

Sam Peckinpah's 1969 hit, *The Wild Bunch*, took the trend a step further. *The Wild Bunch* was humorless in its portrayal of death—unless audiences cared to believe that Peckinpah's entire orgy of slaughter satirized westerns by presenting the ultimate in violent westerns.

There is little fantasy in *The Wild Bunch*: The story is about three characters, a brutal bunch of Texas bandits who had been chased through Mexico by bounty hunters during the early years of the Mexican Revolution. The outlaws reek of dirt, and they use the vocabulary one would expect of mercenary killers. The Mexicans speak untranslated Spanish, and the poverty and hunger of peasants at a time of revolution come across in moving detail. But the greatest stress on reality appears in the violent scenes. Throughout the picture, Peckinpah zeroes in on man's supposedly destructive impulses. The characters do not just kill to knock down the enemy; they act as though they enjoy slaughter. Two super massacres occur in the picture. In the first, a group of lady temperance demonstrators walk straight into the line of fire, and some are crushed to death by horses. In the style of *Bonnie and Clyde*, men fall to their finish in slow motion with blood dripping. The final gundown extravaganza takes two and three-quarter minutes to unfold, during which approximately 170 individuals are liquidated in a variety of ways. For this striking commentary on man's savagery, Peckinpah received great acclaim. Like director Arthur Penn (of *Bonnie and Clyde*), Peckinpah "arrived" through a stylized study of violence.

The shock, humor, art, and realism that characterized aspects of *Psycho, Goldfinger, Bonnie and Clyde,* and *The Wild Bunch* can be found in many of the most popular films of the 1970s. Ultraviolence has achieved respectability, both in the eyes of ordinary moviegoers and intellectual movie buffs. Some of the major ultraviolent movies touch on complicated and controversial themes, stirring excited discussions in academic and artistic circles. For example, Sam Peckinpah examined the idea of manliness in *Straw Dogs*; Stanley Kubrick connected the issue of treating aggressive personalities with an Orwellian nightmare in *A Clockwork Orange*; and Roman Polanski even developed a contemporary version of Shakespeare's *Macbeth*, complete with closeups of bloody knifings and beheadings. By combining realistic violence with sophisticated dialogue and particularly topical themes, some producers have used ultraviolence as vehicles to win coveted Oscar awards. Two fast-action, bullet-packed shows won Academy Awards in 1971 and 1972 for "Best Picture": *The French Connection* and *The Godfather*. In America's most exclusive clubs, nabobs joked with each other about driving their cars like

Gene Hackman or making each other offers they couldn't refuse. A new media style had "arrived"; ultraviolence was chic.

Through these years of ultraviolence's extraordinarily rapid climb to popularity, many cruder, lower-budget films with fewer pretensions to sophisticated dramatic symbolism or irony also cashed in on the new interest. Their *raison d'être* could hardly be called redeeming social value. Hunger for cash from bloodthirsty audiences obviously figured heavily in producer motivation. The so-called Italian Westerns contributed to this revolution in cheap movie sales. These productions, filmed in Europe, offered plenty of shock, killing, and sadism. Directors eagerly added almost any extreme condition to spice up their horror shows. For example, when William Price Fox went to Italy to do a story about Italian Westerns for the *Saturday Evening Post*, actor Hunt Powers revealed one of the latest ideas:

> They are doing a scene about a man with a gold bullet. The doctor was probing for it and the guy was sweating and biting down on a piece of rawhide. All of a sudden the director had a brainstorm. He had the doc find the bullet, hold it up, and shout "Gold!" Then someone else shouted it, and nine men stampeded over and started clawing at the guy's stomach looking for more.[3]

A very appealing star emerged from the Spaghetti Westerns to extend his popular attraction to new films about supercops and superdetectives. In shows like *Play Misty for Me, Joe Kidd,* and especially *Dirty Harry,* Clint Eastwood turned tough and bloody scripts into monetary goldmines. Eastwood's ultraviolent performances helped place his name among the leading ten box-office attractions for five years running, and in 1972 he earned top position.[1]

Many other low-budget films of the 1970s tried to exploit violence for violence's (or was it dollars?) sake. These hard-core ultraviolent shows did not make the respected listings, but they did attract excited audiences, particularly teenagers. Newspaper advertisements betrayed the baseness of their appeal. Publicity for one very forgettable film, *The Losers,* showed, for example, a rifle-wielding bunch on motorcycles with the captions: "It's the Dirty Dozen on Wheels!"; "The Army Handed them Guns and a License to Kill!" Another of the motorcycle genre, *Run, Angel, Run*, featured the following titillating plot summary: "He Squealed on His Gang . . . And the Word Was Out . . . WASTE HIM! . . . The Most Freaked Out Motorcycle Maniac Ever Assigned to Kill! This Is Where the Action Is!" An ad for an obscure favorite called *The Mechanic* showed actor Charles Bronson with a telescopic rifle under banner headlines announcing that the star plays "a professional assassin hired by 'The Family'—He has more than a dozen ways to kill . . . *and they all work!*" A highly detailed picture in ads for *The Taking of Pelham One Two Three* showed thugs aiming machine guns at men and women in a crowded subway train with the caption, "We are going to kill one passenger a minute until New York City pays us one million dollars." Television commercials for another movie, *The Texas Chain Saw Massacre*, hardly needed their explicit film excerpts; the title told enough.

Occasionally, some moviegoers moved from their typical posture of indifference toward these tough films, but after their past insouciance, their sudden expressions of concern led to embarrassment. This was evident in the case of some whites, who, fearing the impact of films on ghetto youth, criticized a spate of new ultraviolent flicks which appealed especially to black audiences. They worried that films like *Shaft Gets His Score*, and *Super Fly* could compound the troubles of a society already disturbed by outbursts from black militants, heroin-related muggings in the inner cities, and sniping against police. The inconsistency, indeed hypocrisy, in their complaints showed glaringly, for except for their black casts the new black-oriented shows were quite close to the James Bond, Clint Eastwood, or Steve McQueen films. Samuel Z. Arkoff, the white director of a leading company producing popular black films, seemed to derive impish delight in his responses to such complaints. "I rather resent and I would think blacks resent the implication . . . that black audiences are somehow not able to recognize something that is degrading to themselves," he commented. Arkoff's defense of ultraviolence was as ludicrous as most typical arguments, but his critics' inconsistency provided an easy opportunity to cry racism. Arkoff had good grounds for complaint, since many among the public failed to question cinema violence per se.[5]

The basic issue involved here, of course, is not racism but how detrimental movie violence can be to American communities—black or white. It would be very sad if black Americans came to believe that criticisms of ultraviolent films appealing to black audiences were nothing more than manifestations of bigotry. The real question about the medium should be: How do movies affect individual attitudes, values, and behavior? Evidence suggests that in the long run the cost of ultraviolent films to any community may be very dear. As for the black community specifically, black civil rights leader Junius Griffin cuts through the doubletalk. Viewing the black-cast ultraviolent shows as a "rip-off," he warns: "We will not tolerate the continued warping of our black children's minds with the filth, violence, and cultural lies that are all-pervasive in current productions of so-called black movies. The transformation from the stereotyped Stepin Fetchit to Supper Nigger on the screen is just another form of cultural genocide."[6]

Indeed, in arguing the potential social consequences of movie themes for all racial and ethnic groups, we should ponder the irony that one of the first extremely controversial films, *The Birth of a Nation* (1915), apparently catalyzed white violence against blacks by conveying the image of a Super White Man. This violently anti-Negro portrayal of Reconstruction after the Civil War helped stir a revival of the Ku Klux Klan and a new wave of lynchings. Producer D. W. Griffith tried to counteract the movie's tragic influence with a later film called *Intolerance*, but the damage had already been done.

As in the cases of individuals modeling their behavior on examples seen on television, there are also numerous indications that movies stimulate violent behavior. Newspaper reports frequently give evidence of the connection. It appeared evident to a police investigator who spoke to Mafia leader Joe Gallo before he was gunned down in a gangland shooting. The investigator warned: "You think you're the Godfather. You shouldn't go to the movies. You're going to get killed one of these days."[7] A similar influence was obvious to the mayor of Gary, Indiana, who worried about news that violent gangs involved in the heroin trade required their members to see and study *The Godfather* for operational tips and pointers.[8] It was evident to the executive director of a drug addiction center in the Bedford Stuyvesant section of New York who complained about the upsurge in cocaine activity among young blacks after they saw the popular film *Super Fly,* which glamorized a black drug pusher.[9]

The movie *Bonnie and Clyde,* with its romanticization of gangster life, seems to have had a uniquely strong impact on viewers. Shortly after it became a hit in Westport, Connecticut, a group of teenagers dressed in 1930s style clothing brandished a snub-nosed revolver when an armored car pulled up outside a local bank. The youngsters, excited by the movie, were out on a "lark," an adventure which ended quickly when the police arrived, arrested them, and confiscated what turned out to be only a toy pistol. For Yancey Morris, a twenty-one-year-old bandit similarly impressed by the film, the lark ended more seriously. Yancey, who liked to think of himself as "Clyde" and called his girl "Bonnie," faced a prison sentence of thirty years for thirty-four robberies inspired by the movie.[10] Still more serious was the case of an eighteen year old who saw the film and, in apparent modeling behavior, killed the owner of a drive-in grocery store just an hour later in what a leading town citizen could only describe as "senseless murder."[11]

As in discussing television's influence, we cannot say with precision that one or another movie cause violence. Such connections on a broad scale can never be proved completely to everyone's satisfaction, although the laboratory experiments of Leonard Berkowitz and many others give strong evidence that films *can* affect viewers' aggressiveness.[12] As laboratory research does not yield proof, it must be supplemented with evidence from actual occurrences, from the record of violence already committed in everyday life. Perhaps one of the most promising means for further investigation, one that has not received adequate attention until now, is in-depth interviewing of a large sampling of people convicted of violent crimes. Through careful and subtle probing of the factors that influenced individual attitudes toward crime and violence, we may be able to understand how much the movies (or television) help foster the mentality that leads to trouble.

Whenever facing the heated issues involved in media violence, however, we should be careful to resist the temptation to call for "More Research," and thus consider the matter closed. One can always avoid responsibility for assessment by claiming the information available is too incomplete to permit comment or interpretation. For those who do finally take a stand after serious study and reflection, probably a solid majority will support the contention that media orgies of bullets and bombs *can* stimulate antisocial behavior. The preponderance of evidence from laboratory research and newspaper stories, combined with good old-fashioned common sense, suggests that the claim can be made with confidence.

We should also be careful not to identify only those who commit violent crimes as the people unfavorably influenced by media violence. If the attitudes of mainstream Americans are becoming more callous toward life, if people are more inclined to accept violence as part of life, if indifference to pain and suffering is affecting the national ethos, media violence may be contributing to this growing malaise. The problem is not just one of media-induced violence; it is also one of media-induced apathy toward violence. Americans have become accustomed to, and indeed expect to be entertained by, a superabundance of beatings and killings on the screen.

Media violence is so prevalent in modern America that citizens find it difficult to ask objectively if entertainment could be otherwise. Even many people suspicious of its influence are uncomfortable about raising criticisms. They risk disapproving glances and mockery from the many who, ironically, subconsciously accept the media's ethics and consider complaints as embarrassing demonstrations of inadequate machismo.

These popular attitudes reveal the very subtle influence of the media. Communications expert George Gerber likens media themes to ballads found in diverse cultures, folk stories that can be much more important as molders of human behavior than people tend to realize. "The ballads of an age are powerful myths depicting its visions of the invisible forces of life, society, and the universe," notes Gerber in pointing out the potentially great force of subtle mechanisms that inculcate values. He reminds us of the words of a Scottish patriot, a thought relevant to any discussion of the influence of television and the movies: "If a man were permitted to write all the ballads, he need not care who should make the laws of the nation."[13] Ballads may carry many different messages. It would behoove Americans to question the kinds of lessons conveyed in their contemporary television and movie ballads.

15
CENSORSHIP?

While Americans have been carrying on a long, tiring debate over whether media violence influences aggressive behavior, they have ignored the most important question: What should be *done* about the potential influence of media violence on aggressive behavior?

To date, very little has been done. Of course, abundant media industry spokesmen have pledged to mend their ways. The movie industry even developed a code rating system which was supposed to give the public some idea of the violence as well as the sex in various movies. Year after year spokesmen repeated these pledges (usually expressing them in the most serious and emotional tones after assassinations), yet media content changed little. Body-counts for television stories still run extraordinarily high, and, as Garrett Epps comments for the movies, if the trend keeps up, "we may soon find screens completely filled with screaming faces, broken teeth, and rivers of red, red blood."[1]

Nobody should be surprised that the media industry's exercises in self-regulation have failed miserably. It could hardly be otherwise, for the core of failure was not in a naturally depraved group of producers but in the fundamental pressures of competitive capitalism. Self-regulation worked about as smoothly for the media as it did for the economic programs followed by Presidents Hoover and Nixon. Like some of the virtually laissez-faire economic "controls," laissez-faire media regulation has not always proved attractive to those involved. Media producers may not really want as many orgies of violence or violence-oriented themes as they offer, but individual voluntary efforts to change direction are too risky. Marching alone to the beat of a different drummer in the media business can bring economic disaster. Let's face it: violence sells. It is immensely popular. Many audiences thirst for adventurous shootouts on the TV screen and realistic blood and guts in the cinema. If one producer, alone, decides to lower the body-count, he can lose soundly to competitors who reap the profits of an ever-ready market for violence and sadism. Self-regulation can never succeed effectively as long as there are abundant ready buyers.

Nevertheless, perhaps we ought to allow self-regulation to mire in its failures, since the issue involves basic human rights. After all, shouldn't audiences be allowed to decide for themselves what they can and cannot see? As many have argued, there should be no interference with the right of viewers to witness whatever they want. In fact, we might say that what is shown is entirely a matter of the producer's imagination.

Let's explore briefly some of the farther reaches of this theory of infinity, the idea that there are no limits. Suppose someone gets the brainstorm of producing a new TV drama series revolving around cases of suicide and the theme catches on quickly to the point of stimulating a "suicide race" between various networks competing energetically to show ever more exciting bridge, shower, and garage scenes? Or imagine that we take clues from the popularity of *Day of the Jackal*, a film about an assassination attempt against Charles DeGaulle, and *Executive Action*, a fictional account of group conspiracy related to President Kennedy's assassination, to create a new film about presidential assassination in the United States. To give this film extra pizzazz and bring it in line with the latest "crime pays" movie genre, let's portray the assassin as successful in both his hunt and getaway. In the course of working toward a suspenseful finish, this adventure show can, with cinemagraphic realism, depict the sniper first going after lesser public figures. We can build up audience excitement with a surprise attack from a balcony in which the assassin sprays bullets down on the floor of a packed United States Senate. We would be wise to feature this memorable episode about half-way through the picture to build up audience tension about the more significant dramatic action yet to come. Then, in the high point of the film, we can show the President of the United States falling in a slow-motion cinematic ballet as bullets riddle his body and blood spurts in every direction.

Are we going a bit far? Are some folks feeling queasy or getting chicken feet? If so, perhaps it is a problem of going *too* far, of crossing the common sense limits of reasonable adventure and stretching into the presentation of sickening, sadistic, and potentially dangerous entertainment. In this case we need not look for someone in the audience to be provoked in the feared way. Just one will suffice to provide a suitable tragedy. If such a thought leads to serious questioning of earlier assumptions about "anything goes," we may be assuming a posture related to the "clear and present danger" concept once elaborated by Supreme Court Justice Oliver Wendell Holmes, Jr. Holmes affirmed the importance of fundamental liberties but recognized there must be outer limits to license. As he noted in a famous illustration of the principle, screaming "Fire!" in a crowded theater ought to be judged out of bounds.[2]

Still, one must ask if regulation of media violence might be inappropriate because it would blind viewers to the realities of life. As mentioned earlier, media defenders point out that the violence shown in TV shows and films *is* a reality in today's world. We must not cover our eyes from portrayals of violent reality, they warn, or we shall not know what to do when we confront it ourselves. Children, especially, must not be shielded from violent stimuli, they note, since children are in the process of learning to cope with aggression. This argument is quite interesting, as it contains a built-in admission that visual media can influence viewers' attitudes and affect people's behavior. Consider, then, some of the lessons about life offered in present media shows. Does the opportunity to see fictional characters try to dispose of other individuals by running them over with automobiles, shooting them, or planting bombs in their cars help the viewer to learn to cope with life? If this is coping, may we be spared from the plagues of adjustment. Furthermore, does it not seem silly to assume there is a need to view violence on television or screen? Would audiences be left so ignorant and sheltered as to have no idea what violence is all about following an abatement of fictional media slaughters?

Perhaps the time has come for working out an effective program of media regulation. Since media industries have failed miserably in regulating themselves with respect to violence, the task may call for ambitious programs of federal regulation.

Just the hint of federal action is enough to give opponents of regulation visions of *1984*. "It's a Skinnerian trend," claims a television network official. "They're gradually setting us up for some kind of Government [notice the capital G] control of TV fiction. It's thought control. . . . It's the kind of thing that can happen when governments decide to become arbiters of truth."[3] Movie producer-director Stanley Kubrick enjoys commenting on the issue with a quotation that calls for action against certain kinds of media rubbish, then identifying its author as Adolph Hitler. Kubrick gives us a Pandora's box warning, pointing out that "To start to ban films—or books, plays, or any medium of free expression—on the grounds of offensiveness is to take the first step on a course that history has shown to end in a suppression of many other liberties." Kubrick gives us an eloquent statement of the Falling Dominoes theory.[4]

This typical response, replete with hyperbolic and hyper-suspicious expressions, tries to raise the bugaboo of censorship as a specter of likely tyranny. It operates on some fuzzy assumptions. For one, the thesis suggests that critics of media violence are hell-bent on destroying civil liberties. According to this view, their attempts to deemphasize portrayals of violence would only be the first major step in an erosion of individual freedom of expression, leading to thought control. This charge seems to evaporate when one considers that most media critics are motivated precisely by the concern for protecting basic liberties, not abridging them.[5] The First Amendment speaks of freedom of speech and freedom of assembly. These freedoms are obviously a major worry behind angry public outcry against media violence following major assassinations or assassination attempts. When the people's choices for leaders are denied by a single gunman, democracy suffers gravely. If media violence contributes to these tragedies, then it behooves the public to do something about such violence. In a larger sense other basic freedoms are involved in the issue too, what we might simply call the freedom to walk down a street at night without fear. Again, if media violence has something to do with threats to this kind of freedom, Americans could profit by action to help secure these rights.

Though media defenders give the matter little thought, diverse limitations on what is depicted on television are already in effect, and hardly a soul identifies the practices as outrageous abuses against fundamental human rights. For example, viewers in most areas cannot see advertisements on television for any alcoholic beverages stronger than beer or wine. Yet, the absence of *Old Grand-dad* on the tube in living color is not considered a terrible abridgement of our basic liberties. More relevant to the issue of violence is the tradition of not showing the killing of animals on television. Organizations like the Society for the Prevention of Cruelty to Animals do not look kindly on such portrayals.[6] When the movie *Patton* made its debut on TV, audiences familiar with the motion picture saw a good example of media irony. The television version cut out a brief but rather detailed scene of Patton shooting a mule, then having the carcass tossed over a bridge. The cinematic slaughter of hundreds of people remained in the TV version, of course.

It is surprising that all the platitudes about freedom and censorship tossed about by media defenders have not been adequately questioned for their fundamental assumptions. The easy associations made between the concept of regulating the depiction of violent action and the idea of thought control are glaring examples of sloppy reasoning. Is just the act of killing someone an idea? Are scenes of beating, stomping, knifing, and shooting ideas? Perhaps movie buffs and TV hounds have been blinded by efforts to blur distinctions between modes of thought and modes of action. Certainly, it should be possible to restrict depiction of some modes of action while still giving maximum liberty to the development of ideas. *Macbeth* does not need vivid and gory displays of dripping blood to be a great play or film. TV producers and moviemakers ought to be able to get their philosophical and artistic points across to audiences without indulging excessively in shows of blood, guts, bullets, and bodies. If they cannot, then perhaps we are getting at a major root of the problem: that some media leaders are preoccupied with selling violence per se rather than developing ideas or perspectives in art form. If violence alone is often the message, then we do have much to worry about.

Why can't we be frank about the popular rhetoric of debate? Censorship is a scare word, frequently invoked to choke off serious discussion of the issues rather than to open up thorough exploration. Professor Jerome Barren states the case bluntly: media spokesmen continually fudge the issue by hollering about censorship and First Amendment rights when really they are trying to say, "You're interfering with our ability to profit maximize."[7]

When all else is lost, media defenders tend to fall back on an extremist argument, assuming that critics of television and screen violence are a bunch of wild-eyed single-causers who think that once we diminish media violence, cruelty and murder will vanish. This assumption is obviously one of desperation. Media violence is only one contributor to a larger problem, as any critic with a modicum of common sense can easily recognize. But just because media violence does not represent the whole picture is no reason to forego attention to it. All problems which contribute to the violence malaise deserve study and action.

Now, let us imagine a very strange situation. Suppose serious acts of violence no longer play a conspicuous part in television and the cinema. What is lost in the new product? Adventure? Exciting action and impressive gymnastics remain possible without excessive bloodshed. Dramatic suspense? We know that thousands of mystery novels have pleased a large and avid readership with a format stressing case-solving rather than crime-committing. Often the trouble has already occurred when our enigmatic detective hero makes his appearance. It is a case of crime in the past tense and suspense in the present tense. Reality? Even in favorite dramatic shows, new episodes of violence can be introduced into the plot without detailed portrayals of the cut and thrust of a knife or the sights and sounds of guns, bullets, and blood. We can understand murder quite well without witnessing an orgy of terror, pain, and death.

In the most fundamental sense, then, the outlines of a program to end media carnage are really not very difficult to imagine. Proposals ought to press for a moratorium on media brutality. Depictions of the killing as well as painful beating or torture of human beings ought to be diminished substantially. All that this policy demands of the media people is that they pledge themselves to do the one significant thing that they have the capacity to do that can help combat violence—namely, to show greater respect for the sanctity of human life.[8]

16

FIREARMS DEMOCRACY

According to popular definition, democracy may imply equality or, more specifically, the absence of hereditary or arbitrary class privileges. If this be democracy, then Americans enjoy a very democratic opportunity for ownership of firearms. No privileged minority monopolizes the supply of guns in the United States. Firearms are abundantly available to all groups who want and can pay for them—from society hill nabobs to the humble classes, from the off-duty policeman to the on-duty criminal. Few are discriminated against: a potential assassin can easily obtain guns as can a member of a juvenile gang or a mentally disturbed individual. Each year domestic manufacturers produce five million new guns to extend opportunities of ownership to a new generation or to enable old-timers to add to their collection. Rather than a matter of privilege, gun possession in the United States is a matter of equal opportunity. Just about any free citizen who wants to put his finger on a real trigger may do so with little effort. Prices are not prohibitive and laws are certainly not prohibitive (in an effective way). The 125 million firearms presently owned by American citizens are impressive evidence of the vitality of this democratic system.[1]

Americans have better opportunities to own guns than people in any other modern industrialized nation in the world. Though a variety of local, state, and federal laws establish permissible ages for gun ownership, provide for licensing, or declare gun possession off-limits in certain places, these prohibitions have little effect. Generally, Americans enjoy considerable freedom to roam city and countryside carrying guns as they carry other personal objects. Along with radios and cameras, guns rank among the most popular portable "small appliances" of the new technological age. They commonly appear in homes, in the glove compartments of cars, and in people's pockets. A 1968 Harris Poll found at least one gun in more than one-half the households sampled.[2] The absolute figure mentioned earlier of 125 million total guns in private possession is only a conservative estimate. The actual figure could be much higher. No statistic on this topic can be precise.

Firearms democracy is indeed partly a product of the affluent society. Thanks to mass production, assembly line techniques, and importation of cheap foreign-made parts, the purchase price for lethal firearms can be less than the cost of a jacket or a decent pair of shoes. Lee Harvey Oswald bought his rifle by mail for just $21.45. During the 1960s imported handguns were on sale at counters across the country for as little as $12.95 and $18.50. Since then prices have escalated somewhat, but not sufficiently to subvert the promise of firearms democracy. Diverse types of guns are still readily available at manageable prices for those who do not want to be left empty-handed or who wish to keep up with the Jones' growing arsenal. True, the discriminating customer who demands prestigious-name goods will pay premium prices. For example, a good American-made revolver may cost more than $100 over the counter. The budget-minded customer will learn, however, that he can limit the purchase price to two figures by selecting one of many foreign-made pieces which have been assembled in the United States to circumvent the firearms laws. Even greater savings can be realized through informal person-to-person purchases. These transactions, easily negotiated on the streets of almost any large American city, frequently involve the popular "Saturday Night Specials," mass-production handguns available at unadvertised bargain prices.

Democratic opportunities for ownership of firearms helped spawn energetic competition for arsenal-building among some groups that few expected to see so well supplied with guns—such as youngsters in the cities. Americans have long been worried about an international arms race, but news of a domestic arms race between juvenile gangs surprised many. Perhaps the suddenness of the problem caught them off-guard. The stereotype of a youthful gunslinging gang member is a special phenomenon of the 1960s and 1970s. As discussed earlier, in the 1950s teenage toughs confronted each other with cruder weapons of advanced technology. In recent years, however, youngsters have been turning to factory-made pistols (22s, 32s, 38s, and 45s) as well as shotguns and rifles. When Gene Weingarten studied gangs in the East Bronx in 1972, for example, he even found machine guns, grenades, and explosives in club headquarters. "The city has never seen so much factory-made firepower in so many youthful hands," reported Weingarten, noting the disquieting implications: "With Bronx gangs, as with nations, arms races tend to lead to disaster."[3] Like the reasons given for energetic armament rivalries among nations, the explanations for weapons buildups among youth groups often lack logic. As the security manager for Kansas City public schools explains, once an arms race gains momentum, it becomes self-propelling; the rationale youngsters invoke to justify it combines offensive, defensive, and even emotional concerns. "Kids carry guns for different reasons," says the security manager. "Some say they have been threatened. Some involve extortion attempts. Some kids just say it's a status symbol."[4]

The idea of keeping up with the "opposition" has greatly encouraged Americans to enlarge their stock of personal firearms. Millions of adult Americans find themselves as pressured by the growing arms race as are teenage gang members. The revolution in firearms ownership continues to draw excited new participants. During the 1960s, many nervous citizens purchased guns in reaction to ghetto violence and sniping and increased burglaries, armed robberies, and muggings. Criminals responded by making better preparations for their confrontation with a more heavily armed citizenry. As the vicious circle widened, armed robberies increased significantly; thus the probability increased for fatal shootings, both accidental and intentional. All groups were now prepared to "defend" themselves. Juveniles had the firepower to demand respect from peers and superiors, and to protect their territory against intruders. Robbers possessed sufficient weapons to produce quick profits while guarding against the dangers of their profession. Mr. Average Citizen owned the instrument he could use to maim himself accidentally, kill relatives or friends irrationally, or, in rare cases, protect himself against an armed violator. In many areas of the nation, Firearms Democracy became extraordinarily egalitarian, a thought that must have crossed the mind of a New York plainclothes policeman who said there were so many guns in the hands of people in one block near the Bowery that he was afraid to enter the street.[5]

As would be expected, homicides escalated with the rise in gun ownership. In Cleveland, for example, a spiraling murder rate coincided with the period of urban confrontations, when many citizens purchased firearms for self-defense. But Cleveland's homicide rate continued to grow significantly after the civil demonstrations and riots waned. The year 1969 marked Cleveland's great leap backward. Cuyahoga County murders jumped from 210 in 1968 to 317 in 1969.[6] For the country in general, many of the great increases in homicide counts occurred somewhat earlier. The FBI reported assaults with guns up 77 percent in just the four years from 1964 to 1967.[7] An Associated Press survey reported even more interesting nationwide jumps for the period 1969 to 1973. Taking a week in March as a sample for each year, the AP found an increase of 70 percent in gun deaths over the period studied. Weekly death totals increased from 206 gun deaths to 350. Regarding gun-related deaths, the AP found homicides up 45 percent, suicides up 33 percent, and accidents up 20 percent. Guns ranked, by far, as the favored instruments of homicide in these deaths.[8] FBI statistics also show the primacy of firearms in homicides. Guns were the death weapon in 65 percent of the FBI's reported murder cases for the 1960-1970 period. "Cutting or stabbing" scored a mere 19 percent to finish in second place, while "other weapons" (clubs, poison, etc.) scored 8 percent and "personal weapons" (hands, feet, etc.) another 8 percent of the cases.[9]

Of questionable comfort is the fact that the victim has a better chance of survival if the attacker holds a knife rather than a revolver. His chances of dying are only about one-fifth as great as they are when the weapon is a gun. As a major study of homicides in Chicago revealed, even though more people were attacked with knives than guns, more people died from guns.[10]

A glimpse at Martin Luther King, Jr.'s experiences with violent attacks illustrates the significant difference between the lethality of two kinds of weapons. In 1958 a deranged woman plunged a Japanese letter opener into King's chest while he was signing autographs in a department store. The knife-like object barely missed his aorta, and King recuperated. A decade later James Earl Ray fired a single shot at King from a considerable distance, killing the civil rights leader immediately. Had the frenzied woman used a gun in her assault ten years before, perhaps American society would have been denied the services of one of its greatest twentieth-century figures just as he was beginning the most active part of his career. Hence, it is the quantum jump in potential lethality that makes the use of firearms an especially prickly issue. Guns are an unusually serious threat because they enable fast, effective, and almost effortless killing.

The presence of guns in one newsmaking riot strikingly illustrates their potential for almost effortless destruction. In southcentral Ohio considerable tension developed in 1971 in a rivalry between students at neighboring Wilberforce College and Central State College. On an October evening trouble began during a rather typical college social event. Students gathered in a local theater to watch a Halloween horror movie and add sufficient hooting and howling to make the entertainment partly participatory. During the show a prankster tossed an egg down from the balcony. Suddenly a soiled and angry victim jumped on the stage and threatened to stop the film unless he learned the egg-thrower's identity. Understandably, no one came forward. The consequent turmoil closed down the show. As people from the audience filed out, representatives of each college broke into separate groups and began taunting each other. While exchanging shouts, they gathered bottles, bricks, sticks, and broken chairs. A few appeared with homemade firebombs. Amid the excitement a shot rang out and twenty-two-year-old Martel B. Crenshaw, a Wilberforce student and Air Force veteran, dropped to the ground. He died of a bullet fired from 174 feet away. One gun turned a college rivalry into a tragic clash. Had a single person not decided to escalate weaponry to the level of firearms, probably all the students could have left the scene in relatively good health. The whole event might have seemed like nothing more than old-fashioned, college-style antics.[11]

Although some can always maintain self-control in heated situations, most people experience at least a few tension-filled moments in their lives when they should not have access to a gun. Fits of rage and outpourings of verbal abuse upon strangers, friends, or family members can sometimes exceed the limits of toleration. "Parents and moralists may not like it," says columnist Max Lerner, "but the fact is that [even] a four or five-year-old child can get into a murderous rage against its parents, with the only thing preventing murder being the lack of means."[12] Statistical data confirm that homicide is usually a crime of emotion. A large number of those who commit homicide in the heat of the moment can also be judged victims: they are victims of Firearms Democracy, people who become criminals, murderers and are perhaps, incarcerated for life because, for a short time, they were lethally uncontrollable.[13]

Firearms Democracy also provides abundant opportunities to commit serious injury or murder for the most absurd of reasons. The wealth of guns in America can turn celebrations into chaos, as in the case of Los Angeles' Jefferson High School homecoming parade. The affair ended in a shootout that left five students wounded, including the Homecoming Queen. Through guns, many participants in petty arguments can settle their disputes dramatically.[14] Even fights over television viewing result in confrontations of this sort. In one incident a mother argued with her two sons over whether they should watch a quiz show. While the three excited family members flicked the channel selector back and forth and grappled for control of the set, the mother grabbed a gun and began firing. All three television watchers were injured. In a more serious incident, a wife made the unforgiveable mistake of trying to change the television channel while her husband was watching a football game. He shot and killed her.[15] The long list of shootings from temporary emotional flareups includes numerous other tragicomic incidents. "They kill each other over bowling machines, over jukeboxes, over pool tables," reports a Cleveland police lieutenant. Other Cleveland murders resulted from arguments about a neighbor's car blocking a driveway and a dispute concerning hot sauce on a man's hamburger. Another detective had covered equally bizarre incidents, noting, "I've seen murders over cigarettes, Cracker Jacks, and a wrong-way look between two guys."[16] A confused search for revenge can also lead to tragic mistakes. Such was the sad irony of Louis Sisler's death. While working in Washington, D.C., as a lobbyist for the National Rifle Association, an angry group confused Sisler for a rapist and shot him at the door of his father-in-law's home.[17]

The mentally disturbed also pose a hazard with guns—both for themselves and for those around them. Each year the newspapers contain many accounts of berserk individuals who slaughter a few, and sometimes many, people in a shooting rampage. While mental derangement is not a peculiarly American problem, its lethal manifestations are more frequent here than in any other developed nation. Where guns are easy to obtain, the mentally ill have numerous opportunities to act out their traumas destructively. In more rational periods these individuals often regret their acts and worry about their unmanageable behavior. Dr. Frank R. Ervin, head of psychiatric research at Massachusetts General Hospital, learned from 200 self-referred patients that more than half owned a weapon and had used it at least once. "These people are concerned about their inability to control their actions," he said. "They find their own behavior puzzling, frightening, depressing. They are asking for help."[18] Apparently,

Firearms Democracy does not provide the kind of help they need.

In sum, the widespread presence of guns stirs deep concern not just because it is a prime cause of violence but because it is the great facilitator of serious violence. Firearms make critical injury or murder easier to accomplish. They raise the stakes in commonplace arguments. It is far more difficult to silence opponents in a dispute with a punch or to commit a robbery with a knife than with a gun. No one can outrun a bullet. Furthermore, guns give their users a sense of distance from the victims. During heated family quarrels, for example, it is fairly common for violence-prone spouses to hurl pots, pans, dishes, or punches at each other, but these weapons are not nearly as likely to provide a final solution to the argument as guns are. Killing without a gun usually demands a more sustained and intensely physical commitment to murder than killing with a gun.

Numerous injuries and deaths by gunshot are accidental. Each year about 20,000 Americans are injured and about 3,000 die from accidental discharges of guns.[19] These cases involve situations familiar to newspaper readers, such as the death resulting from a child playing with his father's revolver or a nervous parent hearing sounds in the night and firing mistakenly. In one of the latter incidents, a Detroit man kept a loaded pistol, which he had bought for protection after the 1967 urban riots, by his bedside. One night he heard footsteps and saw the knob of his bedroom door turn slowly; he fired, turned on the lights, and discovered that he had shot his three-year-old daughter through the head.[20] In another case in Columbus, Ohio, a policeman got a nasty reminder of the dangers of approaching the home of an armed and frightened citizen. Arriving outside a house in response to a burglary report, the officer noticed an open basement window and decided to investigate. While he was leaning down to look through, the tense resident mistook him for the burglar and fired his gun. An exchange of gunfire began and continued until the confused parties could identify themselves. The officer went to the hospital with bullet wounds, while the home defender entered the city prison to await a hearing.[21]

Even robbers are prone to gun accidents. In Washington, D.C., an apparently novice bandit panicked and accidentally discharged his gun, wounding a store proprietor in the arm. The surprised would-be thief ran away without taking a penny.[22] In Philadelphia, a holdup man took $80 from a gas station, then accidentally shot himself as he tried to tuck the gun under his belt.[23] In a more serious case an unsuspecting customer walked into a photography studio in New York while a holdup was in progress. The robbers panicked, shot him fatally, and scurried off.[24]

The police, too, must exercise great caution. Sometimes the tensions of their jobs lead them to overreact. The potential for accidental shootings is especially great when police are nervous about reports of ambushes and sniper attacks. As former police commissioner of New York City Patrick Murphy explained, "No officer can be expected to perform his duty at the high level which the public properly expects if he must be continually apprehensive that even his most routine police assignment will bring him face to face with a senseless killer."[25] That nervousness can lead to the shooting of innocent citizens who are mistaken for highly dangerous criminals. Moreover, policemen sometimes become serious menaces to the communities when they fire warning shots at suspected criminals. In 1972 the Pittsburgh police department decided to halt such practices. According to one of its spokesmen, "A warning shot is more dangerous than firing right at a felon. Often you hit someone not even involved."[26]

Since many residents are now self-appointed armed policemen in defense of their homes, it is worthwhile to question the effectiveness of their protective efforts. As mentioned before, both residents and intruders have become active participants in the arms race. Each seeks to prepare for the other's challenge. But even with both sides armed, the intruder holds a distinct advantage—the element of surprise. If the resident can manage to face his intruder on equal terms, he still takes a serious gamble in trying to protect a few worldly possessions. Guarding some jewelry, a stereo set, or cash with gun in hand can cost him his life. Armed preparedness in defense of the house would seem worthier of the risk if more residents did indeed foil home robberies with their guns. One major study of Detroit showed that only two in a thousand burglaries were aborted by shots fired at the robbers. Although there must be many unrecorded cases of burglars being frightened off by armed residents, it is clear that firearms have not proven to be very effective deterrents. In fact, the escalating burglary figures coincide with the period of escalation in firearms ownership. Only in the protection of businesses is there moderately convincing evidence that guns can foil criminals.[27]

Clearly, Americans have not stocked up on guns solely to defend themselves against other gun wielders. The buildup of private arms arsenals involves positive interest in gun ownership as well as negative reaction to the use of guns by others. As the popular saying goes, many Americans "have a love affair with guns."

The gun cult runs deep in American society, affecting the old and the young, the rich and the poor, the law-abiding and the law-breaking. Owning a gun may foster ego satisfaction and self-confidence; shooting it can inspire a feeling of virility, courage, and leadership. Many Americans, obsessed with gun ownership, look after their personal hardware with great care and pride. They shine, clean, and admire their firearms much as they look after the new family automobile. British observer David English muses: "The obsession with guns of some Americans is one of the most incredible aspects of the country to a foreigner. They talk about their guns the way the British talk about their pets. Rifles, carbines, and shotguns are cleaned and polished and caressed with the same devotion that one gives to dogs and horses."[28]

American culture offers abundant inducements to join the cult. Even before children can verbalize their thoughts well, they begin to simulate gunplay with finger gestures learned from peer group games and television shootouts. A sizable collection of water pistols, capguns, and other toy weapons gathered during childhood also helps to encourage the spirit. With the onset of adolescence many graduate to the real thing. Poor children learn their gun tricks in the streets: mainstream youngsters often receive the benefits of a semiformal education in gunsmanship and gun lore. The mainstream case is particularly interesting for the way it promotes love of guns as an acceptable—indeed, respectable—attitude. In the classroom youngsters learn that the Kentucky long rifle "opened the frontier," that the Winchester repeater "won the West," and the Colt revolver "made men equal."[29] At home fathers proudly show gun collections to their sons, speak enthusiastically about the art of shooting, and instruct them in the techniques of gun care. Community organizations also sponsor the gun cult. For example, local Jaycee organizations once arranged shooting education programs for youths between the ages of seven to fourteen as, according to one report, "part of a national effort to teach gunsmanship to young people across the nation." There was no charge for the BB gun equipment used in this program, thanks to the benevolent contributions of the Daisey-Heddon Company (manufacturers of BB guns, of course).[30] Adults, too, sometimes are given access to a gun by the special promotional efforts of local institutions. For instance, the Dallas International Bank made a special Christmas season offer: a Browning automatic shotgun in lieu of interest for customers purchasing a 30-month, $1,800 certificate of deposit. The gimmick proved immensely successful, attracting a large group of happy new depositors. The spirit of Christmas again prevailed.[31]

Young men outside of mainstream society also learn reverence for the gun, develop marksmanship and skills, and seek to acquire their own guns. They too become converts to the cult. For instance, Black Panther activist Earl Anthony wrote glowingly of "the era of the gun" in reminiscences of his youth experiences, suggestively titled *Picking up the Gun*. "The most essential part of the standard equipment of a [Black Panther] party member was the *gun*," claimed Anthony. Interpreting the value of firearms in attracting an audience when one thought he had something important to say, Anthony asserted that "The gun had overnight [catapulted] the party into the vanguard of the black liberation movement."[32] Mainstream Americans did not like this kind of talk, even though it was principally just another way of expressing a shared interest in the gun cult.

Among the various guntoting youths from poor backgrounds, small-framed individuals, particularly, find ideals of the gun cult highly exciting. The popular association of guns with machismo is very appealing to such youngsters. They view guns as a Great Equalizer, as instruments for attaining unexpected success and prestige. In the past, physical size and strength determined the power of a sidewalk assaulter or gang member. Today, firearms can help a little man achieve status as one of the toughest of the toughs, thus compensating for his physical shortcomings. For instance, Donald E. Newman learned from interviews in California prisons that several short-statured young criminals viewed gunpacking as crucial to their personal confidence. One subject carried a gun only when he went out for entertainment, considering it an especially important part of his attire when he was with women. He wore the gun conspicuously in his belt while talking almost obsessively about manliness. Freudians may do what they wish with this example. It is enough simply to note that most of the men arrested for armed robbery whom Newman interviewed were not very large or strong, a fact leading Newman to conclude that guns provided tremendous psychological uplift for these people. "The most important element in robbery often was not the acquisition of money," observed Newman, "but the one brief moment in which these men held a gun and forced someone to do anything they commanded." He found this attitude especially evident in the alacrity of the small-framed prisoners to work as gunmen back in their working days with other robbers. "It made me king," explained one. Another claimed that holding a gun on people to rob a store made him feel like "president" or "governor."[33]

It is difficult to conclude this discussion without reference to the daring feat of a 5'2" Philadelphia man. He confronted a well-endowed 6'3" German girl, pointed a gun at her stomach, and announced that he was going to rape her. The lass screamed, a policeman nearby responded by releasing his dog on the attacker, and the ill-fated little chap was taken away. He later received a sentence of three to seven years in jail.[34]

Many Americans are troubled by more and more reports of shooting accidents, gun murders in family quarrels, armed robberies, youth gang killings, assassins, and related horrors.

They worry about the way Firearms Democracy keeps the spirit of Dodge City alive in modern American towns and cities. Some of them wonder whether Firearms Democracy is making such a mess of things that it is time to ask the obvious question: Does America now need domestic disarmament?

17
DISARMAMENT

The great debate over gun controls drags on, full of sound and fury but accomplishing little. Pro-gun spokesmen continue to attack control advocates, bringing a full array of forensic weapons to their combat—statistics, parables, historical examples, references to the Constitution, quotations from famous figures, and even some popular jingles. This multifaceted attack makes the entire issue of gun control seem much more complicated than it really is. Accordingly, society's persistent indecision about attempting domestic disarmament appears to be an appropriate response to an extraordinarily complex problem. In reality, indecision on the issue stems from the public's widespread vested interest in guns and its high tolerance for violence, not from unplugable holes in the argument for firearms control.

If the power of pro-gun groups rested solely on the weight of their logic and common sense, the great debate would have ended long ago. The real muscle that determines what America does with its domestic firearms comes from the political force of millions of gun cult enthusiasts. So prevalent is the enthusiasm for guns in American life that even during the periods of angry

230 UNCHALLENGED VIOLENCE

public reaction to assassinations there was little congressional support for effective control proposals.

The most visible political power behind the gun is the National Rifle Association. The NRA has been extremely successful over the years in making politicians aware of its members' aversion for firearms regulation. Robert Sherrill, author of a witty and incisive study entitled *The Saturday Night Special,* calls the NRA "The most effective lobby in Washington."[1] Yet Sherrill shows that the problem of resistance derives from much more than just one organization's political pressures. After all, only a minority of America's gun enthusiasts belong to the NRA. The problem relates more fundamentally to America's love affair with firearms—from the cherished place given to guns in history books as the weapon that won the West to its present place of respect as the preferred instrument for hunting, recreation, and protection of home and person. As long as the cult remains strong, and its popularity seems to be growing rather than waning, gun controls will lack abundant political friends and the idea of Firearms Democracy will continue in vogue. In this environment even the most cockeyed warning about the dangers of gun controls will be accorded great respect. Thus, the great debate will go on and on.

Before considering specific proposals for firearms control, a review of the gun cultists' favorite points in the great debate is in order. Among the many arguments proffered in defense of guns, four major ideas appear most frequently: (1) guns are neutral, (2) guns protect individuals, (3) guns protect the country, and (4) the Constitution protects guns.

Guns Are Neutral

As the familiar saying goes, "Guns don't kill people; people kill people." For a blunter explanation of the idea, consider this cultist's commentary: "A firearm of any description is about as harmless as a piece of molten lead molded into shape." The trouble begins, he explains, when "you get some jerk behind it." In other words, people and their motives are the trouble, not guns. With certain individuals, almost anything may become a dangerous weapon. Baseball bats or automobiles can be lethal when used by madmen or determined killers. Thus, it is silly to distinguish guns from other objects and try to prohibit them. By the same token, society could bar other weapons traditionally associated with murder, such as kitchen knives and nylon stockings.[2]

Perhaps we can clear up the confusion by changing the cliche to read "people with guns kill people," since abundant evidence shows that guns are by far the preferred homicide weapon in the United States. As mentioned in the previous chapter, guns establish a sense of distance between shooter and victim that facilitates murder, minimizing the amount of physical energy necessary to kill. Guns are also much more lethal than any other potential murder weapon. Finally, guns are easier to handle than just about any other instrument. Consider the cultists' repeated reference to the automobile when stressing that a person determined to make trouble can turn anything into a murder weapon. Imagine someone walking into a bank, shouting, "Hand over the money, or I'll drive my car through the door and run you down."

Guns Protect Individuals

Most cultists argue their case by giving guns credit for what they are: instruments designed especially to kill. Therefore, firearms are important for guaranteeing individual security, the cultists tell us. At home, at work, or at play, guns provide valuable means of self-protection.

We need not review the messy record of this kind of protection—numerous accidents and emotional shootouts from the presence of guns in homes, thousands of guns stolen from home or office, and a very tiny percentage of crimes aborted by citizens with guns. Nevertheless, cultists continue to defend this idea fervently and some go so far as to recommend considerable expansion of gun ownership. This, they claim, would make deterrents more effective. Given the direction of their argument, the proposal makes good sense. It merely extends the "guns protect individuals" thesis to a logical conclusion. For example, handgun specialist Jeff Cooper argues very seriously in *Guns and Ammo 1969 Annual* that, "The foolish efforts of our legislators to disarm the public have measurably contributed to the increasing prevalence of vicious, pointless, wanton crimes." Decent citizens need more forceful means to confront life's dangers, thinks Cooper. "Since the urban American is, for all practical purposes, now disarmed, and since the result is rampant crime," he reasons with striking logic, "why not try a totally different approach? . . . if we in the United States not only permitted, but required, the vast majority of our people to master and carry sidearms whenever they left home, we'd have this crime thing licked in six months."[3] Understandably, scenarios like the one Cooper imagined provide rich material for America's humorists. During Pat Paulson's comic presidential campaign in 1968, he recommended giving guns to everybody as a means of combatting crime (at least Paulson offered an imaginative simultaneous countermeasure: to lock up all the bullets). Later, television character Archie Bunker addressed the problem of airplane hijacking in a similar manner, suggesting that all passengers be issued guns before entering commercial planes and turn them in upon leaving.

Guns Protect the Country

A well-armed citizenry also strengthens national security, say the cultists. Through firearms preparedness Americans can defend the Fatherland against a coup d'etat, a military takeover, a presidential plot to grab power through dictatorship, or an insidious Communist plot to take control in a surprise attack. "To be a bit corny about it, we think this is one of the reasons why we remain a free nation," said National Rifle Association spokesman William Gillmore.[4]

We might also press *this* pro-armament idea to its logical conclusion. If some fanatics ever attempted a surprise power grab, the citizenry would need weapons more powerful than handguns, rifles, and shotguns to protect the country. Better they should be kept well stocked with grenades, bazookas, automatic weapons, and jet fighter bombers to maintain effective deterrents. At least that's a reasonable recommendation if we are to distrust the loyalty and competence of the people charged with protecting the country in the first place—members of the armed services.

The whole notion of protecting America by arming citizens to the teeth conveys a very strange assumption about the sources of democracy's strength. Astute observers of American democracy such as Alexis de Tocqueville and Hannah Arendt have associated its vitality with an effective economic, social, and political system, not threats of force and violence.[5] The gun cultists' point of view seems closer to Mao Tse-tung's maxim that "power comes out of the barrel of a gun." It suggests that American democracy is so weak that it can easily be taken over through force by people within the country. If America's democratic system were really being held together primarily by the counterforce of millions of guntoting citizens, it probably would not be worth saving in the first place. Surely there are more civilized factors at play that give strength to the Constitutional system.

The Constitution Protects Guns

Cultists insist, however, not only that guns protect the Constitution but that the Constitution protects guns. At the slightest hint of gun controls, they frequently invoke the Second Amendment to the Constitution. In this part of the Bill of Rights we find the oft-quoted statement: "A well-regulated Militia, being necessary to the security of a Free State, the right of people to keep and bear Arms shall not be infringed." Gun cultists tend to forget this sentence has a dependent clause. Placing great stress on the *right* of people to keep and bear arms, they do not care to delve into the historical significance of the words "a well-regulated Militia, being necessary to the security of a free state."

It does not take much study of history to learn that the Founding Fathers had a military problem in mind when they chose those words. Stated simply, their new nation lacked a standing army. At the time, the Fathers feared a standing army, especially after bitter experiences when the tyrannical British quartered troops and demanded garrison duty from the colonists. Instead of depending on a highly professional military organization for defense of the country, leaders of the new nation relied on the hearty local farmers and townsmen to serve militia duty in times of trouble.[6] The militia concept did not work as well as expected. During the War of 1812 British soldiers easily marched through Washington, D.C., and ravaged the capital. Andrew Jackson's victory at New Orleans (which had no effective impact on the peace settlement, since an agreement had already been worked out in Europe) helped many Americans to overlook the terrible embarrassments suffered during the course of war.[7] For America's military leaders, however, the lessons could not be forgotten. During the following decades they moved toward establishment of a regular, standing army. Today this military machine operates with highly sophisticated equipment and does not depend on a privately armed citizenry for its backbone or muscle.

As for privately owned firearms, the Second Amendment to the Constitution does not prohibit gun control legislation. If it did in an absolute sense, the more than 20,000 local, state, and federal laws now on the books would be, ipso facto, unconstitutional. Actually, the courts have already interpreted the second Amendment specifically as related to collective military preparedness, not individual gun ownership.[8] So dies one more bogus argument—a point of contention that for many years has needlessly exhausted time and energy in the great debate.

The American public, though distracted by the contentions of gun cultists, remains interested in firearms controls. Indeed, contrary to what cultists suggest, the public has generally favored firearms regulation since the United States first began to pass federal firearms possession laws in the 1930s.[9] Later, in the 1960s, polls by the Gallup and Harris organizations showed very strong support for controls. A 1963 Gallup survey found 79 percent agreed that no one should be permitted to own a gun without a police permit. In a 1967 survey they found 84 percent favored gun controls. A Harris sample in 1968 indicated that 71 percent wanted tightened federal laws regarding the sale of guns. While differences in findings depend on the types of questions asked and people's moods at the time of interviews, the main thrust is clear: there has been strong support for gun controls.[10]

The pale forms of control legislation now on the books are a poor response to this strong public interest in better regulation of firearms. In part, these failures are the result of an illusion of action created when popular outrage prompts passage of token control measures by the federal government. After major assassinations or assassination attempts involving a President or presidential contender (e.g., John F. Kennedy, Robert Kennedy, and George Wallace), Congress usually engages in a flurry of activity that produces a weak law. The new legislation serves largely as a palliative to the protestors while providing significant loopholes for the gun lobbyists. In one highly publicized law passed in 1968 Congress seemingly slapped a ban on cheap, foreign-made pistols (the Saturday Night Specials). Gunmakers easily got around the law by purchasing imported parts and assembling them in the United States.[11] In a related, well-publicized decision, Congress barred out-of-state purchase of handguns and banned mail orders of rifles, shotguns, and ammunition. This act merely spurred the sales of neighborhood retailers. Congress also put Form 4473 in the hands of gun dealers—a rather laughable questionnaire that was supposed to screen out dangerous customers. The form requests dealers to describe the purchaser's physical features and list his address. In turn, the customer must swear that he is over twenty-one, a citizen of the state in which the transaction takes place, and is not one of the gunholding undesirables (e.g., a person who is on drugs, a fugitive from justice, or a mental incompetent). The purchaser is as good as his word, and signed testimony of his "honor" goes on to the Treasury Department. As would be expected, the legislation did not pose a serious obstacle to many dangerous individuals. One deranged young man responsible for mass indiscriminate murder in a shopping center easily walked off with a newly purchased gun, even though he had a police record, including two arrests with a deadly weapon.[12]

Many state and local laws give the appearance of controlling firearms much more effectively than federal laws. They certainly are more demanding in what they ask of the customer. In Philadelphia, for example, someone who wishes to purchase firearms in a regular business establishment must face a series of bureaucratic checkouts and maintain a measure of patience. As a clerk in one store explained the procedure to newspaper columnist Sandy Grady: "You leave a deposit on the gun. Then fill out those yellow forms in triplicate. You'll need two passport-sized photos and a driver's license. The police will check for any criminal record. Usually we get a form back from L and I [Licenses and Inspections] in four to six weeks. Then you pick up the gun." Walking out of the store and into a bar, Grady quickly learned how easily one could purchase a pistol without worrying about identification procedures, a waiting period, or producing a sizable bundle of cash. "They're bringing in tons of stuff from down South," a barroom figure told him, referring to unrecorded buying opportunities.[13]

The contrast Grady found in Philadelphia between formal and informal firearms sales illustrates the futility of accomplishing significant regulation when more than 20,000 different federal, state, and local gun laws set the rules. On the basis of the number of gun laws here, America should have the most firearms-regulated society in the world. In actuality, the plethora of laws is extremely confusing and renders most of the legislation ineffective. Many of the most outstanding community members who fancy themselves shooting enthusiasts and gun collectors violate the laws frequently but give their actions little thought. Why should they? There are so many diverse codes on the books that just by traveling across a municipal, county, or state line one may enter a community with a very different set of regulations about firearms ownership, possession, and use. Even a legal specialist would have difficulty keeping his records together while on the road. The limited success of strict firearms legislation attests to this problem of diverse, complex, and contradictory laws. For example, Washington, D.C., had, in the words of Superior Court Judge Charles Halleck, "probably the most stringent gun laws in the country." Yet laws in the Federal District did not prove sufficient to prevent weapons from reaching the hands of thousands of unchecked customers.[14]

While some stringent local gun registration laws effectively screen out troublemakers through the application process, nonregistrants continue to cause difficulty. In a study of New York City, Charles N. Barnard found that over several years only 6 of 60,000 people made criminal use of their guns among those who had been carefully screened through the Sullivan Law and granted permits. But many nonregistrants purchased weapons in unrecorded sales on the streets. Others crossed state lines to buy guns where laws were more permissive, places where a little lying made gun acquisition easy.[15] These out-of-state purchases can pose serious difficulties for states that make strong efforts to solve their problems. A study of Massachusetts (which has strict rules) for a ten-year period revealed that 87 percent of the guns used in crimes came from out of state.[16] In addition, many obtained guns by stealing them from the numerous firearms collections now available in private homes.

After the shooting of George Wallace in 1972, Congress went through another period of excited discussion about gun control laws which as in 1964 and 1968 ended once again in only token changes. While control advocates tried to capitalize on public wrath over the Wallace episode to pass stronger federal legislation, Congress moved sluggishly and made only minor alterations. Limiting their attack largely to a ban on cheap, snub-nosed revolvers, Congress even got support for action from some of the arch political enemies of control legislation. Senator Norman Hruska of Nebraska, hard-core critic of controls, offered valuable support that helped pass the law. His position on the bill gave substance to the control advocates' suspicions about the degree of reform intended. Their skepticism was appropriate. The new restrictions only applied to inexpensive, snub-nosed revolvers known as Saturday Night Specials. It did not even work effectively to check the sale of cheap, easily concealable revolvers, since inexpensive pieces could still be cut down to "convenient" size by sawing off part of the gun. Moreover, the legislation contained other loopholes that still left millions of unregistered handguns in circulation.[17]

Throughout this debate the "law and order" Nixon Administration remained adamantly opposed to anything more than the very minimal laws made inevitable by the highly publicized assassination attempts. The Congress, too, shirked its responsibilities. In the aftermath of Wallace's tragedy, the Senate gave a resounding defeat to proposals for much more significant legislation. It rejected Senator Edward Kennedy's plan for strong gun controls by a vote of 78-11 and knocked down Senator Philip A. Hart's proposal to ban possession of all privately owned handguns within a year by a still more lopsided vote of 83-7.[18]

Strong proposals like Kennedy's and Hart's typically arouse strong opposition, but political leaders even continue to reject more moderate plans for action as well. One frequently discussed "moderate" option involves the idea of "restrictive licensing" of all handguns. Essentially, this approach puts the burden of proving need on the gun owner. It requires him to apply for permission to possess firearms and asks him to explain the reasons for his need. Gun cultists condemn this modest requirement as an encroachment upon individual liberties. Several decades ago Attorney General Homer Cummings offered an appropriate response to such complaints. "Show me a man who doesn't want his gun registered," said Cummings, "and I will show you a man who shouldn't have a gun."[19]

Opposition to restrictive licensing rests more heavily on a desire to avoid any possibility of losing one's gun than objections to registration in principle. For that is the key purpose of such proposals in the first place—to *restrict* the number of guns in circulation, giving ownership permission to those who need weapons and prohibiting ownership to those judged undesirable or unable to demonstrate a reasonable need. Restrictive licensing calls for a thorough check on all applicants. Most high-risk groups—people with criminal records, alcoholics, drug addicts, the brain-damaged, or the feeble-minded—would be denied permission. People from certain occupational categories who would usually receive ownership permission would be police officers, security guards, and owners of small businesses in high crime areas. As for those who fall between these two general groupings, application decisions would depend largely on fitness for ownership and demonstration of need.[20]

Proponents of restrictive licensing emphasize that their

proposals do not rule out the use of handguns for legitimate sporting purposes. Gun enthusiasts who frequent shooting ranges could continue their leisure-time target practice. Indeed, some could obtain permission to keep firearms in their own possession while others could make use of guns on the range premises. Limiting handguns to shooting ranges is not an intolerable imposition. To a degree, the range is analogous to bowling alleys. Some sportsmen arrive at the alleys with their own bowling balls and others borrow them from the establishment. But all recognize that they are to take aim *on* the alleys, not outside in the parking lot. As for hunting with handguns, the proponents of restrictive licensing tend to be more tolerant of target practice on the range than hunting in the field. Pistols are not nearly as effective for hunting as rifles or shotguns, they say, and these small, concealable weapons have too long been associated with shooting humans rather than animals.

On the issue of long guns, spokesmen for restrictive licensing disagree about the preferred scope of coverage. Because many American citizens enjoy hunting wildlife, these controls advocates usually do not recommend restrictive licensing of rifles and shotguns. But they do disagree about whether complete registration of long guns should be required. Some want all long-gun owners to register their firearms through federal authorities, while others advocate more permissive procedures. The latter group recommends identification cards for long-gun owners and some recording procedures for the sale of new or used long guns. They do not, however, wish to burden the owners of rifles and shotguns with registration of their present arsenals.

Gun cultists hurl several severe criticisms at moderate restrictive licensing plans, some of which have some truth. For example, cultists frequently cite high estimates for the dollar cost of restrictive licensing. Actually, costs vary according to differences in the extent of investigatory work. A fairly permissive licensing system that does not put applications through rigid tests would not be very expensive. The report of the President's Commission on the Causes and Prevention of Violence estimated that a program for renewing licenses every three to five years would cost about $1.00 yearly per gun owner. A year before the commission's report, the FBI estimated the cost of researching the most important and expensive part of the application (checking whether an applicant has a criminal record) to be $2.43. Nevertheless, a broadly effective program of restrictive licensing would cost much more. A 1968 study in New York indicated costs could run as high as $72 per gun applicant.[21]

There are less obvious but significant expenses involved. Restrictive licensing would result in the removal of millions of firearms from people declared ineligible for gun ownership. Since so many guns are already in circulation, the price tag for such an operation would of necessity be large. While the Violence Commission estimated the cost of compensation at about $500 million, the figure could very well be higher, given the increases in firearms since 1968 and the likelihood that the commission underestimated the total number of guns in circulation.[22] Still, advocates of controls argue that American society is already paying a tremendous price for its gun problems. From a long-range perspective, they see the price tag as quite a bargain.

Gun cultists level another valid criticism on moderate plans by warning about the perils of making handguns a scapegoat. In reality, heavy restrictions on handguns may *not* effectively reduce violent crimes. If guns per se are as serious a problem as control proponents claim, ask the cultists, what is to stop criminals, assassins, and other undesirables from switching over more fully to rifles and shotguns? Even these weapons can be rendered more concealable simply by sawing off their barrels. With full or shortened barrels, these types of firearms are already a serious menace. An Associated Press survey of gun deaths nationwide in a week in 1973, for instance, found that handguns figured in only 37 percent of the total cases and in 41 percent of homicides. The bulk of fatalities involved long guns.[23] Thus, concentration on handguns obscures the fact that firearms problems relate to all types of guns. The public's myopic inability to see the full length of the barrel leads it to make incorrect assumptions about the size of the problem.

Finally, in one of their most serious and valid warnings, gun cultists speculate that the variety of proposals recommended for moderate licensing and registration laws would ultimately lead to general abolition of firearms ownership. New legislation would whet the controls advocates' appetite for change, they say, and encourage them to call for more complete restrictions. The regulators play politics when they claim they want only moderate controls, argue the cultists, because they know that if they spoke openly about their ultimate hope for a society relatively free of guns they would be lambasted. Behind these charges is the cultists' belief, often kept discreet, that moderate controls would not bring the solutions regulators seek. Since firearms would remain a serious problem after a period of trial, regulators would begin calling for more sweeping programs to rid society of the menace. On this accusation the cultists score a bullseye. They are closer to the truth than most gun critics care to admit.

The cultists know what they are talking about, for they now find themselves the victims of their own historical adamance against controls. Perhaps some years ago moderate programs could have made a difference, because the dimensions of gun ownership were not nearly as large as today. Now it is too late for half-way measures. With 125 million or more guns in circulation, even if a solid moderate plan removed as many as half the domestic firearms, the outcome would prove frustratingly short. Among the 62 1/2 million remaining guns would be numerous weapons readily available for assassins, street criminals, the deranged, the emotionally volatile, and others responsible for adding names to the obituary columns each day. Real headway cannot be made against these threats until the gun becomes an anomaly in American society, until people are genuinely surprised and concerned when they see one in somebody's possession. Without limiting guns to a select minority who have legitimate reason to hold them, it will be almost impossible to halt the violence.

Alas, the painful truth. Deceptive reforms, half-way measures, and holding efforts against controls only lead to more frustration and heightened anxiety. Yet it does not follow that a radical policy is needed. The word *radical* carries a negative connotation for many, suggesting an uprooting of their way of life in order to make extreme changes. But the stated goal, a relatively gunless society, represents a *conservative* policy. It is designed to preserve the quality of American life, to protect the nation's social and democratic traditions from subversion by new, ever larger waves of violence. It aims to *conserve* the quality of American civilization.

And how is the United States going to change to a relatively gunless society? The thought sounds absurd, given present attitudes and political realities. It is an unlikely prospect for the immediate future. From a pragmatic standpoint, Americans seem very far from agreement on the goal of a relatively gunless society, not to mention means to accomplish the aim. Nevertheless, it is appropriate to consider the way such a plan could be accomplished. Imagine, for a moment, that the society has resolved to move ahead, attempting to implement a broadly effective gun control plan. . . .

In brief, the plan calls for restrictive nationwide licensing through federal laws to affect all kinds of firearms: handguns, rifles, and shotguns. In its earlier stages this policy will limit ownership to police officers, security guards, owners of small businesses in high-crime areas, and others in special need of protection. Ultimately, as firearms crimes diminish to significantly safe levels, the society will move as close as possible toward complete prohibition of private ownership and possession of firearms. If, over considerable time, clear evidence can be amassed, through pilot testing in selected areas, to show that police can carry out their work safely and effectively without guns, that measure, too, should be taken. Gun use for sporting purposes can continue, but firearms for this type of activity will be obtained only at specifically designated centers. Sportsmen interested in target practice will use guns provided on the range site. Hunters can check out their firearms at officially licensed public or private stations, or at local and state police offices. They will be expected to return the firearms after a specific length of time. Finally, farmers facing threats to their crops or livestock from wild animals can obtain special permits, the duration of which will depend on the nature of the problem. There are, no doubt, other groups that will request firearms, too. Specific arrangements can be made for these people in accordance with the general principles that guide the program.

That is the plan in a nutshell, a plain, uncomplicated proposal that would, no doubt, be greeted with roars of protest from gun enthusiasts. It is easy to imagine the obvious charges: "grossly simplistic. Terribly superficial. Evading the law would be easy. Soon criminals would monopolize the guns. It would expose the decent population to serious dangers. The people don't want to give up their firearms. They feel a natural infatuation for guns that cannot be eradicated. Laws can't change these emotions. Strict controls are unfairly discriminating against America's gun-lovers. . . ." All of these charges are familiar responses to talk about gun controls in general. Let's examine some of them more closely.

Claims that disarmament plans would encourage widespread evasion of the law is one of the favorite criticisms proffered by gun cultists. The analogy with 1920s-style prohibition laws is especially popular in this argument. Since many people are so strongly attached to firearms, say the cultists, they would use great ingenuity to bypass prohibitive legislation and encourage illicit production and sale of millions of guns each year. The black market would quickly turn into the major market for firearms, fostering widespread disrespect for the law. Everyone knows how miserably liquor prohibition laws failed in the 1920s and how much they created an environment conducive to criminal activities.

This contention prompts an obvious question: Why would people be so intent on breaking a gun prohibition law designed to protect them? Is the love of guns really analogous to the love of liquor? The assumption that people would do anything to get their hands on a gun just as they struggled to get a bottle of booze in the 1920s is an amusing and revealing comparison. Modern science understands some of the principal motivations behind heavy consumption of alcohol. When imbibing goes beyond mere socializing, a physiological as well as an emotional dependency develops. Alcohol, in short, is a drug, and it has addicting qualities. Alcohol addicts suffer withdrawal symptoms when they try to go off the habit. Is this what we have in the case of guns? If so, perhaps society should think about ways to encourage the next generation to avoid the habit.

Perhaps there *is* something physiological about the interest in guns, say the cultists, and we ought to be more tolerant and understanding about this need. It is a matter of human nature, they claim, invoking once again the instinct theory of human aggression. And what is this primal force that explains people's intractable resistance to firearms control? It is man's innate desire to take aim, they tell us, the apparently instinctive drive to shoot at a target, be it a numbered chart or a live animal. The lust for zeroing in on targets, so evident in children's play, is also part of the emotional makeup of adults, say the cultists.

All this makes one wonder how the ancient pre-firearms people got along. Indeed, one wonders what is wrong with the chemistry of the millions of Americans who do not presently practice bullet-popping. More specifically, why does the thrill of hitting targets have to manifest itself in the particular mode that interests the cultists. There is nothing wrong with "taking aim," but why must we relate it solely to the discharge of guns? How about the pleasure of throwing basketballs into a hoop, releasing arrows at an archery range, or rolling bowling balls at a set of pins? Or, perhaps, consider one of the most popular aim-taking exercises of all: the challenge of trying to hit a tiny golfball into a tiny hole more than 500 yards away in only five strokes. There are numerous alternative sports available that reward players for their accuracy. Furthermore, if the sportsmen insist that gun-shooting is their bag, the plan suggested earlier does maintain plenty of opportunities for practice. The gunsman need only check out his instrument at an officially licensed location and use it in the officially designated places.

No, say the cultists, this approach would not be satisfactory because it creates terrible impositions on gun enthusiasts interested in target practice or hunting. Confining the sport to certain locales (within or near officially licensed stations) could ruin the sport, they say. It is difficult to muster feelings of deep sympathy for the gun sportsmen when comparing his problem with similar minor inconveniences tolerated by other sportsmen. Millions of Americans enjoy recreational activities and get along quite well with limitations on opportunities to make use of their equipment anywhere they wish. Bowlers see little use for their ebonite globes until they set their sights on indoor lanes; tennis enthusiasts find the availability of a court and net helps considerably. Most golfers do not take aim on their own course; they usually make hard contact with the ball only on ranges and on private and public fairways. Millions of boating enthusiasts, lacking their own rivers, lakes, and oceans, not to mention mooring places, survive quite well using docking and storage facilities beside the nation's waterways. Very few Americans have their own airfield; flying enthusiasts tend to keep or rent planes at hangers and airports. As for guns, we might add that the plan recommended earlier is already in effect in the nation's military establishments. Personal possession of guns is forbidden in the barracks and officers' quarters. Violators can face a court martial for private gunplay in these environments. When the military resident wants to hunt, he may check out a rifle or shotgun from the armory, then return it when he is finished.[24]

Far from throwing up their hands at this point, cultists turn to the dangers of being left weaponless. If a disarmament plan worked successfully, they warn, criminals would still find ways to obtain guns, leaving the huge noncriminal population unarmed and largely unprotected. As the popular saying goes, "If guns are outlawed, only outlaws will have guns." A very cute jingle, but the message is far from accurate. Gun-toting outlaws can be isolated, too, if the controls plan is sufficiently broad in scope. Effective control of firearms requires a sweeping program, one that isolates the man in private possession of a gun. When possession becomes more and more an anomaly, raising the suspicions of community members (especially when they do not recognize the gunholder as someone who holds special permission for possession), real progress against armed "outlaws" can begin. Once the gun-wielding population is reduced to a small minority, efforts to isolate violators and implement the laws will be much easier to accomplish.

Present-day gun legislation carries very little force. Since violations are so common and widespread, authorities see little value in making extraordinary efforts to crack down on the evasions of a few individual gun owners. Their attempts would make very little impact on the overall problem. What is the value of trying to sweep back the ocean? On the other hand, if these efforts to implement gun laws followed an active and effective campaign to pull millions of guns out of circulation, the task of putting pressure on a minority of violators would be much more manageable.

The time factor can help a great deal in facilitating this kind of progress. Most of society's more troublesome criminal gun wielders are young men in their teens and twenties, not aged professionals with lifetime careers in crime behind them. With deescalation of gun circulation and increasing unavailability of firearms, each new pool of adolescents would find the gun-slinging route to crime more and more difficult.

Obviously, effective domestic disarmament cannot be accomplished overnight. Implementation of certain aspects of the proposal outlined earlier would require patience and caution. As mentioned before (and this cannot be emphasized enough), law-abiding citizens who are particularly vulnerable to criminal violence ought to enjoy extended permission to keep firearms in their possession. Disarmament in their cases would depend on the success of stages of the overall program. Active phase-out of weapons ownership would begin only when experiments in test areas demonstrated that the new policy had brought substantially greater security in the region. Shopowners in high-crime districts and people otherwise subject to danger certainly should not be disarmed prematurely. In short, the program could outlaw guns effectively, including the guns of outlaws. Its purpose is to provide greater real safety, not to frame idealistic laws that only do more harm than good for the citizens it is supposed to protect. The aim is to offer effective security as well as comfort and peace of mind. Immediate, blanket, undiscriminating disarmament would undermine that purpose.

All this talk about planning for effective gun control might sound like a utopian dream if it were not for the relatively success-ful examples of it in other nations of the world. Several modern countries which have strong controls boast comparatively good records in minimizing firearms violence. U.S. statistics for homicides committed with guns provide invidious comparisons with the figures from these nations. For example, the gun homicide rate in the United States is thirty-five times higher than the rate for England and Germany. In 1970 only three people were killed with handguns in Tokyo, a city of 11,400,000 population. In the same year 538 New Yorkers died from handguns out of a smaller population of 7,900,000.[25] After two headline assassinations in 1968, Lyndon Johnson pointed out that guns were involved in more than 6,500 murders a year in the United States compared to 30 for England, 99 for Canada, 68 for West Germany, and 37 for Japan. The combined total of 234 gun murders for England, Canada, West Germany, and Japan is puny against the U.S. record, even though the combined population of the other four well exceeds ours.[26] Incredibly, gun-related homicides in the United States escalated radically in the years following President Johnson's extraordinary comparisons for the late 1960s.

England is a favorite nation for comparison in this respect, especially for American travelers who return from their first trip to London excited by their feelings of safety while walking the streets of London, day or night. Incidence of violent crime, particularly crime at gunpoint, in England is miniscule in comparison to that in New York, Chicago, or Los Angeles. One recent study of criminals arrested in England over three years found that only 159 of 400,000 were carrying guns when caught. London bobbies demonstrate the difference in security daily by patrolling streets with nightsticks rather than guns and bullet-lined belts. To be sure, England has its difficulties with aggressive citizens, as do all nations, but the problem does not usually result in fatalities. As David M. Paul, Her Majesty's Coroner for Greater London, notes, "We do our share of punching, gouging, and kicking, but there isn't an opportunity to grab a pistol and kill somebody, simply because there aren't that many guns around."[27] Author Donald Goddard attributes the difference to criminal etiquette in England. Goddard, who penned *Blimey, Another Book About London*, believes English society views stealing by threat or physical violence "unsporting." The English expect their thieves to get away with a pocketbook or wallet without injuring anyone, explains Goddard. "Criminal virtuosity commends the Londoner's grudging admiration."[28]

Few criminals in England carry firearms, a situation aided considerably by the country's strong gun control laws. Much of the country's success in restricting illegal use of guns can be traced to the strong start of its legal campaign. The Firearms Act of 1937 required every gun owner to obtain police certification. This law and subsequent legislation established a system which allowed gun possession for hunters, sportsmen, farmers plagued by vermin, and people living in hazardous areas or working in dangerous occupations. Every transaction involving guns and ammunition had to be registered. Licenses went only to those who passed extensive police investigations of applications. By the early 1970s the English citizenry had a relatively small arsenal of about one million guns in private hands. Pistols and rifles represented only about a quarter of this arsenal because of tight controls on these two categories of weapons. The remaining firearms, that is, shotguns, constituted about three times as many pieces as pistols and rifles combined. This condition especially developed out of the farmers' demands for firearms to protect their crops and animals, a concern that led to less stringent legal regulation of shotguns in comparison to pistols and rifles.[29]

Despite her generally outstanding modern record of controlling firearms and firearms violence vis-à-vis the United States, England too has begun to run into trouble. In the early 1970s Britons were alarmed by relatively large increases in violent incidents in their own country. Scattered reports pieced together into a disturbing picture that suggested the problems which deeply troubled the United States might begin to spread in England. Reports of violent gang activity (including daring work by some aggressive female muggers), armed robberies, shootouts, and firearms murders provoked many citizens to comment about the "bloody awful violence." Reports also circulated that London's proud bobbies were themselves thinking about supplementing their nightsticks with firearms to prepare for future confrontations. An arms race between criminals, police, and even citizens seemed imminent. By 1973 additional evidence revealed that, indeed, firearms constituted a serious new menace in England and that the British police were, understandably, arming themselves with more powerful weapons. Crimes involving firearms increased about 25 percent for 1971 and 25 percent again for 1972, reaching the high figure of about 2 per day (still small compared to about 500 per day in the United States). The news of one well-publicized armed bank robbery and subsequent shootout particularly shocked Britons. An exchange of gunfire between police and criminals left one bandit dead and another wounded. Politicians capitalized on the incident to point out the validity of their warnings about increased violence. Instead of heaping all their wrath on the criminals, however, some of them demanded to know how many of England's traditionally non-violent policemen had guns. One British observer of the gunfight expressed mixed emotions about the growing controversy. She appreciated the police's need for guns in such situations but did not wish to sanction an armament campaign, saying, "We don't want gun battles between police and criminals as happens in America."[30]

In 1973 Britain's Home Secretary, Robert Carr, called for a campaign to halt the growing problem through a new government plan to enforce stricter gun controls. Carr asked that the same rigid rules which applied to handguns and rifles be applied to shotguns. His proposal, issued through the government, called for a ban on the mail-order sale of guns and closer scrutiny of firearms dealers and shops. It put a freeze on gun collections and provided a narrower legal definition of antique weapons. The Home Office's proposal also suggested stamping all guns with identification numbers. Its plan included an important grace period for those who possessed guns illegally to turn them in with impunity. Similar amnesty periods associated with gun regulation had worked in England before. Britons turned in 79,000 weapons in 1961, 41,000 in 1965, and 25,000 in 1968. The amnesty concept is fundamentally important whenever governments pass extensive gun control laws. In the United States, for example, the Fifth Amendment protects citizens from incriminating themselves, a problem that can easily develop on a large scale unless new legislation provides amnesty for those who turn in weapons presently held illegally. Finally, the Home Office's proposal called for a ban on toy, imitation, and replica guns. This concern was partly spirited by reaction to embarrassing incidents in which the police shot and killed criminals who were holding imitation guns which the police mistook for lethal firearms. Hence, the general thrust of the Home Office's plans placed the blame for England's new troubles squarely on the increased availability of guns. As the Office explained in its formal "Green Paper" statement, "There is evidence that, in a significant number of cases, firearms are used criminally or irresponsibly because they happen to be available rather than because those concerned were determined to obtain them by hook or by crook."[31]

We should point out, however, that England's task of firearms control is much easier than America's because of different historical traditions. The United States has been much more lax in facing the gun problem. Firearms Democracy—the decades of experience with permissive laws—makes gun control a far more prodigious challenge in the United States and one that affects many more people. Because of this difference, attempts to model policies on the experience of other nations cannot provide adequate solutions. Each society must develop its answers in terms of its own reality. For the United States, that reality involves a gun cult so pervasive that it affects a very sizable portion of the population. That reality begs recognition of a harsh fact that gun control advocates find painful to accept and reluctant even to consider. In short, implementing truly effective controls demands substantial sacrifice from millions of Americans whose idea of recreation would be seriously challenged.

Gun owners charge correctly that an attempt to end widespread possession of firearms would place an unequal burden on them. They are right because any strong plan, any proposal that has a chance of effectively decreasing the violence, must demand that gun owners dispose of their prized possessions. Advocates of gun controls too easily forget that many people who own firearms treasure their property. Some gun owners see their pieces as collectors' items or sports equipment, and others view them as means to provide physical protection or psychological comfort. Gunless Americans can talk glibly about clearing houses of firearms, but how cooperative would they be were society to ask them to give up some of their favorite leisure-time possessions?

Suppose social order could be greatly enhanced if each individual agreed to surrender his prized stereo set, garden tools, billiard table, sailboat, or sportscar. It is much easier to appreciate the need for domestic disarmament than it is to appreciate the pain of individual sacrifice involved in executing it. Millions of Americans maintain strong emotional attachment to the gun cult. While that attachment should be questioned, it cannot be laughed at simply as an absurd habit that may easily be obliterated with the stroke of a pen. Generations have been trained in the firearms tradition from youth, and they will not take interference in their love affair with the gun lightly. Many of them take the responsibilities of gun ownership seriously. They know the techniques of firearms safety and care, and they certainly do not intend to use their guns for antisocial purposes. In any case of effective firearms control, the heavy burden of sacrifice will fall squarely on their shoulders. If they squawk at the mere mention of controls, their protestations deserve understanding and sympathy. No group wants to accept quietly a profound change in their leisure-time life-style. Yet the change must be profound if it is to do any good.

Gun owners also levy another appropriate charge—that their critics too often make guns a scapegoat in the attack on violence while downplaying other factors for which they, too, are responsible. A point well taken, for certainly firearms legislation does not get at all the underlying causes of violence. It can be an important step in alleviating the problem, but it does not, by any means, constitute the entire solution. Gun controls alone cannot cure the present national malaise. Nor can one measure guilt or innocence in contributing to violence simply by asking whether a person owns a gun. The problem is too complex to allow gun cultists to become whipping boys in the search for solutions. Responsibility for the problematic course of American civilization is in the hands of all its citizens, including those who never put their fingers on the trigger of a real gun.

Part III
Conclusions

18
CIVILIZATION

If we were to ask what is civilization, we could easily elicit a hundred different answers, each reflecting the special concerns of those proposing a definition. An artist might point out the importance of aesthetic appreciation; a physical scientist could use technological advancement as a major criterion; a social scientist might look for sophisticated patterns of personal interdependence and cooperation. But we should remember that the qualities which give pleasure, refinement, and distinction to civilized life depend on the ability of men to find nonviolent ways in handling their affairs. Without violence the highest potential of civilization becomes attainable; with violence, civilization itself is threatened.

Psychiatrist Frederick Wertham once commented, "The whole fabric of our civilization rests on the avoidance of violence."[1] In its ideal form, civilization offers social, economic, cultural, artistic, scientific, and political amenities to its citizens free of debilitating threats of disruption. To put it another way, we could say that civilization really began when men learned to forego violence for more pacific dealings with each other. As the old aphorism goes, "He who was the first to abuse his fellow man [verbally] instead of knocking out his brains without a word laid thereby the basis of civilization."[2] Viewed in this manner, the absence of destructive violence against one's fellow man becomes a *sine qua non* for civilization. The benefits of civility accrue once people adopt peaceful and sophisticated ways to resolve disagreements among themselves.

Nonviolence as a basis for civilization appears in definitions from ancient times to the present. It is evident even in the word's Latin roots. In ancient times the term *civis* signified life, rights, duties, and moderation of citizenship. To be citizenlike meant to be gracious, affable, courteous, and subject to fair play and the laws of government. In seventeenth-century England the verb "to civilize" carried similar connotations. It signified to make civil, to tame, to bring out of a state of rudeness and barbarism, to enlighten, refine, and polish.[3]

Even for America's antebellum slavocrats, the word civilization carried noble meanings. As one spokesman for the South put it, "the institution of slavery is a principal cause of civilization."[4] That connection may sound strange today, but it made plain sense to nineteenth-century slaveholders. They praised their society for providing a school of civilization for the "savage" Africans. Moreover, they believed slavery helped prevent violent confrontations between classes of whites. Slavery ennobled the status of all Southern whites, they argued, thereby sheltering the South from the kind of destructive class conflicts that troubled their slaveless Northern brothers.[5] This attitude shows that slaveholders, too, modeled their concept of the good society on the ideal of nonviolence. Southerners eventually rejected the connection between slavery and a model of the good society, but they maintained many of the fundamental precepts so long associated with the concept of civilization. In modern America the notion of civilization still reflects the people's world-view, the ethos they strive toward, and the best that is in them. Violence continues to represent an obstacle to the attainment of civilization.[6]

If Americans were asked to state the one word which best conveys the spirit of *their* civilization, many would answer "democracy." The connection has been popular since the 1830s when Alexis de Tocqueville assessed national life in his *Democracy in America*. It is also evident in the titles of popular twentieth-century works such as Leslie Lipson's *The Democratic Civilization* or Ralph Henry Gabriel's *The Course of American Democratic Thought*. When defining democracy, authors often begin with the political implications of phrases that have become household words: majority rule, leadership by consent of the governed, government of, by, and for the people. Yet Americans should ponder how fully these ideas about democracy presuppose the avoidance of violence. In fact, that is precisely what the beauty of democracy is supposed to be: developing rules and establishing institutions whereby conflict can be resolved without violence. "Democracy, by definition, is a political system in which respect for a dissenting minority and government by consent, not by violence, are fundamental premises," insists sociologist Feliks Gross.[7] Only the United States and a few other nations in the modern world have legitimized and institutionalized the concept of democracy successfully enough to handle struggles for freedom and equality by nonviolent, political means, claims Gross. Nonviolence establishes the foundations for achieving the democratic ideal just as it serves as an important prerequisite for achieving the potential of civilization. Democracy, nonviolence, and civilization are related. Democratic means of settling differences enable higher forms of civilization.[8]

Many who trumpet the success of American democracy frequently refer to the importance of nonviolence. They praise the stability of America's democratic system and hold it up as an impressive model for other nations to copy. America has been fortunate to work out an orderly political arrangement, they say. The system offers institutional channels for unhappy people to seek redress of grievances without resorting to armed revolution. Americans settle their differences by the ballot, not the bayonet. Proponents of American-style democracy point with pride to the fact that, after Great Britain, the United States has the longest record of governmental continuity in the world.[9] Political scientist William Nisbet Chambers looks for the roots of this longevity in the troubled early years of the new nation, when Washington,

Adams, and Jefferson helped launch one of the world's greatest political experiments. Chambers suggests that many emerging nations can take some cues from the difficult beginnings of the United States, when the people struggled successfully to work out a participatory democracy and an orderly conduct of government.[10] Historian Henry Steele Commager expands on Chambers' idea, stressing its relevance for all American history. He praises the two-party system for gradually extending its reach to the people over many years, by evolution rather than revolution. In these works and many others we see a mutual dependency among related concepts: stability, democracy, civilization.[11]

Max Lerner connected these concepts in his now classic work, *America as a Civilization.* Published in 1957, Lerner's optimistic study looks like an encyclopedia of great expectations. He traces America's sense of mission from the Puritans' errand into the wilderness and the Founding Fathers' political goals to the achievements of America in the twentieth century. From this record Lerner finds much to be hopeful about. He acknowledges shortcomings in American civilization but argues that, overall, the society has kept alive the spirit of its founders. Perhaps the most important part of this spirit is the persistently hopeful belief that man's difficulties can be overcome and the nation will continue to progress. Americans reject fatalistic notions of determinism, says Lerner. The attitude of defeatism, which burdens so many other societies, does not slow Americans. As for violence, the American system's way of avoiding it represents an important aspect of its success. America has had "an unbroken succession of national administrations without violence," Lerner points out proudly.[12]

The Lerner thesis about American civilization, popular in the 1950s and early 1960s, became known among U.S. scholars as the Consensus School of history. It appeared in popular syntheses of the day such as Louis Hartz's *The Liberal Tradition in America* and Daniel Boorstin's *The Genius of American Politics.*[13] These books stressed America's uniqueness, noting that the country had not suffered from a long feudal past as did European countries. Throughout their history Americans showed little interest in revolutionary ideologies because their country had not been dominated by intransigent, reactionary aristocrats who viewed the masses with fear and contempt and thrived on status inequalities. The German poet Johann Wolfgang von Goethe stated the case well in 1827:

America, thou hast it better than our old Continent. Thou hast no ruined castles, no such geologic chaos. No useless memories of old history and futile strife vex thy inner spirit in this living hour. Use thy present time to the ends of good fortune!

America had experienced some class, ethnic, racial, and sectional divisions, the Consensus School admitted, but natural wealth, democratic institutions, a tradition of liberal thought, and a spirit of compromise among the people combined to make peaceful growth typical. As Louis Hartz describes these impressive qualities, "Even in crisis or stagnation most Americans persisted in their image of America as an unfinished country in which history was the art of the possible, but in which the possible, by experience, seemed to stretch farther than anywhere else."[14] This was a proud message to the rest of the world. It was, in the words of Ralph Henry Gabriel, America's way of saying, "We are the Greeks; the rest of the world is made up of barbarians."[15]

Despite an abundance of optimistic statements, many Americans continued to worry that the barbaric spirit was more prevalent in their culture than commonly admitted. They wondered if their fellow citizens reacted too confidently to the trappings of civilization while ignoring some disturbing signs of danger. Could the record of numerous violent crimes, civil disorders, assassinations, and wars permit smug optimism? In the 1960s a new school of historical interpretation gained prominence which gave expression to these concerns. No, they said, Americans should not be optimistic if they take cognizance of history. Documenting their impressions, revisionist historians uncovered considerable evidence of abrasive confrontations and civil strife in the American record and argued that Americans had not shared common ideals as much as Consensus historians suggested. In fact, they argued, vehement protest against injustices has peppered much of national history. In an environment of widespread unrest and violence through the late 1960s, Conflict history seemed particularly relevant and plausible.[16]

With the passing of dramatic collective violence involving ideological and political disputes in the 1970s and a growing weariness among historians over either/or propositions for interpretation, the Conflict versus Consensus approach lost appeal. The change reflected new directions in academic interest, but it also developed out of changes in issues that concerned the American people in general. Nevertheless, the fundamental questions which stirred the debate—arguments which questioned the character and course of American civilization—remained very much alive. These questions touched on broad interpretations about the rise and decline of societies.

Through the first six decades of the twentieth century, observers tended to apply gloomy associations between the decline of civilization and violence to European countries rather than to the United States. The unexplainable slaughters in World War I, involving Europe's greatest nations, created disillusion and skepticism about purportedly civilized peoples. How could so many Europeans engage in such carnage with each side believing its cause good and noble, people asked? How could nations throw themselves into a holocaust for absurdly flimsy reasons? Americans considered World War I a sorry example of Europe's shortcomings. The United States did its part to bring the fight to an end, they reasoned, but Americans would not get caught again in the madness of European nationalism. In the 1920s and 1930s isolationism flowered in the United States. This standoffish attitude passed with the coming of World War II, but America's feeling of moral superiority over Europe remained. Germany's epoch of fanaticism under Hitler only heightened American skepticism about European civilization. Stories of Hitler's bellicose and genocidal policies aroused American self-congratulation. How different the American *zeitgeist* seemed, so far removed from the German sickness. Americans came to know the war as a battle between democracy and fascism, between those who respected humanity and those who showed contempt for it. The contrast strengthened America's feeling of relative innocence in a world rife with recurrent episodes of violent madness.

The Americans' attitude of civilized superiority suffered hard and shaking blows in the 1960s and 1970s. Beginning particularly with John F. Kennedy's assassination in 1963, confidence and optimism about the future quickly deteriorated. Disturbing news events followed in rapid succession: escalation of a confused and ugly war in Vietnam, riots and violent protests in the ghettoes and on college campuses, more assassinations, and a soaring increase in violent crime. This news barrage deflated those who thought they had been witnessing the glorious American century. Suddenly, the grand, sweeping evaluations of American society swung around 180 degrees. No longer a model of civilization, America was a nation deeply troubled from within. The crises could not be blamed on outsiders; these were homegrown problems. What was wrong? Some spoke of a sick society. Some talked of civil war, anarchy, or Armageddon. To many, a favorite quotation from the cartoon philosopher Pogo tersely explained the difficulty: "We have met the enemy and he is us."

Amid widespread disorders and rising fears in the late 1960s, some began to ask whether America's period of greatness had already passed. Did the outbreaks of violence signal a decline in American civilization? Students of violence claimed they saw such a downward trend, although they were not ready to declare it permanent and irreversible. One excellent anthology on the subject, featuring comments from prominent people in private, public, and academic life, conveyed the new concern in its title: *Violence: The Crisis of American Confidence.*[17] When the National Commission on the Causes and Prevention of Violence drew up its final report, a serious reference to the idea of rising and declining societies appeared in its pages. "When in man's long history other great civilizations fell," the commission warned, "it was less often from external assault than from internal decay."[18]

The hint was unmistakable: Americans had better start thinking seriously about whether their society was moving up or down.

In America's new period of doubt and pessimism, much speculation appeared about the inevitability of cultural decline. Perhaps society's direction could not be reversed, thought the sad skeptics; perhaps recent developments were in keeping with some grand pattern that determines the growth and atrophy of all major civilizations. The concept of internal decay contributing to the fall of society was not new, of course. Edward Gibbon, particularly, helped to popularize this interpretation in *The Decline and Fall of the Roman Empire.* Concluding on the reasons for Rome's fall, Gibbon spoke of "the most potent and forcible cause of destruction, the domestic hostilities of the Romans themselves." In the early twentieth century, Oswald Spengler's *The Decline of the West* became a seminal study of the forces of societal deterioration. Very few Americans had ever read Spengler's difficult prose. Yet the outlines of his thesis were familiar to many Americans as a general approach to history. One did not have to be a student of Spengler to hold a somber view of Western civilization's inner potential for self-destruction. One did not have to be a specialist in historical interpretation to recognize that Spengler's concerns closely approximated many of America's own in the late 1960s.

Oswald Spengler spoke of European problems and disillusionment which now had a familiar ring to those troubled about developments in America. Spengler, a German, wrote during and after World War I. Out of shock and disgust he generalized about the course of Western civilization. Spengler scorned optimistic, nineteenth-century liberalism with its belief in continued progress. Instead of peace and advancement, Spengler reminded his readers, the West was experiencing acts of hysteria, ruthless tyranny, and almost constant warfare. Men continued to delude themselves into believing civilization had advanced considerably since the Stone Age. Yet the old savage seemed ever ready to spring forth. Instead of achieving blissful tranquility, the twentieth-century West already had a sorry history of hunger, wars, conquests, victories, defeats, and masses praying for peace.[19]

Would there be an end to this madness? Could man be protected from destroying himself? Spengler's morphological method left little room for optimism. Each culture was like an organism, he argued, and each went through a life cycle. Like other living things, cultures experienced the stages of birth, growth, maturity, and decay, which he respectively labeled spring, summer, autumn, and winter. Whatever efforts societies might make to hold back their transformations, they could not escape inevitable destiny. Reviewing the history of diverse civilizations, Spengler pointed to supposedly irreversible patterns of rise and decline. "We may marvel at it or we may lament it," he commented stoically, "but it is there."[20]

The temptation to apply a Spenglerian assessment to modern America's crisis is always great. Unblinking acceptance of cyclical theories is comforting, for it relieves anxieties about an uncertain future by removing pressure to find solutions to the problems. If man is incapable of solutions, he may as well sit back and let history take its course. Come what may, let us at least hope that current troubles place us in the autumn rather than winter of our discontent.

Lest we sulk into immobilizing pessimism, we should be aware that Spengler's analysis rests on very tenuous assumptions. Most sophisticated scholars of today do not view Spengler's thesis with awe. They recognize it as a provocative but faulty interpretation that conveniently organizes historical material in ways that serve the grand design of its author.[21] Spengler's explanation is a product of his *zeitgeist*; it came out of a disillusioned age already inclined to accept his neat, compartmentalized theories of the inevitability of societal decline. Numerous writers borrowed Spengler's concepts, translated them into more readable form, and sold them to a market already predisposed to buy the argument. Possibly such a market exists in America today.

Neither Europe's destiny nor America's can be considered so manifestly determined as Spengler suggested. The future is in the hands of men, and men can make of it what they wish. We will do well to remember our freedom of choice. At a time when pervasive violence and fear erode the quality of life, Spenglerian stoicism can be dangerously defeating. If people persist in viewing the difficulties with detached and objective pessimism, they should not be surprised if the result is more of the same. We can expect little improvement when those who are troubled by a problem do not believe they have the capacity to act on it effectively.

19
CITIES

Attitudes about the future of American cities have changed dramatically in the era of growing concern over violence. The public's earlier confidence, which often viewed city life as the brightest example of America's potential for achieving an attractive and sophisticated civilization, eroded significantly in the 1960s and 1970s. Americans increasingly viewed the urban condition as a prime example of spreading deterioration rather than an environment that inspired optimism. Indeed, observations on social problems in the cities now represent some of the most pessimistic commentaries about the direction of American society. For a nation that is presently 85 percent urban, this situation suggests disturbing implications. By population and sentiment, the city, to a large degree, *is* American civilization.

When nineteenth- and twentieth-century commentators praised the promise of American life, often they pointed to the cities as the cultural milieu which gave U.S. civilization its greatest chances for fulfillment. This had been the promise of cities since the Biblical period, they said. In classical times urban life contrasted sharply with conditions in the rural districts, for urban society represented an oasis from violence in the countryside. Cities offered security, order, and liberty from the threats

residents in rural districts found themselves exposed to constantly. Etymologists and historians reminded Americans that even
the origins of words like "urban" and "rural" developed out of
related distinctions. In Greek and Roman times "the well-
mannered *civis* living in urbs was, for that reason, civil and
urbane as well as civic and urban; his manner of life was
epitomized in the very word civilization," pointed out twentieth-
century historian Arthur Maier Schlesinger. "His rude neighbor,
on the other hand, was a pagan or a rustic (from the Latin words
paganus and *rusticus* for peasant, a boor (from the Dutch *boer,* a
farmer) or a heathen (that is, a dweller in the heaths)."[1]

Commentators also saw the cities historically as the centers
for enjoyment of civic culture, the places where men cooperated
and shared in a life far more sophisticated than dreary existence
in the rough countryside. "Memphis, Thebes, Nineveh, Babylon
were the great capitals of early civilized man," noted Schlesinger.
Nineteenth-century theologian Theodore Parker called cities
"the fireplaces of civilization whose light and heat radiated out
into the dark and cold world."[2] Alexis de Tocqueville supported
this contention, commenting that American frontiersmen sometimes resorted to savagery because of harsh conditions in the
countryside, but, nevertheless, they carried with them the ideas
and customs of civilization, habits which, in time, could establish
patterns for a more sophisticated way of life.[3] Twentieth-century
historian Richard C. Wade worked with this concept to revise the
famous "Turner thesis" of American history. Disputing Frederick Jackson Turner's argument that the frontier experience
had the greatest influence in molding values in newly settled
areas, Wade contended that American culture in the open areas
emanated from the attitudes and life-styles set by frontier towns.
Again, it was the city that carried American civilization to the
country folk.[4] Other twentieth-century students of the city
argued in similar manner about the trend-setting role of urban
centers. "What we call civilization . . . has been cradled in the
city," explained Louis Wirth. "The city is the center from which
the influences of modern civilized life radiates to the ends of the
earth."[5] As John R. Seeley summed up the cause-effect relation-

ship, cities are "where the civilization is refined, developed, elaborated, and fed back into the hinterland."[6]

These are just a few of the familiar, optimistic views of cities as a Promised Land. Whether speaking about the history of man's civilizations in general or American civilization in particular, numerous commentators have celebrated the city's contribution to education, literature, science, and art, its provision of opportunities for ambitious, inventive people, its place as a hotbed for new political activities geared to reform and improve man's standard of living, and its role as an environment where people expected that "a finer, more humane civilization" could thrive.

We should also acknowledge, of course, that Americans have long expressed serious skepticism about the city's potential. Thomas Jefferson was one of the first leading citizens to become popularly associated with major qualms about city life. Jefferson viewed "great cities as penitential to the morals, the health, and the liberties of man," and he praised the virtues of simplicity, decency, and freedom in rural living.[7] Later, in the late nineteenth century, agrarian protestors called Populists became closely associated with distrust for urban folk. These troubled farmers blamed their difficulties on people they saw as a despicable assortment of exploiters and undesirables in urban centers: industrial capitalists, big bankers (particularly advocates of the gold standard), foreigners, criminals, and radical socialists.[8] Distrust continued into the twentieth century. The rural-urban hostility broke into the open, especially in the 1920s. The Ku Klux Klan experienced a revival, and members exhorted lovers of country life and "Americanism" to restrict the settlement of city-oriented Catholic and Jewish immigrants. In 1924 the Democratic party suffered a severe schism between rural and urban elements when its national convention broke into camps of Eastern, "wet," pro-immigrant urban elements and Southern and Midwestern "dry," anti-immigrant, pro-Klan, rural elements. Perhaps the "Scopes Monkey Trial" most dramatically demonstrated the tensions of the period. In the small town of Dayton, Tennessee, townsfolk rallied around prairie lawyer William Jennings Bryan in an epic debate with the slick, radical

Chicago attorney Clarence Darrow. The trial represented much more than just a debate over teaching evolution in the schools: it signified a contest between rural and urban attitudes.[9]

Distrust of the city has been common among many of America's leading writers, philosophers, and architects as well as among the common folk. Besides Thomas Jefferson, the list includes Henry David Thoreau, Nathaniel Hawthorne, Herman Melville, Edgar Allan Poe, Henry James, John Dewey, Louis Sullivan, and Frank Lloyd Wright. Henry Adams penned some of the gloomiest observations about the deterioration of city life. In one ultra-pessimistic passage he wrote about the prospects for further violence:

> At the present rate of progression, since 1600, it will not need another century or half a century to tip thought upside down. Law, in that case, would disappear as theory or a priori principle and give place to force. Morality would become police. Explosives would reach cosmic violence. Disintegration would overcome integration.[10]

In modern times Lewis Mumford, noted student of the city, has updated Adams' poignant and troubled observations. In his monumental work, *The City in History,* Mumford claims Adams' prophesy has already been fulfilled. The future will be bleak, he says, unless we contend "with the forces of annihilation and extermination that now, almost automatically, and at an ever-accelerating rate, are working to bring about a more general breakdown." [11]

Intellectual disenchantment has its historic quality, of course, but sentiment apparently has been skewing sharply in the direction of greater discontent in recent years. Earlier statements about a Promised Land are less common now; many of society's most educated and sophisticated thinkers are more inclined to speak in terms of a "crisis." This changing sentiment is evident, for example, in the treatment of urban issues in the journal *Daedalus.* As late as 1961, when the esteemed intellectual organ published a special number about "The Future Metropolis," many authors finished their essays with rather sanguine comments. Their analyses recognized some problems, but the challenges they saw did not seem insoluble.[12] Seven years later *Daedalus* published another special issue on urban life entitled "The Conscience of the City." Through much more somber analysis, contributors wrote about poverty, unemployment, drug addiction, juvenile delinquency, race riots, violence, and speculated about the urban crisis in America, the failure of the cities, and the demise of the city. As in the issues of *Daedalus,* a growing mood of despair began to envelop much of intellectual commentary on the cities.[13]

Until recently, many city residents in America tended to write off suspicious comments about urban life as the uneducated prejudices of country bumpkins and the pessimistic predictions of intellectuals representative of their ultra-critical prejudices on any subject. Gloomy assessments seemed unnecessarily heavy and out of proportion to the problems. They admitted that cities faced traffic congestion, poverty, racial tensions, crime, and the like, but no mass-population environment could be paradise. Cities were nevertheless the places "where the action is," the hub of cultural and civic events, places where the ambitious and talented yearned to go in search of opportunity. Cities represented excitement, progress, and hope.

The confidence of America's millions of urban residents is quickly passing. Like country yokels and intellectual critics, the mass of urban citizens are harboring increasingly negative views of city life. They worry more than before about pollution, traffic, slums, blight, and many other problems. Their most pressing and prevalent worry is the fear of violence, the terror of falling victim to a teenage tough, a mugger, a sadist, or anyone else representing the threat that makes a walk down a dark street, hearing an unexpected knock at the door, or working alone on a night job situations that cause accelerated heartbeats, heightened nervousness, and painful insecurity. Urban Americans worry greatly about becoming victims of violence. They already are victims of the fear of violence.

20
APPLE PIE

Is violence "as American as apple pie?" The apple pie statement is more than just another catchy phrase when we interpret it to mean that violence has had a pervasive influence in American history and represents a particularly serious problem today. In the context of this definition, the idea is anything but cockeyed.

Americans often give the apple pie thesis much more credence as a commentary on history than as a symbolic description of the current scene. They acknowledge a violent historical tradition, admitting that frontier adventures, battles with Indians, foreign wars, civil conflicts, gangster shootouts, and other bloody episodes loom large in the history books. Violence *is* an integral part of the American past, they agree, a factor as natural in the course of national development as good old-fashioned apple pie. Regarding the contemporary situation, however, Americans are more inclined to see the trees of violence than the forest. They concede many specific observations but avoid generalizing about the implications. They will agree that violent crime poses a growing problem and admit that the specter of presidential assassination worries them. Many think television shows and films feature too much violence, and they believe there are too many guns in private hands. And so on. But do these indications suggest that violence has become as American as apple pie? This continues to be difficult to accept because it calls for recognition that the diverse examples of violence that trouble them may be related. It is difficult to accept the notion that something very fundamental is going wrong. Each individual problem in isolation is disturbing enough, but a wide-lens view of the whole mess is downright unnerving.

The broad view is also quite frustrating because it leads to questions about the ad hoc firefighting technique Americans rely upon to handle their difficulties. A strategy that emphasizes specific efforts to put out violent fires when they appear, then settling back to await a new flareup, has obvious shortcomings. Consider, as an example, public reaction to recent changes in manifestations of violence. Over the last two decades, Public Enemy No. 1 on the violence list changed from collective, protest violence to individual, criminal violence. In the late 1960s mainstream Americans were most worried about the behavior of student antiwar demonstrators and black protestors from the ghettoes. They feared that greater anarchy and destruction would spread from the activities of politicized militants. Amid such turmoil and tension the apple pie theory sounded very plausible. Even historians supported this popular concept by showing the new developments were not anomalous, that they were not freak occurrences in a typically tranquil nation. Digging up a long record of civil disorders from the archives, historians demonstrated that the nation's past contained many similar incidents. Then, rather suddenly, civil disorders faded from view. As the situation settled in 1971-1972, many people reconsidered their alacrity to accept the apple pie theory. For those who had reserved their special fear and enmity for ideological protestors, the crisis seemed over. But others understood the persistence of violence. The problem did not really pass away; it took on other forms. Concerns that had been secondary to the civil protest issue in the 1960s now intensified. Cries for law and order continued, but they now pertained more to violent criminals than to civil protestors.

Public reaction to assassination attempts also illustrates vacillations in attitudes to the violence problem. Opinion varied from serious worry (usually around the time of the attacks) to guarded optimism that the nation could progress without suffering more tragic incidents (usually after extended periods when no assassination attempts were being reported). For example, when the King and Kennedy murders shocked the nation in 1968, thousands made table-slamming exclamations about the guilt of all and the need to prevent additional attempts on the lives of our leaders. During those troubled days, violence did indeed seem to be a broad-based, "apple pie" issue. Then the danger appeared to subside over the next four years. News of political assassinations no longer captured newspaper headlines. Relieved by the absence of Sirhan and Ray, some people even conjectured that the rash of assassinations during the 1960s was only a temporary contagion. Now the epidemic had passed, they said. But events during the presidential campaign of 1972 punctured this confidence, providing a harsh reminder of the persistent danger of assassination. The attempt on George Wallace's life showed that the trouble had not passed. Indeed, it seemed to reemerge, almost according to pattern, during presidential campaigns.

Airplane hijackings revealed another manifestation of violence and its shifting forms. The antisocial behavior of disturbed hostage-takers could appear in many guises, again confusing the public about the nature and control of violence. For a short time, during 1971 and 1972 particularly, skyjackings became a costly and seemingly ineradicable menace. Numerous gun-wielding passengers parachuted downward with bags of money, sent planes off to distant "revolutionary" countries, and interrupted airline schedules dramatically. Commercial plane travel became unusually hazardous when media reports made skyjackings sound like daily occurrences. Passengers typically began joking about visiting Cuba or Algeria as they boarded at airports. After thousands of angry letters to airlines, newspapers, and congressmen, the government organized stiff new security procedures at airports. Elaborate and expensive metal detection equipment and an army of special guards and baggage checkers created formidable obstacles for the hijackers, thus bringing the problem under control. When the fuselages of commercial airplanes became one of the few American environments in which stringent gun control regulations were in effect, challenges from eccentrics and criminals diminished significantly.

The basic impulse behind skyjacking did not die, however. Individuals found other ways to take hostages for monetary, ideological, or psychic gain. In the aftermath of a slowdown in skyjackings, armed robbers burst into several banks across the country, holding employees and bystanders as collateral for safe getaways. There were other, similar incidents. In Brooklyn, members of a radical Muslim sect holed up in John and Al's Sporting Goods store for forty-seven hours with a party of hostages and thousands of rounds of ammunition. They vowed to die for "victory and paradise" before their hostages escaped and the police forced them to surrender. In Dallas two escapees from a mental hospital held off police for many hours with guns and held twenty-two hostages for bargaining purposes. These were just a few of the violent threats to hostages. In short, criminals motivated by many of the same reasons as the skyjackers simply found other means and places to vent their hostilities. Like other manifestations of violence, the rise and decline of skyjacking showed how easily the challenges could change form. Efforts to eliminate the threat of violence by bearing down on a specific symptom produced only short-term successes.

The persistence of violence in American society gives force to the apple pie thesis. It makes the hackneyed comment, "America is a violent society," a relevant assessment of the country's situation. This comment must be refined, of course. The label applies quite appropriately as long as the assessor does not lose perspective or blow the issue out of proportion. Certainly other nations have a sorrier record on specific aspects of violence—civil disorders, foreign wars, assassinations, or whatever. Some countries will even surpass the United States in the general competition for ranking as the world's most violent society. Colombia, the home of *la violencia*, is one front-runner in this dubious rivalry. A favorable comparison with Colombia, however, is obviously no cause for celebration. When matched against similar societies—that is, the world's leading developed nations—the United States is a huge, modern-day Dodge City.

America's infatuation with material riches encourages a blindness to these national failures. The inclination is to look past cultural shortcomings and to regard economic development as the foremost criterion of success. With production of material goods as the major yardstick for measuring progress, during the 1960s and early 1970s many people viewed America's affluence as evidence that the country was doing something right. Richard Nixon clearly demonstrated this attitude in his reaction to the widespread domestic violence during his presidency. "There are those who say that this is the worst of times in which to live," said Nixon, complaining, "What pitying nonsense this is." He went on to affirm his optimism about the nation's future, stressing that most of the rest of the world was poor while America was rich. The brightest chapters in American history were yet to come, he promised, if only people wouldn't despair.[1] Just how Nixon's views could be interpreted in the light of continuing economic changes around the globe was not clear. What were the implications of nations like Sweden, West Germany, Switzerland, Japan, or Kuwait possibly achieving higher per capita incomes in the years ahead? How might Americans react to placing first among these countries in rates of violence and low or lowest in material well being per average citizen?

Even now, in a period of America's prominence among the world's richest nations, affluence offers only limited promises in an environment troubled by violence and anxiety. Material wealth loses much of its attraction when for its protection it requires fences, bolts, alarm systems, and guns. The satisfaction of monetary success dampens when well-paid laborers scurry out of the factories at 5 P.M., racing home before nightfall and leaving the industrial environs which turn into favorite mugging places. Certainly millions of poor people find the promise of improved life in an affluent society rather empty when the only neighborhoods they can afford to live in are violent concrete jungles.

Is the "apple pie" mess here to stay? Or can it be cleared up? Might concerted efforts end the pervasive influence of violence in American life? An extraordinarily large proportion of the American population prefers to leave resolution of such questions to fate, to the "natural" course of events. Leave things alone, they say; do not interfere. The problem will work itself out in time.

This laissez-faire approach to the difficulty is similar to the way Americans first handled their problems with big business in the nineteenth century: by worrying excessively about the fumbling hand of human intervention. Interference in social behavior will backfire, they say, warning that attempts to guide people and institutions, and redirect values and behavior bring the end of freedom and the beginning of tyranny. Like those who resignedly tolerated the robber barons, they prefer to leave the troubled environment relatively uncontrolled, unregulated, and in many cases almost uncriticized. Society looks on with resignation, accepting developments as the immutable workings of nature. People appear to be saying, "Violence is as American as free enterprise."[2]

Fatalism is now the ruling popular attitude. When people ask what society can do to diminish the problem of violence, far too often the answer is a variant of "nothing much." Violence is a harsh reality, they claim. You cannot wipe it out of man because it is *inside* him, a fact supported by the history books and daily newspapers. Be especially skeptical of suggestions to condition violence out of man, they warn, because that kind of effort brings a cure worse than the disease. By necessity, they say, it treads heavily on man's precious freedom and dignity.

Such explanations lead straight to the most debilitating implications of accepting an "apple pie" thesis as the last word on violence. When people believe violence is the "American way" and nothing much can change it, they stand immobile in the face of challenges and resigned to accepting their fate. They prepare their minds to live with violence instead of fighting it.

21

ACTION
AND INACTION

Is violence likely to remain as American as apple pie, or can society become more successful in controlling it? Are people capable of alleviating the problem effectively, or is violence so endemic that accommodation is necessary? The current rush of developments is pushing Americans closer and closer to confronting questions as stark as these. The stimuli for violence continue to accelerate at extraordinary rates. Fictional killings multiply on the tube and screen while real killings multiply on streets and in homes. New generations of children find ever larger collections of toy weapons in stores, while adolescents and adults find millions of real weapons available for purchase. And so it goes. *More* violence is likely to challenge Americans in future years. Is *more* resignation their likely response?

Whether Americans act energetically on this challenge depends considerably on how well they can handle the thorny contradictions between freedom and controls. This dilemma is at the heart of their debates over the appropriateness of concerted action. The major stimuli for violence relate to people's private lives and, thereby, relate to their sense of freedom. Americans are properly touchy about their notions of freedom, and they do not want to compromise them. How, then, can they act on the problem?

Consider the issues of media regulation and gun controls as illustrations of this dilemma. Each year millions of citizens receive increasingly detailed lessons in violence from television and the movies. Although we may agree with the goal of trying to show more respect for human life in media shows, any discussion of the means to accomplish this invites a chorus of angry disagreement. Tampering with the media's right to show what they want stirs concern about freedom of speech and excites warnings about censorship. To agree about ways to deal with media violence would be a prodigious achievement. Concerning the second example, we know that millions of Americans consider their ownership of firearms inviolable for two reasons: guns are private property and guns give a great deal of personal pleasure. Again, we are infringing on people's notions of freedom and rights when we talk about removing firearms from private possession.

Similar reactions arise in discussions on controlling any other aspect of violence. Debates usually provoke angry charges about encroachments upon fundamental human liberties. Hence, it is a concern for freedom, a very respectable concern, that represents one of the most formidable obstacles to action against violence.

This dilemma relates directly to the traditional and popular philosophical debate over freedom versus controls. To find some comfort in deciding how far society should go in trying to manage violent stimuli and check violent behavior, the suppositions in this debate ought to be faced squarely. In other words, can freedom and controls work together or are they mutually exclusive? To examine this question, we will briefly probe the ideas of two individuals whose views are, in many respects, diametrically opposed on the subject. Their polemics throw light on some of the most challenging difficulties. The two controversial figures are, not surprisingly, B. F. Skinner and Rollo May.

B. F. Skinner, the Harvard psychologist, does not usually

deal specifically with violence in his writings, but his basic ideas are relevant to the general controversy about violence. Skinner challenges the critics of controls at the most basic level: in their assumption that controls destroy freedom. More than any other individual, Skinner has provoked new questioning about the popular catchwords that people often defend without much thought. The title of his controversial book on the subject, *Beyond Freedom and Dignity*, hints at his explosive thesis. In Skinner's opinion, the popular notions of freedom and dignity are already obsolescent.[1]

Essentially, Skinner advocates the technology of social science to improve man's condition. Scientific approaches can help greatly to encourage positive, constructive behavioral characteristics, he argues. By organizing communities along the lines of sound psychological techniques, experimenting to find which approaches work best for the good of the whole and rewarding behavior judged socially desirable, Skinner believes science can outline a better way of life. For example, effective education of the young or careful conditioning of prisoners (to reward positive attitudes) can help significantly to "control" the characteristics which lead to violent crime.

Skinner does not wince at tough words like conditioning and controls. When used intelligently, he asserts, controls can provide much healthier and happier social environments than society now enjoys. In fact, argues Skinner, we are already under the influence of controls—controls often directed from very questionable sources. Hucksters, advertisers, politicians, demagogues, and others know the tricks of conditioning audiences, and they exploit their knowledge for dubious purposes. Then why not consider conditioning for more commendable goals, he asks? "Controlling" people for positive social purposes will not rob them of their freedom and dignity, he says, since they do not truly experience freedom and dignity anyway. Although people do not realize it, there are innumerable subtle conditioning forces that already very strongly influence their behavior. Thus, in modern times the words freedom and dignity are an emotion-laden phrase that rallies people in defense of what is largely an illusion. Individuals, Skinner asserts, could enjoy much more meaningful freedom and dignity, not to mention happiness, in a controlled environment.

Understandably, Skinner's thesis excites an avalanche of criticism. Many observers see elements of *1984* or a *Brave New World* in his model society. They reject any notion of controlling people, worrying about what kind of individuals would obtain power as controllers. Although Skinner is confident that benevolent philosopher kings would manage the conditioning stimuli, many naturally question whether the controllers might turn out to be men like Adolph Hitler—one of the most notorious controllers from history. Critics also ask how an elaborate conditioning program would affect the people scheduled for controls. They point to Alex's experience in Anthony Burgess's book, *A Clockwork Orange*, as an illustration of the perils of allowing self-righteous social manipulators to make guinea pigs of human beings. When behaviorists in *A Clockwork Orange* tinkered with the psyche of what seemed to be an incorrigibly violent criminal in prison, they stripped him of the few things that were still his own—his individual freedom and dignity. By temporarily conditioning the violence out of Alex, they created the equivalent of a psychological straitjacket. In a sense Alex became as mechanical as clockwork and no more alive, symbolically speaking, than an orange. He could respond reflexively to the signals of his controllers, but he lacked an essential human quality, the capacity to determine his own behavior.

Of course, we don't need elaborate details to imagine the shortcomings of a Skinnerian utopia. Skinner's case is so extreme and its problems are so patent that one wonders whether there might be a little provocative game-playing here.

Although there are some Skinnerian fanatics running about these days who would always defend Skinner's arguments, we should ask: is the master himself so oblivious to reality? Skinner is quite serious in his statements, but it seems likely that the controversial psychologist does not blindly believe his ideas could work to perfection. Perhaps he recognizes the role of the utopian theorizer—to prod, to provoke, and to stir people into questioning popular assumptions. Whether intentionally or inadvertently, Skinner has angered his many critics into responding with precisely the same old conditioned platitudes one would expect to hear. In a sense, the reactions to Skinner are far more instructive than any insights he, himself, offers. These days few philosophical discussions on freedom or free will are conducted without individuals loudly repudiating Skinner's theory and declaring their love for freedom. Announcing one's abhorrence for Skinnerian ideals is a prerequisite for intellectual respectability in these encounters. The eager desire to establish personal distance from Skinner for all to see reveals how sensitive the issue has become. Hardly anyone wishes to appear standing even one step "beyond freedom and dignity."

By taking Skinner altogether seriously, discussants often engage in an absurd exercise. Skinner's thesis can easily be knocked down as a straw man when viewed as a realistic proposal for solutions. But why consider such an extremist argument at face value? Why try to fight a list of absurdities by responding with more absurdities? By taking Skinner as something of a Devil's Advocate, on the other hand, we may find that he sheds some light on today's nagging problems. His answers may not be satisfactory, but his questions may be on the right track. With respect to violence, perhaps popular American thought *is* covered with beclouding clichés about protecting human dignity from the abuses of social experiment and change. Many Americans incessantly proclaim the need for vigilance lest they fall into a Skinnerian-style nightmare, yet they are already dropping deeper and deeper into a whirlpool of violence and bloodshed that is very real. The consequences are likely to be further abridgement of their freedoms, both in their inability to enjoy life free from the threat of violence and in various limitations on their civil liberties as society moves reluctantly toward compromising fundamental human rights in efforts to catch or deter violent criminals.

These credits notwithstanding, we must admit that Skinner's style is too abrasive and his solutions too authoritarian to find popular acceptance. Overall, Skinner is far too much the extremist to offer palatable and workable answers to the problem of violence.

From the other end of the determinism versus free will

spectrum comes the voice of Rollo May, a noted psychiatrist. Through his influential book *Power and Innocence: A Search for the Sources of Violence*, May asks many of the same questions Skinner asks, but proffers very different answers.[2] Predictably enough, initial responses to May's book were very different, too. While many reviewers and readers found Skinner's work offensive and frightening, they greeted May's study as an insightful, helpful treatise on the issues. The tremendously favorable reception accorded May's work shows that America's intellectual community, like the national community in general, remains faithful to many of the old laissez-faire beliefs about handling problems of violence. The popularity of still another sophisticated warning against broadbased social action, this time seasoned with the terminology of psychoanalysis, demonstrates the difficulty of moving a reluctant society toward facing violence head-on.

In *Power and Innocence* May excoriates Skinner's most offensive language and recommendations while phrasing his own interpretation of the issues in terms people like to hear. Beware of utopianism, May warns. Look skeptically at the man who tells us that "when we develop a society which trains us rightly, we'll be in fine shape." With persuasive eloquence, May criticizes the behaviorists' chatter about controlling people as psychologists control rats. A Skinnerian perspective makes light of the human element, of the dignity of individuals, and fails to recognize how appalling it is to compromise that dignity by trying to subject people to subtle and insidious controls. A reviewer of May's book summarized the spirit of this criticism by warning that "many social engineers and behaviorists would like to believe that free will is dead."[3]

To this point, May's critical observations are praiseworthy, though hardly original. Essentially, they are motherhood and apple pie comments endorsing free will and declaring faith in human potential. May's recommendations for long-range goals are also both laudable and familiar. He calls for a more humane society and, in vague terms, endorses a change in values. Nothing to dispute here. In addition, May stresses the importance of a psychiatrist's sense of understanding and tolerance when he deals with violent people in individual therapy. Again, this is fine. But what else should be done about violence? Through all the book's wit and wisdom, charm and eloquence, May finishes by not recommending very much at all. When all is said and done, it is essentially a laissez-faire profile that shows through the rich prose.

May's position becomes manifest in his treatment of a variety of controversial topics about violence that have received attention here. Regarding the fundamental debate over innate versus learned violence, for example, May prefers the Lorenz-Ardrey-Storr approach, rephrasing a now familiar argument. You cannot train aggressiveness out of children, claims May. Aggressiveness and violence have their function: they serve survival purposes. People need to work out their tensions, he says, and it is unhealthy to suppress their drive toward such release. Indeed, there is no use denying "with our minds the 'secret love of violence' which is present in all of us in some form," May asserts.[4]

Applying this thesis to specific issues, May seeks appreciation of the public's thirst for violence in TV programs and movies. It develops out of an interest in the realities of life, he explains, and those realities cannot be denied. "Mass communications hold a mirror up to ourselves," May claims, "and if we break this 'mirror,' we will be left only with ourselves."[5] If some people identify with gangsters in the movies, society should not be disturbed; rather, people should try to understand it. In these situations many movie buffs find vicarious release of their secret dreams of revenge, dreams that develop out of their frustrations within a society that thwarts and oppresses them. We should not make the media scapegoats, since, as everyone should know, violence has long been a focus of fictional commentary, from Sophocles' dramas to Shakespeare's plays and Grimm's fairy tales.

May is interestingly permissive when dealing with the violence of individuals from underprivileged backgrounds or people with grievances over economic, social, or political matters. We should realize that violence offers psychic as well as potential material gains for these groups, he says. Observers of the violence problem have not appreciated this need adequately, argues May. They react almost reflexively to reports of attacks and bloodshed with emotional condemnations of violence. "Why has the positive side of aggression been so consistently repressed and the negative side so emphasized," May asks. In the case of black militants, for example, he wonders why people fail to recognize that "violence is the only way for blacks not only to throw off the yoke of colonial powers but also to develop some unity among themselves."[6] May's interpretation of this problem has a familiar ring, of course. It closely parallels Frantz Fanon's philosophy, the idea that violent expression of anger and frustration often fosters a healthy feeling of self-esteem. If nothing else, an outpouring of aggression helps to affirm oneself and to assert individual freedom and dignity.

The overall thrust of May's analysis suggests that social activism cannot do much about the problem of violence. Regarding individuals, May recommends psychotherapeutic treatment for the most troubled, and public appreciation of the frustrations and inner drives that motivate their behavior. On a more general level, May recites the familiar plea for more attention to problems of poverty and inequality. But the psychiatrist noticeably fails to recommend more direct action against violence. He makes no proposals that go beyond individual therapy to reassess the vast cultural stimuli to violence. He shows little enthusiasm for efforts to counteract machismo standards, the messages of media fiction, the gun cult, or a host of other relevant factors. While paying lip service to the need for changes in the value system, May does not sanction the kind of action that would really make changes count. After all the clever metaphors, psychological examples, and illustrations from history, May's argument leaves us where we started. The old endorsement of laissez-faire biases comes out again, encouraging us to marvel at the irony of things and realize that society cannot do very much to change man's future.

So here we stand, still immobile and still watching the conflict of extremes. But is there no alternative but the cold, calculating activism of Skinner or the compassionate but skeptical inaction of May? Must we choose between social science manipulation and humanistic individualism? Obviously, there are alternatives. Evaluating possible solutions to a major social problem does not require strict adherence to one or another extreme school of thought. Surely the problem of violence can be described in a critical yet optimistic manner, identifying the serious factors that have contributed to the difficulties while, at the same time, suggesting action that can effectively alleviate them.

For an example of such a work, one which combines compassion for individuals with enthusiasm for the potential of society to pull itself together and improve people's lives, there is a long-forgotten book whose ideas have stood the test of time. In the 1920s Raymond B. Fosdick addressed some of the issues under question here with insight and prescience. Fosdick understood the unpleasant consequences of continuing to hide from the problems, yet he did not unquestioningly recommend social science approaches as a panacea. Fosdick stated his case in plain and tolerant language, relatively free of the professional jargon and chauvinistic rhetoric characteristic of today's debate. His book is as relevant to the problems of violence today as it was when it first appeared in 1929. He titled his treatise *The Old Savage in the New Civilization.*[7]

Fosdick stressed the importance of both major ideas in the present debate on violence. He combined the compassion for human dignity with the hope that science could help direct man out of his troubles. Fosdick talked about the phenomenon popularly identified today as cultural lag—people's inability to keep the social components of their civilization apace with fast-moving developments in their technological civilization. Looking sadly over mankind's bloody record, Fosdick emphasized the irony that great failures occurred at precisely the time when prospects seemed especially good for improving the material quality of life. Unfortunately, men persisted in acting like barbarians in an age of technological sophistication. The reasons for this cultural lag were easy to see. While societies could accomplish revolutions in transportation and communications, they continued to glorify "all that is base and brutal in mankind." To continue this brutishness portended serious trouble, thought Fosdick, especially in view of new advances in weapons technology. The tendency of people to capitalize on weapons improvements to become more efficient in destroying each other glaringly showed man's failure to control science for his own benefit.

This pattern prompted a disturbing question about the future. Was man to be the master of the civilization he had created or its victim? Fosdick saw the potential for an optimistic answer to the question. He believed societies could prevent larger orgies of violence in the future, whether the problems involved violent crimes by individuals or wars between nations. Work toward a truly civilized way of life required restrictions on aggressive tendencies and social controls that could provide people with better security against violence.

Fosdick lamented the continuing reluctance of many people even to try to change the course of events. Guidelines for possible action were at hand, he asserted, but people refused to use them. Why not try to put the lessons of social research to work, he asked? Couldn't impressive contributions of the physical sciences be matched, at least to a degree, with implementation of some major contributions from the social sciences? "We eagerly apply to our methods of living the conclusions of the natural sciences," noted Fosdick, but "we scorn rather than apply the conclusions of the social sciences."[8] He attributed much of this reluctance to man's emotional marriage to tradition:

> Man is so lethargic, so suspicious of innovation in everything that is related to himself that only with difficulty can he be persuaded to desert any fraction of his inherited practices and routine. . . . The forces of established order are marshalled in full army against change. It makes no difference how necessary the change be, how essential to the vitality and life of the social order; its foes remain implacable. . . . We raise our hands to invoke the sanctity of old customs and glorify the god of things as they are.[9]

Fosdick's study pinpoints the fundamental problem—the persistently fatalistic, hands-in-the-air attitudes about making progress against violence. In these attitudes violence is made to be something close to original sin; it always has been part of man's nature, always will be, and there is nothing society can do to change it. But Fosdick's entire analysis radiates welcome skepticism for this basic assumption. He raises questions that bring to mind the poignant message in Shirley Jackson's powerful little story, "The Lottery."

Jackson's tale involves an imaginary little town which holds a "lottery" every year. As the dialogue progresses, we learn that some townsfolk have begun to question the annual practice. They cite the example of other villages where citizens talk about giving up the tradition. "Pack of crazy fools," snorts an old man leery of the idea of change:

> Listening to young folks, nothing's good enough for *them*. Next thing you know, they'll be wanting to go back to living in caves, nobody work any more live *that* way for a while. Used to be a saying about "lottery in June, corn be heavy soon?" First thing you know, we'd all be eating stewed chickenweed and acorns. There's *always* been a lottery," he added petulantly. "Bad enough to see young Joe Summers up there joking with everybody."
>
> "Some places have already quit lotteries," Mrs. Adams said.
>
> "Nothing but trouble in *that*," Old Man Warner said stoutly. "Pack of young fools."[10]

At the end of the story, Jackson reveals what the lottery tradition was all about: it involved the annual selection of a townsperson to be stoned to death in public.

If one heeds Jackson's message and stresses the potential for significant change, just what should we do about violence? For Fosdick the answer involved implementing some of the lessons learned in the social sciences. Obviously, social science research has come a long way since he recommended action. After all the work of past decades, we should be capable of testing the implications with a lot more understanding and confidence than even Fosdick could in 1929. American society already has a wealth of research information available from investigations funded by millions of dollars from taxpayers and private foundations. Many of these projects took years to complete. Moreover, conclusions from this research are also available—assessments found in the final pages of hundreds of journal articles and monographs. Beyond that, many committee reports and recommendations from special commissions remain on library shelves as typical examples of the "big study, little action" syndrome. Students of violence often comment in frustration about the similarities of the massive National Crime Commission report to the Wickersham Report of 1931 or the Kerner Commission report to the Chicago Commission on Race Relations' report of 1922.

Obviously, everyone can find much to dispute the recommendations of these commissions or the major articles and books on violence. Such skepticism is a tribute to the finest traditions of scholarly inquiry. There must be continued assessment of all proposed remedies and constant revision of many hypotheses. But speculation about solutions cannot drag on forever. Eventually, some reasonable proposals should be tested in real situations. Certainly enough principal, tentative conclusions emerge from the research to make intelligent large-scale application and experimentation possible. It now seems appropriate to work in earnest to implement some proposals to alleviate violence. After all, the corollary of research is action.

Lest we exalt our social scientists as the heroes of this situation, a few critical words are in order. Many social scientists undermine the idea of action almost as much as the laissez-faire theorists, but for different reasons. The problem often involves preoccupation with professional detachment. Far too many social researchers enjoy boldly challenging the theories of colleagues but are squeamish about challenging the very problems they are theorizing about in the first place. Often, when someone asks them what should be done about a specific problem of violence, they plead an academic version of "no comment." It is not their job to make recommendations, they claim; only observation and interpretation of behavior patterns are appropriate. In their eyes the model of an outstanding social scientist is one who tries to study the problem objectively while eschewing personal recommendation of ways to alleviate it. Toying with policy recommendations brings in their own biases and compromises their role as objective scientists, they say. Besides, they add, social scientists do not have true answers to the problems anyway, since research results are inconclusive, and there is still need for further investigation.

One wonders how anyone could make a single recommendation with all these reservations in mind. When does the social researcher who admirably searches for objectivity expect to find proof positive on his hunches? Is he not likely to find that, when dealing with human relationships, the word proof is a relative term? Social research may produce helpful indications but usually not unanimous verdicts, conclusive evidence, or definitive answers. Somewhere along the way, researchers need to take a stand, basing their judgment on the best level-headed evaluation of the evidence they can muster. Issues can always be avoided with calls for "more study," a recommendation which gives relief to those who fear acting on problems and often leads to deferring excellent opportunities for experimental action. These opportunities are not easily regained. Indeed, many social scientists criticize their colleagues for perpetuating the "more research," pass-the-buck attitude. In *The Coming Crisis in Western Society*, for example, Alvin Gouldner chides his fellow sociologists for their repetitive insistence on detachment and separation from policy decisions. Gouldner sees the present challenges requiring more than simple recording of behavioral patterns accompanied by declarations of neutrality on questions about action.[11] Thomas E. Bittler supports the spirit of this criticism, warning: "No longer can [the behavioral scientist] permit himself to be merely an observer of human events. Increasingly, his energies should turn toward translating information into action. Nowhere is this need for his contribution so urgent as is the control of human violence."[12]

What are those recommendations for action to alleviate violence? Let us conclude with a very general response, because it better focuses on the main issues. Plans for action which are quite specific can easily distract attention from the principal questions, provoking a multitude of disputes about intricacies of execution. The inevitable picayune questions about implementation arise over each small suggestion. To avoid this distraction, let us take a cue from a nineteenth-century reformer who faced similar frustrations. When James G. Birney first campaigned for the abolition of slavery in the 1830s, he had difficulty keeping the discussions on the major issue. His purpose seemed plain and defensible enough: he aimed to impress audiences with the need to abolish slavery. But with almost every appearance his central idea seemed to get lost under an avalanche of questions about the complexities of *executing* abolition. How much would it cost, people asked? Would slaveholders agree to abolition? Might proposals for reform conflict with certain laws and constitutional regulations? Etc, etc. Birney faced the same kinds of tangent-leading questions on the abolition of slavery that today's reformers face on the issue of the mitigation of violence. In time, Birney found a solution, and passed his advice on to a fellow abolitionist, Gerrit Smith:

> Connect with emancipation, any other scheme, which must be made successful, or proved that it will be so, before slavehold-ing is utterly condemned, and you will be fought on *that* ground by the adversary. Then he will foil you, in spite of all you can do. . . . He will meet you on its practicality—he will dispute your facts—he will impeach your testimony—he will bring counter-evidence—he will baffle you to the end of the world, whilst in the whole discussion, the great lever that God has given to move men's hearts, the sin of oppression in any and every form, is utterly unused.[13]

Those who fret about violence could well consider a similar approach when making proposals for action.

And now to those recommendations. In general form they are very simple. They are also quite obvious by now. In brief, we may conclude that Americans should draw back from trying to excuse acts of violence as inevitable consequences of man's innate condition. They should be less tolerant of the sanctions for violence and romanticizing of aggression, especially the associa-tion of it with machismo and heroism. Contemptuous attitudes toward human life and orgies of bloodshed and killing should pass from media tubes and screens. Finally, lethal firearms should be removed from the possession of most citizens.

There is nothing new or unusual about these proposals. If

almost nothing significant has been done to put them into effect over recent years, it is not just because of disputes over the fine points of implementation but also because of indecision about whether anything should be done at all. Laissez-faire sentiment remains strong. The details of action would not be difficult to work out if consensus could be achieved on the fundamental wisdom of going ahead in the first place.

Relatively speaking, the remedies suggested here would not be costly. For example, deemphasizing the destructive aspects of the machismo ethic or removing gratuitous violence from television programming do not require huge dollar expenditures. Even the cost of an effective gun control program is miniscule in comparison to what the use and fear of guns are costing Americans yearly. The monumental obstacles to action on these fronts involve much more than money. Efforts to upgrade the quality of American life by concentrating on economic remedies while neglecting the attitudes that condone violence are likely to fail. For example, effective treatment of urban decay and poverty requires much more than just huge dollar appropriations. Economic improvements will not necessarily usher in an era of domestic peace and tranquility, as some pages from recent American history demonstrate. As students of diverse cultures know (particularly anthropologists), brotherhood and dignity in human relationships can thrive in some of the poorest cultures. The quality of life involves much more than just material wealth. It implies, too, a cultural ethos that stresses respect for other persons. To say that there is much more potential for civilized human relationships than is currently realized even in America's most wretched ghettoes is not to defend poverty. Campaigns against economic inequality deserve the strongest push possible, but it is important to remember that they are far short of constituting a complete answer to the problems. City life in America can be much safer and more satisfying without rehabilitating a single brownstone apartment building or constructing a single new recreation center. Friends of the poor give questionable service when they demand high priority for spending on urban blight and antipoverty programs, yet dismiss appeals to effect changes in the violence ethic as voices of fascism, racism, or police statism. The popular expressions of fear and anger over crime and violence are not just diversionary efforts to draw attention away from more fundamental problems. Law and order *are* fundamental problems. The very success of treating other social ills depends largely on their resolution.

We should be cautious not to lay disproportionately heavy blame on the contribution of the poor to violence. Obviously, mainstream Americans are responsible for the problem too. They are not models for the less privileged when they furnish their own children with abundant toy tanks, bombs, and guns and support the firearms cult. Much too frequently they welcome new media violence without question, and they do little to challenge the general glorification of violence in American culture. Some of "the best and the brightest" among them designed and defended the Vietnam War policy through arguments pregnant with machismo images. Mainstream Americans do not deserve warm sympathy when they grumble about incidents of violence yet at the same time sanction the value system that helps violence to thrive. With notable inconsistency they fret over society's spreading malaise and the way it increasingly threatens to affect them personally.

One can easily conjecture about a bleak and disturbing future if American society continues on its present course. The scenario looks something like this:

> Violent crime will become even more serious. In turn, police departments, courts, and prisons will enlarge and the law will jettison more civil liberties in order to capitalize on opportunities to catch criminals. Guns will become even more common appurtenances of modern living as citizens load up to protect themselves. Over the years there will be more presidential assassinations as angry and deranged men blast more holes in the fabric of democracy as well as in the bodies of leaders. Bomb explosions will rock public buildings as confused individuals plan indiscriminate attacks to call attention to their personal grievances. There will be more wars over petty, emotional matters, and generations following these wars will again look back wondering how the hostilities could have been

justified. In short, many, many Americans will suffer serious injury or die unnecessarily. And many, many others will suffer seriously simply from the fear of violence.

At times these predictions will appear inordinately bleak. Trends do not usually move in a linear direction. There are ups and downs, periods of optimism and periods of despair. We should expect halcyon years aplenty when many will enjoy a temporary sense of relief. It is likely that there will be stretches of time notable for the lack of civil, collective violence and fairly long intervals when there will not be a single attempt on the life of a president or a presidential candidate. Violent crime rates may even dip significantly. But the roots of trouble are too deep for these hopeful signs to prevail over the tendency toward violence, fear, and cultural deterioration. Over the long haul this condition will seriously undermine the quality of American life. In a more dramatic sense, it will bring a veritable decline in American civilization.

Perhaps this scenario is too melodramatic. Certainly the situation does not have to turn out this way. A civilization's future is not inevitable. People make it, and people are capable of directing it for their own benefit. American history, as we know it, is a rich and exciting saga of people who allowed problems to creep up on them but, eventually, developed the determination to overcome them. The task now is for Americans to refuse to excuse violence and accommodate to it. They must stop trying to live with the problem and start wrestling with it. Leo Tolstoy understood their difficulty long ago when he said, "Men *are* sincere in their hatred of cruelties, but they don't know how to abolish them or lack the courage to alter their mode of life."[14] Nowadays we know a lot more about ways to abolish cruelties, and, hopefully, we have not run short on courage.

NOTES

Chapter 1: The Problem

[1]*Circus*, August 1972.
[2]*Philadelphia Bulletin*, June 13, 1972.
[3]*The New York Times*, October 9, 1973.
[4]*Newsweek*, November 27, 1972.
[5]Lewis Yablonski, *The Violent Gang* (New York, 1972), p. 7.
[6]*The New York Times*, May 16, 1972.
[7]*Philadelphia Bulletin*, June 14, 1972.

Chapter 2: Fear

[1]*The New York Times*, March 27, 1964; A.M. Rosenthal, *Thirty-Eight Witnesses* (New York, 1964).
[2]Ibid., March 28, 1964; Bibb Latané and John M. Darley, *The Unresponsive Bystander* (New York, 1970); Stanley Milgram, "The Experience of Living in Cities," *Science* (1970): 167, 1461-1468; David Abrahamsen, M.D., *Our Violent Society* (New York, 1970), pp. 38-39.
[3]*The New York Times*, March 28, 1964.
[4]Ibid.
[5]Ibid., May 25, 1972.

[6]*Philadelphia Bulletin,* March 17, 1972, March 18, 1972.

[7]Ibid., March 30, 1972.

[8]Ibid., March 17, 1972.

[9]Ibid.

[10]*The New York Times,* April 23, 1972. Also see Donald J. Mulvihill and Melvin M. Tumlin (co-directors) and Lynn A. Curtis (assistant director), *Crimes of Violence,* II. A Staff Report Submitted to the National Commission on the Causes and Prevention of Violence (Washington, D.C., 1969), p. 220.

[11]*Crime in the United States: Uniform Crime Reports—1970* (Washington, D.C., 1970), pp. 2-3.

[12]*The New York Times,* June 24, 1970.

[13]Ibid., November 19 and 20, 1972.

[14]See, for example, the listings under the section called "Crime and Justice" in the *Washington Post.*

[15]*Philadelphia Bulletin,* April 19, 1972.

[16]Ibid., June 9, 1972.

[17]*Newsweek,* March 8, 1971, p. 29.

[18]*The New York Times,* May 28, 1972.

[19]For examples of murder cases involving witnesses of crimes, see: *Philadelphia Bulletin,* March 28, 1972, June 7, 1972; *Cleveland Plain Dealer,* November 15, 1971; *The New York Times,* March 31, 1972, April 25, 1972.

[20]Morton Hunt, *The Mugging* (New York, 1972), p. ix. In a poll conducted in New York City by Daniel Yankelovich, Inc., during the last two weeks of November 1973, respondents called crime the problem of greatest personal concern. Sixty-three percent of the respondents named crime. Second was drugs (28 percent). Inflation and the high cost of living scored 20 percent. *The New York Times,* January 16, 1974.

[21]*The New York Times,* February 4, 1972.

[22]Ibid., May 25, 1972.

[23]Ibid., December 31, 1970.

[24]Ibid., January 30, 1973.

[25]Ibid., February 1, 1973.

[26]Ibid., December 22, 1971.

[27]*To Establish Justice, To Insure Domestic Tranquility,* Final Report of the National Commission on the Causes and Prevention of Violence (New York, 1970), pp. 38-39.

[28]*Newsweek,* March 8, 1971, p. 29.

[29]Ibid., February 8, 1971, p. 31.

³⁰*The New York Times,* January 1, 1972.

³¹Ibid., January 1, 1972, April 21, 1974.

³²Ibid., January 1, 1972, October 9, 1972.

³³*Newsweek,* September 25, 1972.

³⁴Charles N. Barnard, "The Fortification of Suburbia Against the Burglar in the Bushes," *Saturday Review of Society* (May 1973).

³⁵*Cleveland Plain Dealer,* November 25, 1971; Carlo M. Sardella, "Will America Become a Land of Electric Gates and Guard Dogs?" *Family Weekly,* January 14, 1973.

³⁶U.S. President's Commission on Law Enforcement and Administration of Justice, *The Challenge of Crime in a Free Society* (Washington, D.C., 1967), p. v; "Walled Suburbs," *Newsweek,* September 5, 1972.

³⁷Ovid Demaris, *America the Violent* (New York, 1970), p. 332.

³⁸*Cleveland Plain Dealer,* November 24, 1971.

³⁹*The New York Times,* May 24, 1973.

⁴⁰Mulvihill and Tumlin, *Crimes of Violence,* p. 405.

⁴¹Ramsey Clark, *Crime in America: Observations on Its Nature, Causes, Prevention and Control* (New York, 1970), p. 16.

⁴²*To Establish Justice, To Insure Domestic Tranquility,* p. 16.

Chapter 3: Crime

¹Carl Bridenbaugh, *Cities in the Wilderness: The First Century of Urban Life In America, 1625-1742* (New York, 1971), pp. 69-70.

²Charles Lockwood, "Crime—100 Years Ago," *The New York Times,* June 5, 1972, p. 31. Arthur Meier Schlesinger, *The Rise of the City: 1878-1898* (New York, 1933), p. 434.

³Daniel Bell, *The End of Ideology: On the Exhaustion of Political Ideas in the Fifties* (New York, 1960), pp. 151-154, 170-174. Fred P. Graham comments on the implications of popular doubts about increases in crime in Hugh Davis Graham and Ted Robert Gurr, "A Contemporary History of American Crime," in *The History of Violence in America* (New York, 1969), p. 488.

⁴Bell, *The End of Ideology,* pp. 138-151.

⁵*Newsweek,* June 7, 1971, p. 28; Gay Talese, *Honor Thy Father* (New York, 1972); Francis A. Ianni, *A Family Business: Kinship and Social Control in Organized Crime* (New York, 1972).

⁶*Newsweek,* July 12, 1971, p. 30; *The New York Times,* April 20, 1972, August 13, 1972, January 18, 1973.

[7]*Crime in the United States: Uniform Crime Reports—1970* (Washington, D.C., 1971), pp. 2-21.

[8]"Increases in the crime rate as reported by the FBI for the first three months of 1974 were particularly large. The figures for serious crime (murder, forcible rape, aggravated assault, robbery, burglary, larceny-theft and automobile theft) were 10 percent in cities of 100,000 or more, 22 percent in suburban areas, 18 percent in rural areas, and 29 percent in small towns with 10,000 or fewer inhabitants. *Houston Post,* July 15, 1974.

[9]Hugh Davis Graham (ed.) and Stephen Paul Mahinka and Dean William Rudoy (associate eds.), *Violence: The Crisis in American Confidence* (Baltimore and London, 1971), pp. 54-59, 69.

[10]"Face to Face on the Issues: Law and Justice," *Life,* June 9, 1972, 56., Hunt, *The Mugging,* pp. 403-404.

[11]*Newark* (Ohio) *Advocate,* February 5, 1973.

[12]*Miami Herald,* January 4, 1973; *The New York Times,* September 20, 1972. One senator barricaded his doors at home at night for fear of murders. *Newark* (Ohio) *Advocate,* February 5, 1973.

[13]Donald J. Mulvihill and Melvin M. Tumlin (co-directors) and Lynn A. Curtis (assistant director), *Crimes of Violence,* II. A Staff Report Submitted to the National Commission on the Causes and Prevention of Violence (Washington, D.C., 1969), pp. xxvi-xxvii, 7-19; James S. Campbell, Joseph R. Sahid, and David Stang, *Law and Order Reconsidered,* Report of the Task Force on Law Enforcement to the National Commission on the Causes and Prevention of Violence (Washington, D.C., n.d.), pp. 266-269; Ramsey Clark, *Crime In America: Observations On Its Nature, Causes, Prevention and Control* (New York, 1970), p. 45; U.S. President's Commission on Law Enforcement and Administration of Justice, *The Challenge of Crime in a Free Society* (Washington, D.C., 1967), p. v; *The New York Times,* May 15, 1972; *Newsweek,* February 8, 1971, p. 60. During this period of disputes over the figures, public suspicion that crime was increasing significantly went against the grain of trends in the FBI reports. *The New York Times,* January 14 and 16, 1973. Also see *Time,* October 23, 1972, and *The New York Times,* November 23, 1972, March 7, 1973.

[14]*The New York Times,* July 25, 1971.

[15]Ibid, April 19, 1973, April 27, 1973.

[16]*Philadelphia Bulletin,* April 15, 1974; *Newark* (Ohio) *Advocate,* April 15, 1974.

[17]*Houston Chronicle,* September 10, 1974.

[18]*The Challenge of Crime in a Free Society,* p. x.

[19]Milton S. Eisenhower, "Introduction and Overview," in Graham, Mahinka, and Rudoy, *Violence*, p. viii.

[20]George M. Carstairs, "Overcrowding and Human Aggression," in Hugh Davis Graham and Ted Robert Gurr, *The History of Violence in America* (New York, 1969), pp. 755-763.

[21]Desmond Morris, *The Human Zoo* (New York, St. Louis and San Francisco, 1969), Introduction and pp. 8-12.

[22]Ibid., p. 39; Desmond Morris, *The Naked Ape: A Zoologist's Study of the Human Animal* (New York, 1968), pp. 238-240.

[23]Elton B. McNeil, "Violence and Human Development," in Marvin E. Wolfgang (ed.), *Patterns of Violence*, The Annals of the American Academy of Political and Social Science (March 1966), p. 151.

[24]Carstairs, "Overcrowding and Human Aggression," p. 752.

[25]Mulvihill, et al., *Crimes of Violence*, II, p. xxvii.

[26]*Cleveland Plain Dealer*, November 10, 1971.

[27]*The New York Times*, July 26, 1970. Associated Press Special Correspondent Hugh A. Mulligan notes that many American visitors compliment Londoners on living in "the most civilized city in the world," *Newark* (Ohio) *Advocate*, January 17, 1973.

[28]Mulvihill, et al., *Crimes of Violence*, II, p. xxvii.

[29]*Newsweek*, June 21, 1971, p. 24.

Chapter 4: Law and Order

[1]Richard Maxwell Brown, "The American Vigilante Tradition," *The History of Violence in America: Historical and Comparative Perspectives* (New York, Toronto, and London, 1969), pp. 154-217. James S. Campbell, Joseph R. Sahid, and David Stang, *Law and Order Reconsidered,* Report of the Task Force on Law Enforcement to the National Commission on The Causes and Prevention of Violence (Washington, D.C., n.d.), p. 359; "Political Violence in the United States," in James F. Kirkham, Sheldon G. Levy, and William J. Crotty, *Assassination and Political Violence*, A Report to the National Commission on the Causes and Prevention of Violence (New York, 1970), pp. 214-218; George R. Stewart, *Committee of Vigilance: Revolution in San Francisco, 1851* (New York, 1964).

[2]*The New York Times*, November 17, 1971; *Newsweek*, August 16, 1971.

[3]*The New York Times*, August 21 and 23, 1971.

[4]Ibid., April 16, 1968, p. 32.

[5]Ibid., July 23, 1973.

[6]Ibid., November 14, 1972.

[7]*Newsweek,* January 15, 1973; *The New York Times,* January 12, 1973.

[8]*Report of the National Advisory Commission on Civil Disorders* (New York, 1968), pp. 40-108.

[9]"The Powderkeg in the Cities," *U.S. News and World Report,* July 5, 1971.

[10]James S. Campbell, et al., *Law and Order Reconsidered,* pp. 291, 298-299, 336. Also see Jerome H. Skolnick, *The Politics of Protest* (New York, n.d.), p. xxiv.

[11]Daniel Walker, *Rights in Conflict* (Washington, D.C., 1969).

[12]Alphonso Pinkney, *The American Way of Violence* (New York, 1972), pp. 116-127.

[13]Paul Chevigny, *Police Power: Police Abuses in New York City* (New York, 1969), pp. 277, 283.

[14]U.S. President's Commission on Law Enforcement and Administration of Justice, *The Challenge of Crime in a Free Society* (Washington, D.C., 1967), p. ix. Also see William A. Westley, *Violence and the Police: A Sociological Study of Law, Custom and Morality* (Boston, 1971), and *Task Force Report: The Police,* The President's Commission on Law Enforcement and Administration of Justice (Washington, D.C., 1967).

[15]*The New York Times,* August 13, 1973. Also see Robert Daley, *Target Blue: An Insider's View of the N.Y.P.D.* (New York, 1973).

[16]*Newsweek,* June 7, 1971, p. 28; Quinn Tamm, "The Police," in Hugh Davis Graham (ed.) and Stephen Paul Mahinka and Dean Rudoy (associate eds.), *Violence: The Crisis of American Confidence* (Baltimore and London, 1971), p. 71.

[17]*The New York Times,* February 4, 1973, March 25, 1973.

[18]Ibid., October 1, 1973. Police in many sections of the country were also increasingly using .357 magnum revolvers loaded with deadly, hollow-nosed, expanding bullets, even though the bullets were prohibited by the U.S. military as "inhumane and cruel," *Houston Chronicle,* July 1, 1974.

[19]*Newsweek,* March 15, 1971.

[20]Ramsey Clark, *Crime in America: Observations on Its Nature, Causes, Prevention and Control* (New York, 1970), p. 328.

[21]Graham, et al., *Violence,* p. 69. For a general discussion of the issue, see Campbell, et al., *Law and Order Reconsidered,* pp. 469-495.

[22]Graham, et al., *Violence,* p. xxvii. The quotation is from Lloyd Cutler.

[23]*The Miami Herald,* January 7, 1973.

[24]*The New York Times,* March 6, 1972, March 2, 1973; *Newsweek,* January 15, 1973.

[25]*Newark,* (Ohio) *Advocate,* March 27, 1974.

[26]*The New York Times,* January 16, 1973.

[27]*Task Force Report: Corrections,* The President's Commission on Law Enforcement and Administration of Justice (Washington, D.C., 1967); Jessica Mitford, *Kind and Usual Punishment: The Prison Business* (New York, 1973).

[28]Morton Hunt, *The Mugging* (New York, 1972), pp. 146-147, 181, 192-193, 285-286, 429-432.

Chapter 5: Blacks and Whites

[1]Fred P. Graham, "A Contemporary History of American Crime," Hugh Davis Graham and Ted Robert Gurr, *The History of Violence in America* (New York, 1969), p. 504; Donald J. Mulvihill and Melvin M. Tumlin (co-directors) and Lynn A. Curtis (assistant director), *Crimes of Violence,* II. A Staff Report Submitted to the National Commission on the Causes and Prevention of Violence (Washington, D.C., 1969), pp. xxvi-xxvii, xxxv; Milton S. Eisenhower, Letter in *Harper's* (December 1970): 6-10.

[2]Arthur Meier Schlesinger, *The Rise of the City: 1878-1898* (New York, 1933), pp. 111-114.

[3]Mulvihill, et al., *Crimes of Violence,* pp. 406-407; "Face to Face on the Issues: Law and Justice," *Life,* June 9, 1972, p. 55.

[4]*Newsweek,* August 16, 1971, p. 70.

[5]*The New York Times,* August 9, 1970.

[6]*The New York Times,* November 15, 1971.

[7]Robert Coles and Jon Erikson, *The Middle Americans* (Boston, 1971). Of course, blacks suffer greatly by having to live in the high crime areas. For evidence of their disproportionately high rates as victims of violent crimes, see *The New York Times,* August 5, 1973, April 28, 1974.

[8]*The New York Times,* October 20, 1974.

[9]Ibid., June 24, 1964.

[10]William Brink and Louis Harris, *Black and White: A Study of U.S. Racial Attitudes Today* (New York, 1967), pp. 100-124.

[11]Peter Goodman, *The Death and Life of Malcolm X* (New York, Evanston, San Francisco, and London, 1973), pp. 13-22.

Chapter 6: Youths

[1]*The New York Times*, November 4, 1974; November 7, 1974.

[2]*Newsweek*, January 15, 1973; *The New York Times*, April 27, 1972; October 14, 1974.

[3]*The New York Times*, May 28, 1972.

[4]Ibid.

[5]Ibid., October 25, 1972.

[6]Ibid., February 13, 1972, April 16, 1972. By 1974, the New York City school system had 950 security guards handling its 96 high schools. *The New York Times*, July 21, 1974.

[7]Malcolm W. Klein, "Violence in American Juvenile Gangs," in Donald J. Mulvihill and Melvin M. Tumlin (co-directors) and Lynn A. Curtis (assistant director), *Crimes of Violence*, II. A Staff Report Submitted to the National Commission on the Causes and Prevention of Violence (Washington, D.C., 1969), pp. 1429-1439; *The New York Times*, January 16, 1973; Lewis Yablonski, *The Violent Gang* (New York, 1962), pp. 1-6, 149-153; Walter B. Miller, "Violent Crimes in City Gangs," in Marvin E. Wolfgang (ed.), *Patterns of Violence,* The Annals of the American Academy of Political and Social Science (March 1966), p. 98.

[8]*The New York Times*, August 16, 1972.

[9]Gene Weingarten, "East Bronx Story—Return of the Street Gangs," *New York*, March 27, 1972, p. 34.

[10]*The New York Times*, June 11, 1973.

[11]Ibid., January 13, 1973.

[12]Ibid., June 11, 1973.

[13]Weingarten, "East Bronx Story," pp. 31-37; Yablonski, *The Violent Gang*, p. 157.

[14]*The New York Times*, April 16, 1972; Weingarten, "East Bronx Story," p. 35; *Philadelphia Bulletin*, May 25, 1972.

[15]*The New York Times*, May 28, 1972.

[16]Ibid., June 11, 1973.

[17]For important theories on the motivation of youth gangs, see Albert Cohen, *Delinquent Boys: The Culture of the Gang* (Glencoe, Ill., 1955); Richard A. Cloward and Lloyd E. Ohlin, *Delinquency and Opportunity: A Theory of Delinquent Gangs* (Glencoe, Ill., 1960); Herbert Bloch and Arthur Niederhoffer, *The Gang* (New York, 1958); *Task Force Report: Juvenile Delinquency and Youth Crime,* The President's Commission on Law Enforcement and Administration of Justice (Washington, D.C., 1967).

Chapter 7: Assassinations

[1]The author was an observer at the convention and was present when the Doral Hotel incident occurred.

[2]*Philadelphia Bulletin,* June 8, 1972; *The New York Times,* June 8, 1972.

[3]*The New York Times,* June 8, 1972, August 4, 1972.

[4]Janet M. Knight (ed.), *Three Assassinations: The Deaths of John and Robert Kennedy and Martin Luther King* (New York, 1971), p. 13; James F. Kirkham, Sheldon G. Levy, and William J. Crotty, *Assassination and Political Violence,* A Report to the National Commission on the Causes and Prevention of Violence (New York, 1970), pp. 73, 77.

[5]Kirkham, et al., *Assassination and Political Violence,* pp. 73-77.

[6]Ibid., pp. 71-73.

[7]Ibid., p. 61.

[8]Knight, *Three Assassinations,* p. 192.

[9]Ibid., p. 194.

[10]Richard Drinnon, "The War on Violence," *Wilson Library Bulletin* (September 1970): 76.

[11]Ibid., p. 69.

[12]Kirkham, et al., *Assassination and Political Violence, pp. 83-88.*

[13]Ibid, pp. 118-120.

[14]*The New York Times,* May 20, 1972.

[15]Knight, *Three Assassinations,* p. 11.

[16]*Philadelphia Inquirer,* May 17, 1972. David English and the Staff of the London Daily Express, *Divided They Stand* (Englewood Cliffs, N.J., 1969), p. 252. Kirkham, et al., *Three Assassinations,* p. 93.

[17]Kirkham, et al., *Assassination and Political Violence,* pp. 93, 117. The idea of accepting the single-man theory seemed so unpalatable to many that conspiracy theories abounded. Yet, a decade later Daniel W. Belin's excellent study, *November 22, 1963* (New York, 1974) supported the essential findings of the Warren Commission. Also see the original commission report: President's Commission on the Assassination of President John F. Kennedy, *Report* (Washington, D.C., 1964).

Chapter 8: Protest

[1]Richard Hofstadter, "Reflections on Violence," in Richard Hofstadter and Michael Wallace, *American Violence: A Documentary History* (New York, 1971), pp. 3-43.

[2]*Report of the National Advisory Commission on Civil Disorders* (New York, 1968), pp. 22-23.

[3]Quoted in Hugh Davis Graham (ed.) and Stephen Paul Mahinka and Dean William Rudoy (associate eds.), *Violence: The Crisis of American Confidence* (Baltimore and London, 1971), p. 67.

[4]For an informative general review of the problem, see Seymour Martin Lipset, *Rebellion in the University* (Boston, 1972).

[5]Hofstadter, "Reflections on Violence," p. 31.

[6]Samuel Eliot Morison, Frederick Merk, and Frank Friedel, *Dissent in Three American Wars* (Cambridge, Mass., 1970).

[7]Clarence Darrow, *Crime: Its Causes and Treatment* (New York, 1922), pp. 215-218.

[8]*Handwriting on the Wall*, #4.

[9]Raymond Tanter, "International War and Domestic Turmoil: Some Contemporary Evidence," in Hugh Davis Graham and Ted Robert Gurr, *The History of Violence in America* (New York, 1969), pp. 555-566. Also see Ivo K. Feierabend, Rosalind L. Feierabend, and Betty A. Nesvold, "Social Change and Political Violence: Cross-National Patterns," and Robin Brooks, "Domestic Violence and America's Wars: An Historical Interpretation," pp. 530-545, in the same volume; Ted Robert Gurr, *Why Men Rebel* (Princeton, 1970).

[10]August Meier and Elliott Rudwick, "Black Violence in the Twentieth Century: A Study in Rhetoric and Retaliation," in Graham and Gurr, *The History of Violence in America*, pp. 399-411.

[11]James C. Davies, "The J-Curve of Rising and Declining Satisfactions as a Cause of Some Great Revolutions and a Contained Rebellion," in Graham and Gurr, *The History of Violence in America*, pp. 690-730. John Chowning Davies, *When Men Revolt—and Why: A Reader in Political Violence and Revolution* (New York, 1971).

[12]Crane Brinton, *Anatomy of a Revolution* (New York, 1957). Also see William A. Westley, "The Escalation of Violence Through Legitimation," in Marvin E. Wolfgang (ed.), *Patterns of Violence*, The Annals of the American Academy of Political and Social Science (March 1966), p. 120; Barrington Moore, Jr., "Revolution in America?" *The New York Review of Books*, January 30, 1969, p. 6.

Chapter 9: Sanctions

[1]Richard Hofstadter, "Reflections on Violence," in Richard Hofstadter and Michael Wallace, *American Violence: A Documentary History* (New York, 1971), p. 30.

[2]Frantz Fanon, *The Wretched of the Earth* (New York, 1968); Earl Anthony, *Picking Up the Gun: A Report on the Black Panthers* (New York, 1970), p. 2; Jerome S. Skolnick, *The Politics of Protest* (New York, n.d.), p. 141.

[3]Alphonso Pinkney, *The American Way of Violence* (New York, 1972).

[4]Ibid., p. 126.

[5]Ibid., p. 194.

[6]Ibid., p. 26.

[7]Ibid., p. 201. For research data on the popularity of related opinions among people representing various positions in the political spectrum, see Monica Blumenthal, Robert L. Kahn, Frank M. Andrews, and Kendra B. Head, *Justifying Violence: Attitudes of American Men* (Ann Arbor, Mich., 1972).

[8]Thomas Rose (ed.), *Violence in America: A Historical and Contemporary Reader* (New York, 1970), pp. xix-xxviii, 26-51.

[9]Kingsley Widmer, "Living-Room Confrontation: The Rage Against Violence," *The Nation,* July 20, 1970.

[10]Barrington Moore, Jr., "Revolution in America?" *The New York Review of Books,* January 30, 1969, pp. 6-12; Hofstadter, "Reflections on Violence," p. 32.

[11]Hannah Arendt, *On Violence* (New York, 1969).

[12]Eugene Goodheart, "The Rhetoric of Violence," *The Nation,* April 6, 1970.

[13]For interesting commentary on the role of the "myth of regeneration through violence" in early American history, see Richard Slotkin, *Regeneration Through Violence: The Mythology of the American Frontier* (Middletown, Conn., 1973), pp. 3-7, 558-565. Also see Hofstadter, "Reflections on Violence," p. 32.

[14]Quoted in *U.S. News and World Report,* September 28, 1970, pp. 27-28.

[15]Irving Howe, "Political Terrorism: Hysteria on the Left," *The New York Times Magazine,* April 20, 1969.

[16]*The New York Times,* December 25, 1970.

[17]Skolnick, *The Politics of Protest,* p. 77.

[18]James F. Kirkham, Sheldon G. Levy, and William J. Crotty, *Assassination and Political Violence,* A Report to the National Commission on the Causes and Prevention of Violence (New York, 1970), p. 521.

[19]Quoted in Janet M. Knight (ed.), *Three Assassinations: The Deaths of John and Robert Kennedy and Martin Luther King* (New York, 1971), p. 128.

[20]*The New York Times,* April 13, 1968.

[21]Ibid., May 13, 1973, May 30, 1973, June 3, 1972, November 16, 1973.

[22]Ibid., October 16, 1972, October 23, 1972.

[23]Ibid., January 23, 1973.

[24]Carlos Marighela, *For the Liberation of Brazil* (New York, 1971).

[25]Maria Esther Gilio, *The Tupamaro Guerrillas* (New York, 1973).

[26]Daniel James, *Che Guevara: A Biography* (New York, 1968).

[27]*Time*, November 2, 1970.

[28]Similarly, the bombing at Haymarket Square in Chicago in 1886, associated in the public mind with the work of anarchists, undermined the cause of organized labor.

[29]Stanley Coben, "The American Red Scare of 1919-1920," in *Conspiracy: The Fear of Subversion in American History* (New York, 1972).

[30]David Brody, "The Emergence of Mass Production Unionism," in John Braeman, Robert Bremner, and Everett Walters, *Change and Continuity in Twentieth-Century America* (New York, 1966), pp. 221-262.

[31]Philip Taft and Philip Ross, "American Labor Violence: Its Causes Character, and Outcome," *The History of Violence in America* (New York, Toronto, and London, 1969), pp. 281-395.

[32]Joseph E. Finley, *The Corrupt Kindom: The Rise and Fall of the United Mine Workers* (New York, 1973).

[33]See, for example, Lerone Bennett, Jr., *Before the Mayflower: A History of the Negro in America, 1619-1964* (rev. ed., New York, 1966).

[34]Joanne Grant (ed.), *Black Protest: History, Documents, and Analyses, 1619 to the Present* (New York, 1968), pp. 281-282.

[35]Knight, *Three Assassinations*, p. 123. Also see August Meier and Elliott Rudwick, "Black Violence in the Twentieth Century: A Study in Rhetoric and Retaliation," in Hugh Davis Graham and Ted Robert Gurr, *The History of Violence in America* (New York, 1969), pp. 399-411.

Chapter 10: Aggression

[1]Sigmund Freud, *Civilization and Its Discontents* (New York, 1930), p. 138.

[2]Ibid., pp. 60, 85-86, 90, 102-103.

[3]Ibid., pp. 143-144; Sigmund Freud, "Letter to Albert Einstein, September, 1932," in Arthur and Lila Weinberg (eds.), *Instead of Violence: Writings by the Great Advocates of Peace and Nonviolence Throughout History* (Boston, 1963), pp. 208-210.

⁴Quoted in Leo Tolstoy, *Tolstoy's Writings on Civil Disobedience and Non-Violence* (New York, 1967), pp. 323-324.

⁵Quoted by Jerome D. Frank in "The Psychology of Violence," in Hugh Davis Graham (ed.) and Stephen Paul Mahinka and Dean William Rudoy (associate eds.), *Violence: The Crisis in American Confidence* (Baltimore and London, 1971).

⁶Niko Tinbergen, "On War and Peace in Animals and Man: An Ethologist's Approach to the Biology of Aggression," *Science,* June 28, 1969, p. 1416.

⁷Dan Behrman, "Understanding Man's Aggressiveness," *UNESCO Courier* (August-September 1970): 4-6.

⁸See, for example, the explanation of Erich Fromm in *The Anatomy of Human Destructiveness* (New York, Chicago, and San Francisco, 1974), p. xv. Also Terry Maple, "Introduction to the Scientific Study of Aggression," in Terry Maple and Douglas W. Matheson (eds.), *Aggression, Hostility, and Violence: Nature or Nurture?* (New York, 1973), pp. 1-5.

⁹Desmond Morris, *The Naked Ape: A Zoologist's Study of the Human Animal* (New York, 1968), pp. 238-241.

¹⁰Robert Ardrey, *African Genesis* (New York, 1961); Robert Ardrey, *The Territorial Imperative* (New York, 1966).

¹¹Quoted in Sally Carrighar, "War Is Not in Our Genes," *UNESCO Courier* (August-September 1970): 42. Also see Ardrey, *The Territorial Imperative,* pp. 18-31.

¹²Konrad Lorenz, *On Aggression* (New York, 1966; 1971).

¹³Ibid., pp. 271-273. For evidence of Lorenz's flexibility in working with this interpretation, see the interview with him in *Psychology Today* (November 1974), 83-93.

¹⁴William James, "The Moral Equivalent of War," in Weinberg, *Instead of Violence,* pp. 301-304.

¹⁵Freud, "Letter to Albert Einstein," in Weinberg, *Instead of Violence,* p. 208.

¹⁶Tinbergen, "On War and Peace in Animals and Man," p. 1417.

¹⁷Anthony Storr, *Human Aggression* (New York, 1968; 1970), pp. 132-133.

¹⁸Bruno Bettelheim, "Violence: A Neglected Mode of Behavior," in Marvin Wolfgang (ed.), *Patterns of Violence,* The Annals of the American Academy of Political and Social Science (March 1966), pp. 52, 55-56.

¹⁹Storr, *Human Aggression,* pp. 1-22.

²⁰Donald J. Mulvihill and Melvin M. Tumlin (co-directors) and Lynn A. Curtis (assistant director), *Crimes of Violence,* II. A Staff Report Sub-

mitted to the National Commission on the Causes and Prevention of Violence (Washington, D.C., 1969), p. 1128.

[21]Discussion of the work of H. Kaufmann in Roger N. Johnson, *Aggression in Man and Animals* (Philadelphia, London, and Toronto, 1972), p. 157.

[22]Leonard Berkowitz, "The Case for Bottling Up Rage," *Psychology Today* (July 1973): 26-28.

[23]John Channing Davies, *When Men Revolt—And Why: A Reader in Political Violence and Revolution* (New York, 1971), pp. 183-184.

[24]Mulvihill, et al., *Crimes of Violence,* p. 430.

[25]John Dollard, et al., *Frustration and Aggression* (New Haven, 1939).

[26]Alexander Allard, Jr., *The Human Imperative* (New York and London, 1972); M. F. Ashley Montagu (ed.), *Man and Aggression* (New York, 1968).

[27]Rodger N. Johnson, *Aggression in Man and Animals* (Philadelphia, London, and Toronto, 1972), pp. 1, 18-19.

[28]Frank, "The Psychology of Violence," p. 82.

[29]Wolfgang, "A Preface to Violence," in *Patterns of Violence,* p. 5.

[30]Alberta E. Spiegel, "Violence and the Mass Media," in David N. Daniels, M.D., Marshall F. Gilula, M.D., and Frank M. Ochberg, M.D., *Violence and the Struggle for Existence: Work of the Committee on Violence of the Department of Psychiatry, Stanford University School of Medicine* (Boston, 1970), p. 223.

[31]Quoted in Staughton Lynd (ed.), *Nonviolence in America: A Documentary History* (Indianapolis, New York, and Kansas City, 1966), p. 157. Also see Clarence Darrow, *Crime: Its Cause and Treatment* (New York, 1922), pp. 275-278.

[32]For critical commentary on the instinct arguments of zoologists and ethologists, see Alland, *The Human Imperative;* Hannah Arendt, *On Violence* (New York, 1968), p. 59; Montagu (ed.), *Man and Aggression;* R. Charles Boelkins and Jon F. Heiser, "Biological Bases of Aggression," in Daniels, et al., *Violence and the Struggle for Existence,* pp. 21-38.

[33]See, for example, Elliot S. Valenstein, *Brain Control* (New York, 1974). Vernon H. Mark and Frank R. Ervin, *Violence and the Brain* (New York, 1970).

[34]K. E. Moyer, "The Physiology of Violence," *Psychology Today* (July 1973): 35.

[35]Johnson, *Aggression in Man and Animals,* pp. 77-79.

[36]Kenneth B. Clark, "The Pathos of Power," *American Psychologist* (December 1971); 1047-1057.

[37]Vernon H. Mark, "A Psychosurgeon's Case *for* Psychosurgery," *Psychology Today* (July 1974): 28-33, 84-86.

[38]For informative discussions of the force of Social Darwinism on late nineteenth-century thought, see Richard Hofstadter, *Social Darwinism in American Thought* (Boston, 1955); Eric F. Goldman, *Rendezvous With Destiny: A History of Modern American Reform* (New York, 1956), pp. 66-124.

[39]Carrighar, "War Is Not in Our Genes," p. 45.

[40]*Women's Wear Daily,* October 24, 1973.

[41]Leo Tolstoy, *Tolstoy's Writings on Civil Disobedience and Non-Violence,* p. 338.

[42]D. Yergin, "Peckinpah and Scenes from His Films," *The New York Times,* October 31, 1971.

[43]Craig McGregor, "Nice Boy From the Bronx?," *The New York Times,* January 30, 1972.

[44]Fred M. Hechinger, "The Liberal Fights Back," *The New York Times,* February 13, 1972.

[45]Quoted in Frederick Wertham, *A Sign for Cain: An Exploration of Human Violence* (New York, 1966), p. 220.

[46]Ibid., pp. 16-17.

Chapter 11: Ethos

[1]Donald J. Mulvihill and Melvin M. Tumlin (co-directors) and Lynn A. Curtis (assistant director), *Crimes of Violence,* II. A Staff Report Submitted to the National Commission on the Causes and Prevention of Violence (Washington, D.C., 1969), p. 480; David English and the Staff of the London Daily Express, *Divided They Stand* (Englewood Cliffs, N.J., 1969), p. 252.

[2]Max Lerner, *The Unfinished Century: A Book of American Symbols* (New York, 1969), p. 364.

[3]Janet M. Knight (ed.), *Three Assassinations: The Deaths of John and Robert Kennedy and Martin Luther King* (New York, 1971), p. 25.

[4]*The New York Times,* April 26, 1972, p. 10.

[5]*Time,* December 28, 1970.

[6]The original version read "perilous fight" rather than "night."

[7]General David M. Shoup, "The New American Militarism," *The Atlantic* (April 1969); Robert N. Bellah, "Evil and the American Ethos," in Nevitt Sanford, Craig Comstock, and Associates, *Sanctions for Evil:*

Sources of Social Destructiveness (Berkeley, Calif., 1971), pp. 186-190; Robert Jay Lifton, *Home From the War* (New York, 1973); *The New York Times Book Review*, December 17, 1973; *Miami Herald*, January 7, 1973; Arthur Schlesinger, Jr., *Violence: America in the Sixties* (New York, 1968), p. 25.

[8]*The New York Times*, April 26, 1971, p. 4.

[9]Ibid., May 1, 1974, p. 1.

[10]Stanley Milgram, *Obedience to Authority: An Experimental View* (New York, 1974), pp. 179-189.

[11]*The New York Times*, June 7, 1972.

[12]Hans Toch, *Violent Men: An Inquiry into the Psychology of Violence* (Chicago, 1969), p. 213.

[13]*The New York Times*, May 20, 1972.

[14]Quoted in Mulvihill, et al., *Crimes of Violence*, II, pp. 1080-1084.

[15]*The New Yorker*, March 22, 1969, p. 31.

[16]J. William Fulbright, "Militarism: Impact of the Military Upon American Democracy," An Address Delivered at Denison University, Granville, Ohio, April 18, 1969.

[17]Frederick Wertham, *A Sign for Cain: An Exploration of Human Violence* (New York, 1966), p. 129.

[18]For related comments showing serious concern about the value system, see Richard Maxwell Brown, "Historical Patterns of Violence in America," in Hugh Davis Graham and Ted Robert Gurr, *The History of Violence in America* (New York, 1969), p. 76; Janet M. Knight (ed.), *Three Assassinations*, p. 192; William Westley, "The Escalation of Violence Through Legitimation," in Marvin E. Wolfgang (ed.), *Patterns of Violence*, The Annals of the American Academy of Political and Social Science (March 1966), p. 125; Walter M. Gerson, "Violence as an American Value Theme," in Otto N. Larsen (ed.), *Violence and the Mass Media* (New York, Evanston, and London, 1968), p. 154.

Chapter 12: Machismo

[1]For example, see: Lola Romanucci-Ross, *Conflict, Violence, and Morality in a Mexican Village* (Palo Alto, Calif., 1973); John P. Gillin, "Some Signposts for Policy," in Richard N. Adams et al., *Social Change in Latin America Today* (New York, 1960), pp. 29-33; Oscar Lewis, *The Children of Sanchez* (New York, 1961), passim.

For comments on manifestations of the machismo-style spirit in North America culture, see Hans Toch, *Violent Men: An Inquiry into the*

Psychology of Violence (Chicago, 1969), pp. 47, 53-55, 190, 213; Gregory Rochlin, *Man's Aggression: The Defense of the Self* (Boston, 1973), pp. 1-5.

[2]Winston Churchill, *My Early Life: A Roving Commission* (New York, 1930).

[3]Henry Scott-Stokes, *The Life and Death of Yukio Mishima* (New York, 1974).

[4]The double standard is especially evident in Lewis, *The Children of Sanchez.*

[5]Jorge Amado, *Gabriela: Clove and Cinnamon* (New York, 1962).

[6]Lewis, *The Children of Sanchez.*

[7]Carolina Maria de Jesus, *Child of the Dark* (New York, 1962). Examples of lower class machismo standards appear throughout the diary.

[8]Jackson Toby, "Violence and the Masculine Ideal: Some Qualitative Data," in Marvin E. Wolfgang (ed.), *Patterns of Violence*, The Annals of the American Academy of Political and Social Science (March 1966), pp. 19-27.

[9]*Crime in the United States: Uniform Crime Reports, 1970* (Washington, D.C., 1970), p. 9.

[10]Joseph Morgenstern, "A New Violence," *Newsweek*, February 14, 1972, p. 68.

[11]Speech to the American Legion, August 30, 1966, in *Vital Speeches of the Day.* September 15, 1966, p. 707. Also see April 15, 1965, and the speech of General Harold K. Johnson in the September 1, 1965, issue.

[12]Ibid., June 1, 1967, p. 511.

[13]*Women's Wear Daily*, October 30, 1972.

[14]David Halberstam, *The Best and the Brightest* (New York, 1970), pp. 24, 43, 75, 590, 655.

[15]*Newark* (Ohio) *Advocate*, November 24, 1972.

[16]Marvin A. Block, *Alcohol and Alcoholism: Drinking and Dependence* (Belmont, Calif., 1970), pp. 1-6.

[17]*The New York Times*, April 22, 1972.

[18]Donald E. Newman, M.D., "Firearms and Violent Crime: Conversations with Protagonists," in George D. Newton and Franklin E. Zimring, *Firearms and Violence in American Life*, A Staff Report Submitted to the National Commission on the Causes and Prevention of Violence (Washington, D.C., n.d.), p. 183; Lewis Yablonski, *The Violent Gang* (New York, 1962), pp. 8, 151.

[19]Newman, "Firearms and Violent Crime," p. 187.

[20]*The New York Times*, May 28, 1972.

[21]For research evidence on the presence of guns working as a stimulus for aggressive behavior, see Leonard Berkowitz and Anthony

LePage, "Weapons as Aggression Eliciting Stimuli," *Journal of Personality and Social Psychology* (1967): 202-207.

[22]Max Lerner, *The Unfinished Century: A Book of American Symbols* (New York, 1959), pp. 364-365.

[23]James F. Kirkham, Sheldon G. Levy, and William J. Crotty, *Assassination and Political Violence*, A Report to the National Commission on the Causes and Prevention of Violence (New York, 1970), pp. 79-88.

[24]Walter C. Langer, *The Mind of Adolph Hitler* (New York, 1972).

[25]Rollo May, *Power and Innocence: A Search for the Sources of Violence* (New York, 1972).

[26]Frank Tannenbaum, *Ten Keys to Latin America* (New York, 1964), pp. 136-160; Frank Tannenbaum, *Mexico: The Struggle For Peace and Bread* (New York, 1950), pp. 81-90.

[27]Wilbur J. Cash, *The Mind of the South* (New York, 1941), p. 44.

[28]Clement Eaton, *The Growth of Southern Civilization: 1790-1860* (New York, 1961), pp. 275-277.

[29]Gene Weingarten, "East Bronx Story—Return of the Street Gangs," *New York*, March 27, 1972, p. 31.

[30]Walter B. Miller, "Violent Crimes in City Gangs," in Marvin E. Wolfgang (ed.), *Patterns of Violence*, The Annals of the American Academy of Political and Social Science (March 1966), p. 112.

[31]*Vital Speeches of the Day*, September 1, 1965.

[32]*Vital Speeches of the Day*, February 1, 1966. Also see March 15, 1966, July 15, 1966, and August 1, 1966. For the "Number One Nation" statement, see *The New York Times Book Review*, June 11, 1972, p. 3.

[33]*The New York Times*, April 27, 1972, May 9, 1972, May 11, 1972.

Chapter 13: Television

[1]Comments by Jack Valenti in *Mass Media and Violence*, Vol. 9A, Mass Media Hearings, A Report to the National Commission on the Causes and Prevention of Violence (Washington, D.C., 1969), p. 192.

[2]Comments of Robert D. Wood, president of CBS in *Philadelphia Bulletin*, June 5, 1972.

[3]Rollo May, *Power and Innocence: A Search for the Sources of Violence* (New York, 1972), p. 241.

[4]*Mass Media and Violence*, Vol. 9A, p. 205. Also see Earnest Callenbach's comments in *Film Quarterly* (Fall 1968): 77-79.

[5]Norman A. Zinberg and Gordon A. Fellman, "Violence: Biological

Need and Social Control," in Renatus Hartogs and Eric Artzt, *Violence: Causes and Solutions* (New York, 1970), pp. 223-239.

⁶Anthony Storr, *Human Aggression* (New York, 1970), pp. 42-54.

⁷Ibid. For a review of some of the important research which casts doubt on the impact, see Seymour Feshbach and R. D. Singer, *Television and Aggression* (San Francisco, 1971).

⁸*Mass Media and Violence,* Vol. 9A, pp. 176-177.

⁹Ibid., pp. 20-25. For earlier comments by Klapper, see Joseph T. Klapper, "The Impact of Viewing Aggression: Studies and Problems of Extrapolation," in Otto N. Larsen (ed.), *Violence and the Mass Media* (New York, Evanston, and London, 1968), p. 138.

¹⁰*Newsweek*, December 13, 1971.

¹¹*TV Guide*, November 25, 1972, pp. 8-35.

¹²*Newsweek*, March 6, 1972, pp. 55-56.

¹³*Television and Growing Up: The Impact of Televised Violence*, Report to the Surgeon General, United States Public Health Service from the Surgeon General's Scientific Advisory Committee on Television and Social Behavior (Washington, D.C., 1972), pp. 8-19, 189-190.

¹⁴*Newsweek*, March 6, 1972, pp. 55-56; *The New York Times*, February 16, 1972.

¹⁵*Newsweek*, March 6, 1972, p. 55.

¹⁶*The New York Times*, March 31, 1972.

¹⁷*To Establish Justice, To Insure Domestic Tranquility,* The Final Report of the National Commission on the Causes and Prevention of Violence (New York, 1970), p. 166.

¹⁸Albert Bandura, Dorothea Ross, and Sheila Ross, "Transmission of Aggression Through Imitation of Aggressive Models," *Journal of Abnormal and Social Psychology* 63 (1961): 575-582; Albert Bandura, Dorothea Ross, and Sheila Ross, "Imitation of Film-Mediated Aggressive Models," *Journal of Abnormal and Social Psychology* 66 (1963): 3-11.

¹⁹*Mass Media and Violence,* Vol. 9A, p. 37. For a review of Berkowitz's research on these issues, see Leonard Berkowitz, *Roots of Aggression* (New York, 1969).

²⁰*Television and Growing Up,* pp. vii, 184. Also see the comments of Nicholas Johnson, former commissioner of the Federal Communications Commission, in *Mass Media and Violence*, p. 245.

²¹*Television and Growing Up,* pp. 166-169, 185-186.

²²*Mass Media and Violence,* Vol. 9A, p. 47.

²³*The New York Times*, September 15, 1971. Studies show that by the time an average child enters kindergarten he has already spent more

hours learning about the world from TV than he would from a college classroom earning a B.A. degree. *Newark* (Ohio) *Advocate,* September 30, 1973.

[24]*To Establish Justice, To Insure Domestic Tranquility,* pp. 160-162; Nicholas Johnson, *How to Talk Back to Your Television Set* (Boston and Toronto, 1967; 1970), pp. 24-34.

[25]*Mass Media and Violence,* Vol. 9A, pp. 118, 127. One British Broadcasting Corporation study found American-made television productions to contain about twice as many violent incidents as British productions. The growth of violence in British programming provoked the BBC to try to reverse the trend, particularly in programs that glorified violence. Also see *Philadelphia Bulletin,* March 31, 1972.

[26]Quoted in Arthur Schlesinger, Jr., *Violence: America In the Sixties* (New York, 1968), pp. 54-55.

[27]*Television and Growing Up,* pp. 5-6.

[28]*Newark* (Ohio) *Advocate,* September 30, 1973.

[29]Frederick Wertham, *A Sign for Cain: An Exploration of Human Violence* (New York, 1966), p. 210.

[30]*Mass Media and Violence,* Vol. 9A, p. 37.

[31]Albert Bandura, "What TV Violence Can Do to Your Child," in Otto N. Larsen (ed.), *Violence and the Mass Media* (New York, Evanston, and London, 1968), p. 128.

[32]*To Establish Justice, To Insure Domestic Tranquility,* pp. 165-166.

[33]Wertham, *A Sign for Cain,* pp. 285-287.

[34]Roger N. Johnson, *Aggression in Man and Animals* (Philadelphia, London, and Toronto, 1972), pp. 152-153.

[35]*Newark* (Ohio) *Advocate,* October 5, 1973; October 22, 1973; Ted Morgan, "Remembering René: Behind the Immolators in Boston," *The New York Times Magazine,* November 11, 1973.

[36]*Miami Herald,* January 3, 1973; Alberta Spiegel, "Violence in the Mass Media," in David N. Daniels, M.D., Marshall F. Gilula, M.D., and Frank M. Ochberg, M.D., *Violence and the Struggle for Existence: Work of the Committee on Violence of the Department of Psychiatry, Stanford University School of Medicine* (Boston, 1970), p. 213.

[37]*Columbus* (Ohio) *Dispatch,* April 5, 1972.

Chapter 14: Movies

[1]*The New York Times,* March 17, 1974.

[2]François Truffaut, *Hitchcock* (New York, 1967), p. 205.

[3]William Price Fox, "Wild Westerns, Italian Style," *Saturday Evening Post*, April 6, 1968, p. 55.

[4]*Columbus* (Ohio) *Citizen-Journal*, January 23, 1973.

[5]*Newsweek*, August 28, 1972.

[6]Ibid.

[7]*The New York Times*, August 17, 1972; *Saturday Review of Society*, February 1973.

[8]*The New York Times*, August 13, 1972.

[9]Ibid., December 22, 1972.

[10]*Newark* (Ohio) *Advocate*, June 26, 1971.

[11]*Violence and the Mass Media*, Vol. 9A, Mass Media Hearings, A Report to the National Commission on the Causes and Prevention of Violence (Washington, D.C., 1969), p. 202.

[12]Leonard Berkowitz, "The Effects of Observing Violence," *Scientific American* (February 1964): 35-41; Leonard Berkowitz and Edna Rawling, "Effects of Film Violence on Inhibitions Against Subsequent Aggression," *Journal of Abnormal and Social Psychology* 66 (1963): 405-412.

[13]George Gerber, "Communication and Social Environment," *Scientific American* (September 1972): 153-158.

Chapter 15: Censorship

[1]Garrett Epps, "Does Popeye Doyle Teach Us How to Be a Fascist?," *The New York Times*, May 21, 1972.

[2]See the testimony of Leon Jaworski and Nicholas Johnson in *Mass Media and Violence*, Vol. 9A, Mass Media Hearings, A Report to the National Commission on the Causes and Prevention of Violence (Washington, D.C., 1969), pp. 252, 260.

[3]*TV Guide*, November 11, 1972, p. 35.

[4]*The New York Times*, April 27, 1972.

[5]For some insights into the thoughts of these media critics regarding individual liberties, see: Epps, "Does Popeye Doyle Teach Us How to Be a Fascist?"; Frederick Wertham, *A Sign for Cain: An Exploration of Human Violence* (New York, 1966), p. 221; Arthur Schlesinger, Jr., *Violence: America in the Sixties* (New York, 1968), p. 61; comments of Otto N. Larsen in *Mass Media and Violence*, Vol. 9A, p. 72; Walter Lippmann as quoted in John E. Twomey, "New Forms of Social Control Over Mass Media Content," in Otto N. Larsen, *Violence and the Mass Media* (New York, Evanston, and London, 1968), p. 175.

[6]Charles Winick, "Censorship and Sensibility: A Content Analysis of the Television Censor's Comments," in Larsen, *Violence and the Mass Media*, p. 258.

[7]Quoted in *Mass Media and Violence*, Vol. 9A, p. 137.

[8]In the spring of 1974, some interesting but uneven developments gave evidence of growing public frustration and desire for change. The Senate Communications Subcommittee held hearings on the subject of violence on television which brought out much additional critical commentary. Later, major networks announced that the violent content in their new programs scheduled for fall would be toned down. Moreover, some individuals tried to combat the problem singlehandedly. For example, Leo S. Singer, founder of Miracle White Company, transferred his $3 million annual television advertising budget away from programs that contained violence. "I can't really explain what happened," said Singer of his reaction to finding four television channels featuring a man with a gun at the same time. "It just hit me. I resolved right there and then that we would no longer be part of a potentially injurious syndrome." *Newark (Ohio) Advocate*, April 10, 1974.

Chapter 16: Firearms Democracy

[1]Robert Sherrill, *The Saturday Night Special* (New York, 1973). Estimates vary greatly, and Sherrill's guess may well be an understatement. Millions of guns are owned illegally and are unrecorded.

[2]J. Christian Gillin, M.D., and Frank M. Ochberg, M.D., "Firearms Control and Violence," in David N. Daniels, M.D., Marshall F. Gilula, M.D., and Frank M. Ochberg, M.D., *Violence and the Struggle for Existence: Work of the Committee on Violence of the Department of Psychiatry, Stanford University School of Medicine* (Boston, 1970), p. 242.

[3]Gene Weingarten, "East Bronx Story—Return of the Street Gangs," *New York*, March 27, 1972, pp. 31-37.

[4]*Newark (Ohio) Advocate*, February 1, 1973.

[5]*Columbus (Ohio) Dispatch*, January 11, 1973; *The New York Times*, August 26, 1971.

[6]*Columbus (Ohio) Dispatch*, January 11, 1973.

[7]Arthur Schlesinger, Jr., *Violence: America in the Sixties* (New York, 1968), p. 41.

[8]*The New York Times*, March 30, 1973.

[9]*Crime in the United States: Uniform Crime Reports—1970* (Washington, D.C., 1971), p. 8.

[10]George D. Newton and Franklin E. Zimring, *Firearms and Violence in American Life*, A Staff Report Submitted to the National Commission on the Causes and Prevention of Violence (Washington, D.C., 1969), p. 44.

[11]*Cleveland Plain Dealer*, November 2, 1971.

[12]Max Lerner, *The Unfinished Century: A Book of American Symbols* (New York, 1959), p. 380.

[13]Ramsey Clark, *Crime in America: Observations on Its Nature, Causes, Prevention, and Control* (New York, 1970), p. 108. For some fascinating analysis of the stimulus potential of guns in anger-arousing conditions, see Leonard Berkowitz and Anthony LePage, "Weapons as Aggression Eliciting Stimuli," *Journal of Personality and Social Psychology* 7 (1967): 202-207.

[14]Rollo May, *Power and Innocence: A Search for the Sources of Violence* (New York, 1972), pp. 189-191.

[15]*Philadelphia Bulletin*, March 28, 1972; *Columbus* (Ohio) *Dispatch*, January 11, 1973.

[16]Ibid.; Peter Hellman, "Seven Days of Killing," *New York*, August 28, 1972, p. 26.

[17]*The Houston Post*, July 11, 1974.

[18]Quoted in Alan Rosenthal, "Violence Is Predictable," *Today's Health* (November 1970): 57, 71.

[19]During the twentieth century, more than 800,000 Americans have been killed by civilian gunfire—more than all American military fatalities from the Revolutionary War to the Vietnam War. *The New York Times*, May 18, 1972.

[20]Ovid Demaris, *America the Violent* (New York, 1970), p. 331.

[21]*Columbus* (Ohio) *Dispatch*, December 18, 1972.

[22]*The Washington Post*, April 6, 1972.

[23]*Philadelphia Bulletin*, May 5, 1972.

[24]*The New York Times*, May 31, 1972.

[25]Ibid., October 3, 1971.

[26]*Philadelphia Bulletin*, May 31, 1972.

[27]Newton, et al., *Firearms and Violence in American Life*, pp. 61-70, 140; *Newark* (Ohio) *Advocate*, November 23, 1973.

[28]David English and the Staff of the London Daily Express, *Divided They Stand* (Englewood Cliffs, N.J., 1969), p. 254.

[29]Newton, et al., *Firearms and Violence in American Life*, pp. 1, 191; *The New York Times*, June 6, 1968. Also see Dale T. Schoenberger, *The Gunfighters* (Caldwell, Idaho, 1971).

[30]*Newark* (Ohio), *Advocate*, January 11, 1973.

[31]*The New York Times,* December 12, 1971.

[32]Earl Anthony, *Picking Up the Gun: A Report on the Black Panthers* (New York, 1970), p. 95.

[33]Donald E. Newman, M.D., "Firearms and Violent Crime: Conversations With Protagonists," in Newton, et al., *Firearms and Violence in American Life,* pp. 183-194. Also see May, *Power and Innocence,* pp. 189-191.

[34]*Philadelphia Bulletin,* June 5, 1972; Newton, et al., *Firearms and Violence in American Life,* pp. 187-191.

Chapter 17: Disarmament

[1]Robert Sherrill, *The Saturday Night Special* (New York, 1973). For an earlier, highly critical review of the gun cult in America, see Carl Bakal, *Right to Bear Arms* (New York, 1966).

[2]Paul Good, "Blam! Blam! Blam! Not Gun Nuts, But Pistol Enthusiasts," *The New York Times Magazine,* September 17, 1972; *The American Rifleman* (August 1971), editorial.

[3]Jeff Cooper, "Handgunning: A Sport of Many Facets," *Guns and Ammo 1969 Annual,* pp. 22-23.

[4]David English and the Staff of the London Daily Express, *Divided They Stand* (Englewood Cliffs, N.J., 1969), p. 256.

[5]Hannah Arendt, *On Violence* (New York, 1969), pp. 50-53.

[6]George D. Newton and Franklin E. Zimring, *Firearms and Violence in American Life,* A Staff Report Submitted to the National Commission on the Causes and Prevention of Violence (Washington, D.C., 1969), p. 113; Richard Hofstadter, "Reflections on Violence in the United States," in Richard Hofstadter and Michael Wallace, *American Violence: A Documentary History* (New York, 1971), pp. 24-25.

[7]John Ward, *Andrew Jackson: Symbol for an Age* (New York, 1955), pp. 1-54.

[8]Newton, et al., *Firearms and Violence in American Life,* pp. 259-265.

[9]Ibid., pp. xiv, 90-101.

[10]Ibid., p. 104; English, *Divided They Stand,* p. 255; Arthur Schlesinger, Jr., *Violence: America in the Sixties* (New York, 1968), p. 46.

[11]*The New York Times,* August 26, 1971; Janet M. Knight (ed.), *Three Assassinations: The Deaths of John and Robert Kennedy and Martin Luther King* (New York, 1971), pp. 191-192.

[12]Good, "Blam! Blam! Blam!"; *The New York Times,* June 2, 1972; *Newark* (Ohio) *Advocate,* May 30, 1972.

[13]*Philadelphia Bulletin,* May 21, 1972.

[14]*The Washington Post,* April 6, 1972.

[15]Good, "Blam! Blam! Blam!"; *The New York Times,* August 26, 1971.

[16]Newton, et al., *Firearms and Violence in American Life,* p. 91.

[17]*The New York Times,* May 18, 1972; *Newark* (Ohio) *Advocate,* February 12, 1973.

[18]*The New York Times,* August 8, 1972.

[19]Schlesinger, *Violence,* p. 46.

[20]U.S. President's Commission on Law Enforcement and Administration of Justice, *The Challenge of Crime in a Free Society* (Washington, D.C., 1967), p. vii.

[21]Newton, et al., *Firearms and Violence in American Life,* pp. xv, 127-131.

[22]*To Establish Justice, To Insure Domestic Tranquility,* The Final Report of the National Commission on the Causes and Prevention of Violence (New York, 1970), p. 156.

[23]*The New York Times,* March 30, 1973.

[24]Ibid., May 31, 1972.

[25]Ibid., May 18, 1972; Knight, *Three Assassinations,* p. 213.

[26]Knight, *Three Assassinations,* p. 213.

[27]Quoted in *Cleveland Plain Dealer,* November 10, 1971.

[28]Quoted in *The New York Times,* June 28, 1972.

[29]Ramsey Clark, *Crime in America: Observations on Its Nature, Causes, Prevention and Control* (New York, 1970), p. 105; English, *Divided They Stand,* p. 254; Newton, et al., *Firearms and Violence in American Life,* pp. 124-125.

[30]*Miami Herald,* January 4, 1973; *Time,* October 16, 1972.

[31]*Newark* (Ohio) *Advocate,* May 30, 1973.

Chapter 18: Civilization

[1]Frederick Wertham, *A Sign for Cain: An Exploration of Human Violence* (New York, 1966), p. 14.

[2]James S. Campbell, Joseph R. Sahid, and David Stang, *Law and Order Reconsidered,* Report of the Task Force on Law Enforcement to the National Commission on the Causes and Prevention of Violence (Washington, D.C., 1969), p. 565.

[3]Charles and Mary Beard, *The American Spirit: A Study of the Idea of Civilization in the United States* (New York, 1942), pp. 60, 66-68.

[4]The defender of slavery was Thomas R. Dew.

⁵George Fitzhugh, *Cannibals All: Or, Slaves Without Masters* (Cambridge, Mass., 1960).

⁶Max Lerner, *America as a Civilization* (New York, 1957), pp. 946, 949.

⁷Feliks Gross, "Political Violence and Terror in Nineteenth and Twentieth Century Russia and Eastern Europe," in James F. Kirkham, Sheldon G. Levy, and William J. Crotty, *Assassination and Political Violence*, A Report to the National Commission on the Causes and Prevention of Violence (New York, 1970), p. 591. Also see R. G. Collingwood, *The New Leviathan, or, Man, Society, Civilization and Barbarism* (London, 1958), pp. 283, 292.

⁸Leslie Simpson, *The Democratic Civilization* (New York, 1964), pp. 14-15.

⁹*To Establish Justice, To Insure Domestic Tranquility*, The Final Report of the National Commission on the Causes and Prevention of Violence (New York, 1970), p. 52.

¹⁰William Nisbet Chambers, *Political Parties in a New Nation: The American Experience, 1776-1809* (New York, 1963), Foreword.

¹¹Henry Steele Commager, "The History of American Violence: An Interpretation," in Hugh Davis Graham (ed.) and Stephen Paul Mahinka and Dean William Rudoy (associate eds.), *Violence: The Crisis of American Confidence* (Baltimore and London, 1971), p. 4.

¹²Lerner, *America as a Civilization*, pp. 40-42, 50, 946-949.

¹³Louis Hartz, *The Liberal Tradition in America: An Interpretation of American Political Thought Since the Revolution* (New York, 1955); Daniel Boorstin, *The Genius of American Politics* (Chicago, 1953).

¹⁴Quoted in Lerner, *America as a Civilization*, p. 50.

¹⁵Ralph Henry Gabriel, *The Course of American Democratic Thought: An Intellectual History Since 1815* (New York, 1940), pp. 19-24.

¹⁶For a review of the issues, see Allen F. Davis and Harold D. Woodman (eds.), *Conflict or Consensus in American History* (Boston, 1966). One of the important books which described a long record of violent confrontations was Hugh Davis Graham and Ted Robert Gurr, *The History of Violence in America* (New York, 1969).

¹⁷The work by Hugh Davis Graham, et al., cited in note 11.

¹⁸*To Establish Justice, To Insure Domestic Tranquility*, p. xxxiv.

¹⁹H. Stuart Hughes, *Oswald Spengler: A Critical Estimate* (New York and London, 1952), pp. 1-13, 32-36, 91-92, 164-165.

²⁰Oswald Spengler, *The Decline of the West: Perspectives of World History,* (New York, 1928), II, p. 435.

[21]Hughes, *Oswald Spengler*, pp. 1-10.

Chapter 19: Cities

[1]Arthur M. Schlesinger, *The Rise of the City: 1878-1898* (New York, 1933), pp. xiv-xv, 1, 78-79.

[2]Ibid., pp. 78-79. Also see Constance McLaughlin Green, *American Cities in the Rise of the Nation* (New York, 1956; 1965), p. 1; Dixon Ryan Fox, "Foreword," in Schlesinger, *The Rise of the City,* pp. xiv-xv; Christopher Tunnard, *The Modern American City* (Princeton, 1968), pp. 11-15, 81, 101-103; Kenneth E. Boulding, "The City as an Element in the International System," *Daedalus* (Fall 1968): 1116.

[3]Quoted in Charles and Mary Beard, *The American Spirit: A Study of the Idea of Civilization in the United States* (New York, 1942), p. 172.

[4]Richard C. Wade, *Urban Frontier: PNEER Life in Early Pittsburgh, Cincinnati, Lexington, Louisville, and St. Louis* (Chicago, 1964).

[5]Quoted in Charles N. Glaab and A.heodore Brown, *A History of Urban America* (New York and London, 1967), p. 307.

[6]John R. Seeley, "Remaking the Urban Scene: New Youth in Old Environment," *Daedalus* (Fall 1968): 1126. Also see Leonard Reissman, *The Urban Process: Cities in Industrial Societies* (New York and London, 1964), pp. 1-2.

[7]Morton and Lucia White, "The American Intellectual Versus the American City," *Daedalus* (Winter 1961): 174; Lewis Mumford, *The City in History: Its Origins, Its Transformations, and Its Prospects* (New York, 1961), p. 576.

[8]Richard Hofstadter, *The Age of Reform* (New York, 1955), pp. 23-93.

[9]William E. Leuchtenberg, *The Perils of Prosperity, 1917-1932* (Chicago, 1958), pp. 204-224.

[10]Quoted in Mumford, *The City in History*, p. 558.

[11]Ibid., p. 560.

[12]"The Future Metropolis," *Daedalus* (Winter 1961).

[13]"The Conscience of the City," *Daedalus* (Fall 1968).

Chapter 20: Apple Pie

[1]"Nixon on Violence: A Cancerous Disease," *U.S. News and World Report*, September 28, 1970.

²For examples of the "hands off," nineteenth-century philosophy, see Richard Hofstadter, *Social Darwinism in American Thought* (Boston, 1944; 1955); and Eric F. Goldman, *Rendezvous With Destiny; A History of Modern American Reform* (New York, 1952; 1956), pp. 66-81.

Chapter 21: Action and Inaction

B. F. Skinner, *Beyond Freedom and Dignity* (New York, 1971). For a fascinating exchange of ideas on related controversies, see "Some Issues Concerning the Control of Human Behavior: A Symposium," *Science* (November 30, 1956): 1057-1064.

²Rollo May, *Power and Innocence: A Search for the Sources of Violence* (New York, 1972).

³*Time*, November 13, 1972.

¹May, *Power and Innocence,* p. 166.

⁵Ibid., p. 241.

⁶Ibid., p. 151.

⁷Raymond B. Fosdick, *The Old Savage in the New Civilization* (New York, 1929).

⁸Ibid., pp. 41-43.

⁹Ibid.

¹⁰Shirley Jackson, "The Lottery," in Adrian H. Jaffe and Virgil Scott (eds.), *Studies in the Short Story* (New York, 1960), pp. 232-240.

¹¹Alvin Gouldner, *The Coming Crisis in Western Society* (New York, 1970).

¹²Thomas E. Bittler, M.D., "The Choice of Collective Violence in Intergroup Conflict," in David N. Daniels, M.D., Marshall F. Gilula, M.D., and Frank M. Ochberg, M.D., *Violence and the Struggle for Existence: Work of the Committee on Violence of the Department of Psychiatry, Stanford University School of Medicine* (Boston, 1970), p. 190.

¹³Dwight L. Dumond (ed.), *Letters of James Gillespie Birney* (New York and London, 1938), I, p. 202.

¹⁴Leo Tolstoy, *Tolstoy's Writings on Civil Disobedience and Non-Violence* (New York, 1967), p. 340.

Index

Muggings, 22, 24-25, 30, 43, 47, 49, 50, 69, 73, 76, 79, 185, 219, 269
Mumford, Lewis, 268
"Murder in America," 9
Murders: bizarre, viii, 7-9, 16
Murphy, John, 189
Murphy, Patrick, 224
My Lai massacre, 162

NAACP. *See* National Association for the Advancement of Colored People
NASA, 28
Nagasaki, 160
Naked Ape, The, 140
Nanna, Dominick, 20
Nation, The, 115
National Anthem, 158
National Association for the Advancement of Colored People, 73
National Broadcasting Corporation, 9, 189, 197
National Commission on the Causes and Prevention of Violence, 26, 31, 47, 52, 185, 190, 192-193, 196, 240, 261
National Crime Commission, 287
National Guardsmen, 106
National Labor Relations Act, 129
National Rifle Association, 222, 230, 232
Nazi concentration camps, 48
Nazis, 155, 162
NBC. *See* National Broadcasting Corporation
Nebraska, 237
Neighborhood Youth Corps, 84
Neo-Darwinism, 141
Neopolitan Noodle Restaurant, 34
New Brunswick, New Jersey, 24
New Deal, 84, 129
New Jersey, 122
New Left, 118, 120
New Orleans, 234

New York, xix, 18, 20, 23-25, 33, 38-39, 48, 85
New York Academy of Trial Lawyers, 49
New York City, 47, 49, 52, 55, 70, 73, 76-78, 108, 206, 219, 224, 237, 247, 273
New York City Police Department, 28, 56
New York State, 61, 65, 240
New York State Lottery, 26
New York Times, 6, 26, 82, 186
Newark, 99, 108
Newman, Donald E., 227
Newsweek, 74
Newton, Huey, 113, 122
Nichols, Police Commissioner John F., 51
Nigeria, 139
1984, 212, 279
Nineveh, 266
Nixon, Richard, 35, 88, 119-120, 133, 161, 180, 210, 274
Nixon Administration, 36, 38, 165, 237
Nobel, Alfred, 165
NRA. *See* National Rifle Association

Oakland, 123
Ohio National Guard, 119
Old Savage in the New Civilization, The, 284
On Aggression, 141
On Violence, 116
Orange County, California, 42
Oswald, Lee Harvey, 88, 90-91
Ottawa, 88, 125

Palestinian guerillas, 126
Paris, 110
Parker, Bonnie, 201
Parliament Hill, 126
Patriotism, 158
Patton, 213
Patton, General George S., 10